D0327001

362.2 S                    78-04202

Schrag, Peter.

Mind control

✓

DEC 8 7

CENTRAL ARKANSAS LIBRARY SYSTEM
LITTLE ROCK PUBLIC LIBRARY
700 LOUISIANA
LITTLE ROCK, ARKANSAS

# MIND CONTROL

*Also by Peter Schrag*

*Voices in the Classroom*
*Village School Downtown*
*Out of Place in America*
*The Decline of the WASP*
*The End of the American Future*
*Test of Loyalty*
*The Myth of the Hyperactive Child* (with Diane Divoky)

# Mind Control

Peter Schrag

Pantheon Books, New York

Copyright © 1978 by Peter Schrag

All rights reserved under International and Pan-American Copyright Conventions. Published in the United States by Pantheon Books, a division of Random House, Inc., New York, and simultaneously in Canada by Random House of Canada Limited, Toronto.

Library of Congress Cataloging in Publication Data

Schrag, Peter.
  Mind Control.

  Includes bibliographical references and index.
  1. Psychiatry—United States—Philosophy.
2. Behavior modification—United States.   3. Public
welfare—United States.   4. United States—Politics and government—1969–     5. Social control.   I. Title.
RC443.S37      362.2'0973      77–15077
ISBN 0–394–40759–8

*Designed by Irva Mandelbaum*

Manufactured in the United States of America

First Edition

# Contents

# Acknowledgments

I am grateful to many individuals and organizations for their help. Many of them are named in the text or cited in the footnotes. Among those who are not or whose assistance is inadequately indicated are Pauline B. Bart; Donna G. Bass; Gail Bensinger; Peter R. Breggin; Sarah C. Carey; Carl D. Chambers; Richard A. Cloward; Joan Cole; Lee Coleman; James Dahlgren; Tom Dixon; Matthew P. Dumont; Bruce J. Ennis; Nancy Fernandez; Leonard R. Frank; Ira Glasser; Don Goldmacher; Henry Goldman; James Gordon; Lester Grinspoon; George Hagglund; Amanda Hawes; Carmen Hellisten; Mary C. Howell; Fred L. Hunter; Joel Kaufman; Terry A. Kupers; Robert Kuttner; Douglass Lea; Henry Lennard; Perry London; Paul Lowinger; Bruce Margolis; Robert Maronde; Reed Martin; Rollo May; Stanley Murphy; Susan Nelson; Bob Nicholson; Michael Parkhurst; Roger M. Patton; Gerald Platt; Robert Plotkin; Andrea Sallychild; Sheldon Samuels; Edward Scott; John R. Seelye; Milton Silverman; Karl U. Smith; Robert E. Smith; Roger Smith; Paul Steel; Thomas S. Szasz; Sharland Trotter; Luke, Shari, and Steven Tullberg; Frank White; and Shirley Willner.

I am also indebted to the Alameda County (California) Mental Health Services, the American Civil Liberties Union, the American Management Association, the American Polygraph Association, the American Psychiatric Association, the American Psychological Association, the California State Department of Health, the Conference Board, the Mental Health Law Project, the Network Against Psychiatric Assault, Health Applications Systems, Inc., the Industrial Union Department of the AFL-CIO, the National Library of Medicine, the Pacific Telephone Co., the Peninsula Community Mental Health Center, the Pharm Chem Research Foundation, the Psychological Corporation, the School for Workers at the University of Wisconsin, the U. S. Food and Drug Administration, the National Institute of Mental Health, the Law Enforcement Assistance Administration, the U. S. Senate Subcommittee on Constitutional Rights, and the West Side Community Mental Health Center.

My greatest debts are to André Schiffrin and, as always, to Diane Divoky.

# Introduction

In the past generation, there has been a fundamental shift in the way government and other organizations control the lives and behavior of individuals. No single method and no single phrase adequately describe it—it is both too subtle and too pervasive—but it represents a radical change in the way people are treated and in the relationship between the citizen, his employer, the state, and the state's institutions. In general, it is a shift from direct to indirect methods of control, from the punitive to the therapeutic, from the moralistic to the mechanistic, from the hortatory to the manipulative. More specifically, it is reflected in the replacement of overt and sometimes crude techniques—threat, punishment, or incarceration—with relatively "smooth" methods: psychotropic drugs; Skinnerian behavior modification; aversive conditioning; electronic surveillance; and the collection, processing, and use of personal information to institutionalize people outside the walls of institutions. Those technologies, all developed or introduced during the past twenty-five years, have made it possible to extend intervention—much of it well intentioned—to millions of people who had never been subject to intervention before. They have made it possible to change the nature of that intervention so that instead of dealing with a specific act—the breaking of a law or a rule in school or a social convention—they deal with generalized behavior and a growing list of reified pseudo-medical abstractions: "aggressiveness," "maladjustment," "personality disorder," "mental illness." In many situations, these technologies have made it possible to convert the official rationale for that intervention from the protection of the state and community to individual therapy or "service" designed ostensibly to benefit the individual. Although they are professedly more humane and less capricious than what they replace or supplement, they are far more intrusive into the life, thought, feelings, and behavior of the individual than anything which existed previously. Collectively, these technologies are conditioning a growing segment of the society to regard all deviance as sickness and to accept increasingly narrow standards of acceptable behavior as scientifically normative.

Each year there are more subjects, clients, and patients; more people in treatment; more officially certified problems to justify it. Local, state, and federal agencies have created an enormous network of institutions and programs to identify clients and "serve" them: a community mental-health system, almost nonexistent twenty years ago, which now treats some 5 million people a year, most of them with drugs; mandatory medical and psychological screening of all of the nation's 13 million poor (Medicaid-eligible) children and, in some places, of all children, which includes family histories and the collection of extensive personal data about parents and siblings; sophisticated data systems which are used to exchange personal information among schools, welfare departments, the courts, and other agencies, and which are also used to track clients through the social-service system; as well as scores of others. Concern for serious child abuse, estimated to run to a few thousand cases a year, has fostered vast child-abuse reporting systems, which require every teacher, social worker, physician, and in some states, every citizen to report suspected abuse or neglect to a social agency or a central register; these systems are producing more than a million reports each year and imposing "services" on hundreds of thousands of parents whose only crime is sloppy housekeeping, failure to cooperate with welfare workers, or lifestyles of which their neighbors disapprove.

*          *          *

This book is about some of these methods of control, about how and on whom they are used, the organizations which use them, the ideology on which they are based, and the extensive effects—personal and social—which they create. For the most part, it does not deal with the now-notorious MK Ultra program and similar CIA-sponsored experiments in mind control and behavior modification, or with prisons, mental hospitals, and other closed institutions, where inmates have always been subject to demeaning rituals of mortification. (And where, as Erving Goffman said, each rule, each specification "robs the individual of an opportunity to balance his needs and objectives in a personally efficient way and opens up his line of action to sanctions.") Rather, the book deals with what appears to be a growing tendency to employ new methods of intervention, to create wholly new systems of "treatment," and to promote a new ideology of control in which society itself becomes more and more like a closed institution. Different agencies frequently employ the same methods, including, as one CIA report summarized them, "drugs, electro-shock, psychology, psychiatry, sociology, anthropology, harassment substances, and paramilitary devices and materials." What makes them significant is that they are no longer confined to covert or clandestine experimentation or to closed institutions. Each year more people outside institutions are drugged, screened, tested, questioned, watched, and followed—and more are subject to those rituals of mortification—as if they were inmates. Some are volunteers; some are conscripts; and some fall into a grey area where no one can be certain whether they are one or the other. Impositions before or which had been possible only within closed institutions now become possible in the community at large. The vision is of a kind of sanitized social efficiency; its language is clinical; its most important symbol is mental health.

The most common subjects are the growing numbers of economically superfluous or socially marginal people—the young, the old, the poor, the difficult—who, in some measure, are exempt from the conventional discipline of the marketplace; but they also include a great number of ordinary middle-class individuals: housewives drugged or treated with electroshock for "menopausal syndromes," middle-class parents reported and investigated for child abuse, workers—perhaps as many as a half million—administered polygraph or other "lie detector" tests as a condition of employment, Valium and Librium junkies who use the drugs to cope with stress and "psychic tension," and among others, several million people of all descriptions who are invited or forced into the proliferating agencies of mental health for everything from suicidal thoughts to problems with the landlord. Beyond the drugs there is electroshock and psychosurgery; and beyond them, the practitioners and the researchers, many of them backed with federal money, are experimenting with even grander methods of predicting, monitoring, and controlling deviance through screening of populations "at risk," prenatal testing, and computer-linked remotely controlled brain implants. All these techniques are founded on an ideology of intervention based not on rules, responsibility, and punishment, but on continuing surveillance and on a medical-model idea of early diagnosis and preventive treatment.

At the heart of the change lies a transcendent faith that with the proper environment or the proper methods, any individual can be reshaped, reformed, or at the very least, controlled with psychological or chemical methods, and, alongside that faith, the chemical, mechanistic, behavioristic view of man that sustains it. The new technologies liberated that view from its institutional, legal, moral, and economic restraints. Where punishment creates resentment and resistance and often involves trials or other elements of due process, where incarceration and psychotherapy are expensive, and where social reform and institutional change are slow and politically difficult, drugs and other forms of behavior modification are relatively cheap; since they are used in the name of therapy, they involve no due process, require no fundamental social change, and obviate the overtly invidious distinctions of race, class, inheritance, or character which often characterized cruder methods.

Given the changes in technology and American society over the past few decades, the new modes of control may have been inevitable. But at a time when government accepts an official unemployment rate of 7 percent, not only for the present but for the indefinite future; when real unemployment, particularly among the old, the young, and minorities, is substantially higher; and when budgets for conventional forms of social service and welfare are curtailed, it becomes almost imperative for government to find new means of controlling and disciplining that growing army of superfluous people, and new categories to convert what is essentially a political and an economic dilemma into a "problem" of mental illness, age, or other forms of individual inadequacy.

There are few cures for the formally sanctioned categories of psychiatric illness—the various forms of schizophrenia or depression, for example—let alone for the vast number of other medicalized problems which have been created in their image. These illnesses usually elude definition: they are not organic ailments; there is no agreement on their symptoms. For the most part, they represent labels for acts which someone or some agency finds offensive, disturbing, or disruptive, or for behavior which fails to satisfy social convention or cultural expectation. Yet while there are no cures, there are programs and technologies of maintenance: drugs to keep the clients docile; behavior modification to keep them cooperative in schools, prisons, and mental hospitals; tests and questionnaires to reinforce the authority of the agency over the client and the scientific legitimacy of the label which it gives him; data banks to record his behavior and to follow him through the system.

Although there is no evidence that drugs cure most forms of mental illness, they clearly have an effect in tranquilizing those who get them. One shot of Prolixin, a heavy tranquilizer introduced in the past decade, is effective for as long as four (and in some instances, six) weeks. There is no evidence that behavior modification can reform prisoners or help children learn school subjects or cure psychotics, however diagnosed; but it is often useful in maintaining order. There is little evidence that screening picks up many problems that weren't already apparent and even less that the treatment (if any) which follows offers any remedy; yet every one of the children tested in the federally mandated screening programs, and his parents, now have their "symptoms," idiosyncracies, and family histories detailed in a data system accessible to almost every social agency which wants to see them, and all know that the state is interested in their thoughts and feelings. And, with the possible exception of the most brutal cases, there is no evidence that any sort of intervention improves the situation of the abused child, but every one of the million families reported annually for suspected abuse is subject to investigation by the police or social workers, and everyone gets a record in a central register, even if the report is unfounded, and everyone learns he is being watched. The promise is cure, but what's usually delivered is maintenance and control.

Together the new programs and technologies are part of a burgeoning establishment involving welfare institutions, universities, hospitals, the drug industry, government at all levels, and organized psychiatry (itself in large part a creature of government). There is no conspiracy here, no master plan of control, but there is clearly a set of interlocking relationships and a community of interest. The ideology of medical-model intervention, psychiatric evangelism, legislative pressure, economic necessity, professional ambition, corporate self-interest, social fear, and the most noble intentions to provide humane treatment themselves conspire to create a climate in which each element of intervention reinforces all the others and in which the total effect is far greater than the sum of its constituent parts. If the drug works, it verifies the diagnosis which, in turn, verifies the scientific validity, however dubious and undefined, of the "ailment" for which it is given. The language and "science" of mental health validates a similar language in welfare, education, and penology. At every level intervention is justified as a more humane and more effective form of treatment than what would be required at the next level: the outpatient clinic as against the closed hospital, drugs as against electroshock or psychosurgery, programs to find and treat "pre-delinquents" or "borderline schizophrenics" or people suffering from "parapsychiatric events" as against later therapy for serious disorders or imprisonment.

Each new level of "humane" treatment and every refinement in behavior technology makes intervention easier; each gets around more legal, economic, or ethical objections; each enhances the authority of the institution that employs it. The ideal, in the view of the behaviorists, is the paranoid's dream, a method so smooth that no one will know his behavior is being manipulated and against which no resistance is therefore possible. Presumably there is no such technology (if there were, few people would know about it), but those which do exist have, at the very least, moved in that direction. In sustaining the ideology of medical-model treatment, they are gradually blurring the distinctions between social and medical problems, between sickness and crime, and between those who are volunteers in the great network of therapy, behavior modification, and social service and those who are its conscripts. It is a subtle, seductive process, a process of mystification, which teaches every individual that his mind and behavior are subject to chemical or other organic processes not fully within his control; that there are professionals who frequently know more about him than he knows about himself and who can better understand his real interests; that it is normal to be watched, tested, and questioned by the agents of social service; and that many of the problems growing out of poverty, inferior schools, poor housing, or simply out of the everyday conditions of human existence are really medical ailments subject to manipulation. Most significantly, it teaches that institutional demands and arbitrary social standards are themselves part of the natural order. It is no longer the cop or the schoolmaster telling the individual what to do; it is science. The individual is no longer being punished; he is being treated. There is no longer a set of impositions which he can regard as unjust or capricious and against which he can dream of rebelling. To entertain such dreams would be madness. Gradually, even the ability to imagine alternatives begins to fade. This is, after all, not only the best of all possible worlds; it is the only one. In an open society formally committed to due process and civil liberties, the consequences of such conditions are beyond calculation.

# MIND CONTROL

# ONE

# The Behavior Complex

## I

For Dr. Louis Jolyon ("Jolly") West, chairman of the Department of Psychiatry at the University of California at Los Angeles and director of its Neuropsychiatric Institute, the winter of 1973 was the headiest of seasons. He had been working for months drafting and refining proposals for one of the most ambitious ventures ever conceived in his field—the creation of an extensive, lavishly financed multidisciplinary Center for the Study and Reduction of Violence; he had written funding proposals to state and federal agencies; and he had secured the approval of senior officials of the state's Health and Welfare Agency. On January 11, the Violence Center became part of Governor Ronald Reagan's formal message on the State of the State. "This center," Reagan had said, "will explore all types of violent behavior, what causes it, how it may be detected, prevented, controlled, and treated." And on January 22, eleven days after Reagan's speech (and two days after Richard M. Nixon's second inaugural), West followed up with a friendly letter to his friend J. M. Stubblebine, M. D., then the state's director of Health:

Dear Stub:

I am in possession of confidential information that the Army is prepared to turn over Nike missile bases to state and local agencies for non-military purposes. They may look with special favor on health-related applications.

Such a Nike missile base is located in the Santa Monica Mountains, within a half-hour's drive of the Neuropsychiatric Institute. It is accessible but relatively remote. The site is securely fenced, and includes various buildings and improvements making it suitable for prompt occupancy.

If this site were made available to the Neuropsychiatric Institute as a research facility, perhaps initially as an adjunct to the new Center for the Prevention of Violence, we could put it to very good use. Comparative studies could be carried out there, in an isolated but convenient location, of experimental or model programs for the alteration of undesirable behavior.

Such programs might include control of drug or alcohol abuse, modification of chronic antisocial or impulsive aggressiveness, etc. The site could also accommodate conferences or retreats for instruction of selected groups of mental-health related professionals and of others (e.g., law enforcement personnel, parole officers, special educators) for whom both demonstration and participation would be effective modes of instruction.

My understanding is that a direct request by the Governor, or other appropriate officers of the State, to the Secretary of Defense (or, of course, the President) would be most likely to produce prompt results.[1]

Although West's letter did not specify precisely what sorts of "undesirable behavior" he had in mind, how the "alterations" were to be accomplished, or why a "securely fenced" Nike missile site would be appropriate, the general objectives of the Violence Center had been extensively outlined in West's earlier proposals. Among the programs planned for the center were genetic, biochemical, and neurophysiological studies of violent individuals, including prisoners and "hyperkinetic" children; experiments in the "pharmacology of violence-producing and violence-inhibiting drugs"; studies of "life-threatening behavior during the menstrual cycle"; studies on "hormonal aspects of passivity and aggressiveness in boys"; surveys "to discover and compare norms of violence among various ethnic groups"; and most significantly, the development of tests "that might permit detection of violence-predisposing brain disorders prior to the occurrence of a violent episode."[2] If such tests could be found, then it would be possible to try out the so-called Schwitzgebel Machine, a means of "implanting tiny electrodes deep within the brain," connecting them to small radio transmitters, and monitoring (perhaps even controlling) the behavior of violence-prone individuals or probationers—or indeed, anyone else—by remote control.[3] Here again space and missile technology would be useful, since a modified missile-tracking device could be adapted to follow the brain-implanted subjects. West later denied that the center also contemplated experiments in psychosurgery—neurosurgical operations to alter behavior—but the inclusion of a project that would make possible "large-scale screening" to detect "violence-predisposing brain disorders," California's recent prison experiments in psychosurgery, and the addition of Dr. Frank R. Ervin to the proposed Violence Center staff made the denials less than persuasive. Dr. Ervin, a vocal proponent of psychosurgery and co-author of a popular book entitled *Violence and the Brain*, had advocated just the kind of studies that West now planned to conduct.

In the book, written with Vernon H. Mark, associate professor at Harvard Medical School and director of neurosurgery at Boston City Hospital; and in a letter to the *Journal of the American Medical Association* written with Mark and William H. Sweet, also professor at Harvard and director of neurosurgery at Massachusetts General Hospital, Ervin had argued that people with "encephalographic abnormalities in the temporal region" have a much higher propensity for violence and other "behavioral abnormalities" than those with normal brain-wave patterns.

The tool we need the most is a satisfactory method of predicting a given individual's threshold for violent acts. That is, we should develop tests for limbic brain function and dysfunction. This development, in turn, will be dependent upon thorough-going investigations of violent individuals who are known to have disease of the limbic brain.

Two kinds of facilities are necessary for any such investigation. One is a place to house the individuals being studied; the other is a medical center staffed with specialists in the field [sic] of neurology, psychology and genetics. . . .

In their letter, Ervin, Mark, and Sweet profess concern about urban riots, raising the question of whether there was something peculiar about the "violent slum dweller" that distinguishes him from "his peaceful neighbor." They were certain that there was such a thing, and that, with the proper research, it could be detected and treated, in some instances with "chemical agents and drugs," in some with psychosurgery. "Even with these new psychotherapeutic and medicinal tools," said Mark and Ervin in their book, "some people with brain disease may still require surgical treatment for the control of violence."[4]

The proposals for the Violence Center went considerably beyond research, however, involving not only physicians, psychologists, pharmacologists, and sociologists, most of whom were already on staff at the Neuropsychiatric Institute; the center would also include lawyers, police officers, clergymen, and probation officers, who would be the beneficiaries of what was described as the center's "basic thrust": "the development and demonstration of practical applications of models for the detection, prevention, control, and treatment of violent individuals." Among those applications were "behavioral indicators, profiles, scales, biological correlates, and social and environmental predictors of life-threatening behavior. These detectors will be structured into transportable models for use by teachers, clergy, social workers, counselors, physicians, penologists, etc." The center was to be heavily engaged in producing films and other "educational" materials for dissemination to the police, schools, mental-health workers, corrections officers, and the general public.

West had ample reason to expect support. He had the backing of the governor and the state's Health and Welfare Agency; he had received promises of cooperation from a number of California prisons and mental institutions; he had many staff members who had long pursued independent research programs on "life-threatening behavior"; and he had secured tentative approval for a grant of $750,000 from the U. S. Law Enforcement Assistance Administration (LEAA) through the California Council on Criminal Justice, and for another $250,000 from other sources. He was also hopeful that other funds would be provided by the National Institute of Mental Health (NIMH), which, like LEAA, had become increasingly interested in developing effective technologies of behavior control.

West was riding a tide of interest in the possibilities of behaviorism and technological behavior control, which had been rising for at least a generation. B. F. Skinner of Harvard had been conducting experiments in operant conditioning since the late thirties and was, by 1970, undoubtedly the best-known psychologist in America. Through the forties and fifties, there had been a wave of lobotomies on "intractable" mental cases, which involved some 40,000 or 50,000 operations; and the procedure known as electroconvulsive therapy (ECT), which had begun with the use of insulin or other chemically induced comas—the original shock treatments—became, until the introduction of tranquilizers, an increasingly popular mode of treatment for the so-called depressive disorders.[5] (It also turned out later that in the early sixties, when he was at the University of Oklahoma, West himself had conducted LSD experiments funded by the CIA, but he apparently did not know the source of his funds.)

Yet it was not until the ghetto riots, the Vietnam protest movement, and the student uprisings of the mid- and late sixties that concern about violence, deviance, and "undesirable behavior" prompted serious proposals for the creation of extensive state and federally funded programs of technological behavior research, screening, control, and "treatment." In *Physical Control of the Mind: Toward a Psychocivilized Society* (1969), Jose M. R. Delgado proposed an "effort" which "must be promoted and organized by governmental action declaring 'conquering of the human mind' a national goal at parity with conquering poverty or landing a man on the moon."[6] Delgado, who was experimenting with brain implantations at Yale, favored the creation of "neurobehavioral institutes" very much like the UCLA Violence Center "with the specific purpose of investigating the mechanisms of the behaving brain," and ultimately the establishment of "a scientific foundation for the creation of a future psychocivilized society based on a better understanding of mental activities."

A few months later, the U. S. Department of Health, Education and Welfare was studying the now notorious plan of Dr. Arnold M. Hutschnecker to curb urban violence by screening all 8-year-old children for "delinquent tendencies," "treating" those who failed the test, and incarcerating "hard-core" individuals in special camps. And in 1970, Mark and Ervin called for the development of an "early warning test of limbic brain functions to detect those humans who have a low threshold for impulsive violence" and for "more effective methods of treating them once we have found out who they are."[7] If such a test had existed at the time, they said, Lee Harvey Oswald, who "had a history of repeated episodes of uncontrolled assaultive behavior," might have been stopped before assassinating John F. Kennedy.[8]

The Great Society and the New Frontier had given way to Law and Order; and the lofty hope of social reform was replaced by sterner invocations to detect, control, punish, and "treat" deviant individuals. "The urgent needs of underprivileged urban centers for jobs, education, and housing should not be minimized," wrote Mark, Sweet, and Ervin in their letter to the medical profession, "but to believe these factors are solely responsible for the present urban riots is to overlook some of the newer medical evidence about the personal aspects of violent behavior."[9]

The federal and state governments had, in the meantime, become increasingly committed to the effort. By 1973, the federal government, through LEAA, NIMH, the Bureau of Prisons, the CIA, and other agencies, was operating or funding scores of behavior modification programs in prisons, schools, and hospitals; NIMH was funding research projects on the possible relationship between chromosome abnormalities and violence, on drug treatment of violent or aggressive behavior, and on aversive shock treatment of homosexuals; the Department of Health, Education and Welfare was gearing up to operate a massive national program to screen all Medicaid-eligible (i. e., poor) children for developmental and psychological problems; and countless studies were under way to test the feasibility of using psychoactive drugs to "treat" killers, sex offenders, and a variety of other deviants.[10] Among the beneficiaries of those programs were Mark, Sweet, and Ervin, whose Neuro-Research Foundation in Boston received $500,000 from NIMH for studies in psychosurgery and related procedures.[11] At the same time, the state of Connecticut was "treating" child molesters at its Somers Correctional Facility with aversive shock, Michigan and California initiated psychosurgery experiments on prisoners, the state of Iowa injected inmates who broke prison rules—the offenses included use of abusive language—with a vomit-inducing drug called apomorphine, and at least one state (California) administered the terror drug Anectine as a means of "suppressing hazardous behavior." Used in small doses in medicine, Anectine works as a muscle relaxant; administered in massive amounts to prisoners, it produces a prolonged seizure of the respiratory system and a sensation that one of the prison subjects called worse than dying. The chief researchers who used the drug at the Vacaville (California) Medical Facility described their work as

> an attempt to evaluate the effectiveness of an aversive treatment program as a means of suppressing . . . hazardous behavior (e.g., suicide attempts and assaults). The drug was

selected for use as a means of providing an extremely negative experience for association with the behavior in question. [Anectine], when injected intramuscularly, results in complete muscular paralysis including temporary respiratory arrest. . . . It was hypothesized that the association of such a frightening consequence with certain behavioral acts would be effective in suppressing those acts. . . . How severe is the Anectine experience from the point of view of the patient? Sixteen likened it to dying. Three of these compared it to actual experiences in the past when they had almost drowned. The majority described it as a terrible, scary experience.[12] [Deletions made by the author]

And yet, despite all that, the Violence Center never really managed to get under way, never got the Nike missile site, and never got its funding. The proposal was too ingenuously blatant; and the timing, which seemed so right in the winter of 1973—the season of Nixon's last and greatest triumph—appeared all wrong a few months later. Protests that began early in 1973 among students and faculty on the UCLA campus—among them several members of Jolly West's own staff at the Neuropsychiatric Institute—reached the California legislature, which threatened to investigate and which blocked the state funding, which had been so certain a few months earlier. The decision, said Earl Bryan, Reagan's secretary of Health and Welfare, represented a "callous disregard for public safety." Meanwhile, partly as a consequence of pressure from civil-liberties organizations, LEAA announced that it had banned the use of its funds "for psychosurgery, medical research, behavior modification—including aversion therapy—and chemotherapy."[13] A number of prominent psychologists, Skinner among them, challenged the announcement, Skinner holding that the behavior of prisoners is always modified by the prison environment, and that it might as well be done right. There was, indeed, no way to understand the meaning of "behavior modification" in the LEAA announcement: the agency's entire mandate, after all, was to support and encourage changes in behavior. Yet when it came to projects like the Violence

Center, the LEAA announcement was clear enough: almost everything UCLA planned to do ran afoul of its specific prohibitions. As late as April 1974, two months after the LEAA announcement, West still hoped to obtain major federal funding through NIMH; but as the high season of Watergate drew toward its conclusion, the official climate in Washington was, at least for the moment, too unfavorable to permit any bureaucrat to take the risk.[14]

# II

The controversy over the Violence Center probably reflected the limits of what America would then tolerate in the realm of overt government-sponsored behavior-control experiments, but it hardly touched—and probably helped conceal—the subtler and much more pervasive techniques and practices that had developed since World War II and that now deeply affect virtually every aspect of American life: on the job, and in the economy generally; in the social-service system—schools, welfare, mental health; through the various agencies of the police and criminal justice systems; and in a vast and almost uncontrollable network of record systems and data banks, which help link all the others. A great part of post–World War II technology has been applied not merely, and often not even primarily, to the control of things, but more significantly to the control of human beings; and that, in turn, has generated a fundamental shift in the ideology of control: from the overt to the (hopefully) subtle, from punishment to "treatment," from moral and civil law to the "natural" order of things, the tyranny of the normative.

Behaviorists like Skinner are fond of saying that there has always been behavior modification, that they are merely trying to make it better, gentler, more humane, more scientific, and more successful. Isn't it better to practice operant condi-

tioning—to systematically reinforce desirable behavior—
than to spank, to imprison, to punish? Isn't it better to be
systematic than to leave the control of behavior to chance or
impulse? "My image in some places," Skinner said, "is of a
monster of some kind who wants to pull a string and manipulate people. Nothing could be further from the truth. People
are manipulated; I just want them to be manipulated more
effectively."[15]

The measure of Skinnerian effectiveness is the absence of
resistance and counter-control: ideally, the technique will be
so elegant, so smooth, that the manipulated will not suspect,
let alone object, that someone or something is trying to shape
their behavior; and a growing number of people, Skinner
among them, are certain that the moment is at hand. "Means
are being found," wrote Perry London, one of the more sober
writers in the field, "that will soon make possible precise
control over much of people's individual actions, thoughts,
emotions and wills. . . . Some people may be surprised at the
extent to which it is now possible to manipulate people systematically."[16] Such assertions are highly questionable. The
precision of which London speaks—that smoothness—is still
a long way off. Virtually every one of the genuinely powerful
techniques developed since World War II is beset with what
physicians and pharmacologists would call "side effects":
toxic or otherwise undesirable physical (or psychological or
political or economic) reactions that generate resistance. In
addition, even the relatively smooth techniques depend in
large measure on cruder and more traditional forms of control: the power of the police, the employer, the schoolteacher.
Nonetheless, the newer methods have become increasingly
powerful, sophisticated, and extensive; they have developed
to the point where they have produced a wholly new attitude
about control, and where, among other things, a growing
number of people have become willing recruits for behavior
modification—volunteers for "behavior therapy" in alcohol,
drug, smoking, sex, and diet clinics, and for programs pro-

fessing to teach self-manipulation with biofeedback, drugs, megavitamins, and other devices. Thus, the self becomes a mechanical object subject to repair and tuning, and "self-control" gets a wholly new meaning.

Considering the scope of the practices, it's hardly surprising that the nation reacted as passively as it did to reports of FBI, CIA, and police surveillance and to casual violations of civil liberties in the years before Watergate: what the cops were doing in their investigations had been going on as a matter of routine in factories, offices, schools, hospitals, and welfare agencies. For at least a generation, the country had been taught to accept as necessary, and perhaps even beneficial, the ordinary intrusions of welfare workers and credit investigators, of personnel directors and school psychologists.

The significance of the new forms of control transcends the impact of the varying and seemingly distinct technologies, many of them with their own schismatic sects of true believers, their own lobbies, journals, and professional associations: Skinnerian behaviorists; druggers; industrial psychologists; motivation researchers; members of the American Association for Electro-Convulsive Therapy, the National Association of Human Services Technologists, and the Society of Biological Psychiatry; testers; screeners; biofeedback freaks; operators of aversive puff-zap smoking, sex, or diet clinics; experts in job enrichment and job enlargement, in "motivation hygiene" and Theory Y. Despite their apparent disparity, they have become part of an organic whole in which each lends credibility to the others and in which every level of intervention is defended as a humane or more efficient means of averting something more severe. Thus, deviant behavior has grown its own branch of preventive medicine with its own institutions—counseling centers, diversion programs, behavior clinics—and its own set of anticipatory syndromes, which, if not cured, will lead to something worse. Although many practitioners vehemently disdain the practices of many of the others, nearly all of them have that

insatiable appetite for information—they cannot tolerate uncertainty and do not recognize the private, the ineffable, and
the unpredictable—and all of them share the common faith
in a behavioral "science" and in the concomitant view of the
individual as a medical, chemical, mechanistic, electronic
organism who may not understand his own real interests.
When Skinner declared, in 1971, that "the outlines of a
technology [to shape the entire culture] are already clear,"
—it is, perhaps, his most-quoted statement—he offered no
new "science," nothing, indeed, that he hadn't written himself nearly twenty years before; but he was raising the banner
of the new ideology of control in which nearly all of the
practitioners more or less believed. The overwhelming reception accorded the publication of *Beyond Freedom and Dignity*—the cover story in *Time*, the book's selection as *The
New York Times'* most important book of the year, and the
torrent of wide-eyed books and articles about "behavior
mod" and "the brain changers" which followed—made it
abundantly clear that behaviorism in America had reached
a critical mass, and that its spirit, if not its methods, had
become part of the conventional sensibility.[17] Everywhere
teachers began to talk routinely about "behavior modding"
their students; the believers began to sign up for behavior
therapy clinics; and the jailers began to play with "reinforcement schedules." "The main question," Skinner would say
in 1976, "is not whether we have a behavioral science but
when we're going to use it. It won't be used as long as people
go on with the idea that it's all a matter of thoughts, feelings
and acts of will."[18] That was, and is, the essence of the faith;
and while Skinner's complaint may have betrayed some basic
confusion about the power of the technology—how else
could an "idea" about thoughts and feelings stand in the way
of the technology?—he was confident that his method had
taken hold. Skinner and his disciples abjure many of the
practices that come under the banner of "behavior modification," and many of the medical-model interventionists who
regard all forms of deviance as disease reject the charge that

they are trying to control behavior; but in their allegiance to the new ideology, all the practitioners—the self-manipulators and those who try "scientifically" to "treat" or manipulate others—are part of the movement.

# III

The principle of Skinnerian operant conditioning is simple enough. At its core is the systematic reinforcement—the rewarding—of behavior that the shaper regards as desirable, and the "extinction," through the withdrawal of the reinforcers that might have sustained it, of undesirable behavior. It does not concern itself with inner states, which Skinner calls mentalism and which he regards as unscientific, but rather with the creation of an environment that systematically provides the proper reinforcement. There is little that Skinner has been able to do with his rats or with those famous pigeons he taught to play ping-pong that P. T. Barnum didn't know a century before. What Skinner did do was to make the process self-conscious, measurable, and systematic; he broke it down into the smallest and most discrete "behaviors"— made them subject to measurement and quantification—and moved it out of the laboratory and into the clinic and classroom. Its power inevitably depends on the extent to which the shaper can control the environment—depends, that is, on the power he already has over his subject: it is always more effective in prisons and mental hospitals than in schools, more effective with children than adults. In his study of mental hospitals, Erving Goffman pointed out that

> punishments and privileges are themselves modes of organization peculiar to total institutions. Whatever their severity, punishments are largely known in the inmate's home world as something applied to animals and children; this conditioning, behavioristic model is not widely applied to adults.

. . . The very notions of punishments and privileges are not ones that are cut from civilian cloth.[19]

Behavior modification is an attempt to apply the style and techniques of total institutions (and of factories) to the world outside. As such, the current fashion of behavior mod says a great deal about contemporary society.

The dream of behavior control—the ability to get "someone to do one's bidding"—is as old as mankind, a primal fantasy of spells cast and demons controlled, the stuff of witchcraft and magic potions, the happy hunting ground of inquisitions and tests of loyalty. Through the centuries it has manifested itself in diverse, though generally crude and brutal ways: Tristan and Isolde were accidental victims of a mood-altering drug, and Hamlet ran the conscience of the king through a lie-detector test; but in daily practice the rack and the chain were the typically effective instruments. In modern industrial societies, however, the problem has been not merely to find effective means of control but, equally important, to produce controllable people and, at least in the democracies, to invent rationales of authority to justify the means. Although Skinner quite properly names Pavlov, the Russian psychologist, and Edward L. Thorndike, one of the American pioneers of intelligence testing, as two of his principal intellectual forebears, contemporary behaviorism is rooted much more deeply in the prosaic soil of rationalized factory production and in the empirical imaginations of Frederick Winslow Taylor, Frank and Lillian Gilbreth, and Elton Mayo than it is in psychological or scientific theory. It was on the shop floor that "scientific" behavior control was first instituted on a large scale (and where it remains endemic); and it was in the work of Taylor, the father of "scientific management" and among the apostles of "human engineering" who followed him, that the attitudes and ideology of self-conscious behaviorism were first articulated.

The essence of Taylor's system, developed at the turn of the century and published in 1911, was what the Skinnerians would call behavior analysis. Every job was broken into its smallest components ("behaviors" in Skinnerian), which were then measured, analyzed, and restructured for (it was hoped) the greatest efficiency. Everything was timed with a stopwatch, all "false movements, slow movements and useless movements" eliminated, and the remains assembled "into one series [of] the quickest and best movements."[20] Taylor's prototypical case was that of a pig-iron handler named Schmidt, "a man of the type of the ox . . . so stupid that he was unfitted to do most kinds of laboring work, even"; whose job was so crude "that it would be possible to train an intelligent gorilla" to do it efficiently.[21] Schmidt, who worked for Bethlehem Steel loading 92-pound ingots of pig iron into railroad cars, was taught to increase his "production" from 12½ to 47½ tons a day. Taylor tells the story:

> Schmidt was called out from among the gang of pig-iron handlers and talked to somewhat in this way:
>
> "Schmidt, are you a high-priced man?"
>
> "Vell, I don't know vat you mean."
>
> ". . . Oh, come now, you answer my questions. What I want to find out is whether you are a high-priced man or one of those cheap fellows here. What I want to find out is whether you want to earn $1.85 a day or whether you are satisfied with $1.15, just the same as all those cheap fellows are getting."
>
> "Did I vant $1.85 a day? Vas dot a high-priced man? Vell, yes, I vas a high-priced man. . . ."
>
> "Well, if you are a high-priced man, you will do exactly as this man tells you to-morrow, from morning till night. When he tells you to pick up a pig and walk, you pick it up and you walk, and when he tells you to sit down and rest, you sit down. You do that straight through the day. And what's more, no back talk. . . . Now you come on to work here to-morrow morning, and I'll know before night whether you are really a high-priced man or not."
>
> This seems to be rather rough talk. And indeed it would be if applied to an educated mechanic, or even an intelligent laborer. With a man of the mentally sluggish type of Schmidt, it is appropriate and not unkind, since it is effective in fixing

his attention on the high wages which he wants and away from what, if it were called to his attention, he would probably consider impossibly hard work.

Schmidt started to work, and all day long, and at regular intervals, was told by the man who stood over him with a watch, "Now pick up a pig and walk. Now sit down and rest. Now walk—now rest, etc." He worked when he was told to work and rested when he was told to rest, and at half-past five in the afternoon had his 47½ tons loaded in the car.

Taylor goes on at length about Schmidt's stupidity and his native sluggishness, and he writes extensively about the benefits in skills and wages that workers derive from scientific management. But the real objective was exactly the reverse. Taylor himself had once supervised the work of factory machinists, not "sluggish" laborers like Schmidt, and had realized that "although he was the foreman of the shop, the combined knowledge and skill of the workmen under him was certainly ten times as great as his own."[22] It was thus almost impossible to assess the efficiency of the work, let alone make the workers do it faster. The task was therefore to arrogate the worker's skill to the company—the "gathering in on the part of those on the management's side of all knowledge which in the past has been kept in the heads of the workmen"—and thus to replace the employee's control of the job, and hence his power over production, with management's. Schmidt may or may not have been working at the greatest efficiency; but what concerned Taylor most was what he called soldiering, the ability of workers to slow down production in an attempt to preserve jobs.

The essential idea of the ordinary types of management is that each workman has become more skilled in his own trade than it is possible for anyone in the management to be, and that, therefore, the details of how work shall be done must be left to him. The idea, then, of taking one man after another and training him under a competent teacher into new working habits until he continually and habitually works in accordance with scientific laws, which have been developed by someone else, is directly antagonistic to the old idea that each workman can best regulate his own way of doing work.[23]

The problem lay in the old method of "initiative and incentive" ("mentalism" in Skinnerian), where the attitude of management was that of "putting the work up to the workmen." For even if those workmen knew best how to select themselves for the right jobs, and even if they understood how to do them most efficiently, they would never be willing to put "their friends or their brothers" into a position where they would "temporarily be thrown out of a job." Under the new system, all the planning, analysis, and evaluation—all the thinking—would be done by management in separate offices removed from the shop floor, and the results broken down into small "tasks," which would be taught, step by step, to the workers ("programmed instruction" in Skinnerian).[24] The objective was not merely to downgrade the worker's skill—to wrest it away from him—but to give management the mystifying paraphernalia, the watches, slide rules, and time sheets, with which to enhance the legitimacy of control.

To achieve his results, Taylor advocated not only his by now banal time-and-motion studies to analyze and restructure jobs and to control the work, but also "the accurate study of the motives which influence men."

> It is true that the laws which result from experiments of this class, owing to the fact that the very complex organism—the human being—is being experimented with, are subject to a larger number of exceptions than is the case with laws relating to material things. And yet laws of this kind, which apply to a large majority of men, unquestionably exist, and when clearly defined are of great value as a guide in dealing with men.[25]

What was required were "accurate, carefully planned and executed experiments, extending over a term of years." Taylor, of course, already understood the basic principle of operant conditioning, which, in his words, involves not only fixing for each man his daily task, but also paying him a large bonus, or premium, each time that he succeeds in doing his task in the given time.... The remarkable and almost uniformly good results from the *correct* application of the task and bonus must be seen to be appreciated.

What Taylor was advocating was endless measurement and testing, and the development of a behavioral science to control all of the work. The most wonderful part of his system, he would say, was that

under scientific management arbitrary power, arbitrary dictation, ceases; and every single subject, large and small, becomes the question for scientific investigation, for reduction to law. . . . The man at the head of the business under scientific management is governed by rules and laws which have been developed through hundreds of experiments just as much as the workman is. . . .[26]

That was the very essence of the Skinnerian spirit.

Although Taylor was far more interested in the control of sophisticated craft skills, and particularly in his machinists, the "sluggish" Schmidt was the perfect example. The work on Schmidt produced the most obvious results—an increase of nearly 400 percent in production (for which Schmidt got a 60 percent raise)—and Schmidt himself, as described by Taylor, was among the most controllable of people, a man with no factory craft and thus no real means of resisting or sabotaging scientific management. (Similarly, contemporary behavior modification appears to be most successful with young children, mental retardates, and other relatively powerless people.)

In the generation following the publication of *The Principles of Scientific Management,* its practices were rapidly extended to increasingly skilled jobs—the most famous example was Henry Ford's assembly line—and ultimately became, in Peter F. Drucker's words, "the concept that underlies the management of worker and work in American industry."[27] It habituated two generations of Americans to the idea that skill reduction and behavior control are inherent in production technology; that it is normal to be subject to the management and surveillance of an impersonal system (and that such a system is often less capricious than the individual foreman); and that while submission is not necessarily the law of nature, it is, at the very least, the price of the job. The base of control had always been the employer's power to hire and fire, to promote and suspend; but as raw, overt, arbitrary power became more circumscribed by government regulation, union contract, and court decision, and as smoother techniques were introduced, punitive discipline and direct employer-employee coercion tended to become residual elements—ultimate weapons which are generally unnecessary and sometimes ineffective—and the foreman himself became merely an adjunct to a system in which his work was controlled just as precisely as that of his subordinates. Yet Schmidt remained the ideal, the person who was not only controllable but who could easily be seen as the ox, the gorilla, who required control. (The hard facts that Taylor provides make it quite clear that Schmidt was neither stupid nor sluggish. On wages of $1.15 a day "he had succeeded in buying a small plot of ground . . . and was engaged in putting up the walls of a little house for himself in the morning before starting work and at night after leaving." Given that description, it becomes even more apparent that it was necessary for Taylor to see him as stupid, that he had to be made stupid to justify intervention and control.) There was no chance whatever that all workers would ever be seen in such terms; but to the extent that their skills—or their confidence in their skills—could be reduced, and to the extent that the "science" of management could be subject to mystification, absolute control could be attained and defended. "In the past," Taylor wrote, "the man has been first; in the future the system must be first."

# IV

The institution of Taylorism in American industry brought in its wake a great army of efficiency experts, motivation researchers, testers, and psychologists—people who would properly select, place, and train the work force and keep it functioning happily on the job—and, along with them, a growing faith in the powers of applied behavioral science which spread quickly from industry to education and other fields. Through the twenty years after World War I, the individual came increasingly to be regarded as a conglomerate of traits subject to measurement, the test increasingly important as a way of justifying school and job placement, and the methods of industrial selection and control increasingly common in other institutions. "Every manufacturing establishment that turns out a standard product or a series of products," wrote Professor Ellwood P. Cubberley of Stanford, a leading philosopher of public education in the first decades of the twentieth century, "maintains a force of efficiency experts to study methods of procedure and to measure and test the output of its works." A similar system had to be adopted in the schools:

> Our schools are, in a sense, factories in which the raw products [children] are to be shaped and fashioned into products to meet the various demands of life. The specifications for manufacturing come from the demands of twentieth-century civilization, and it is the business of the school to build its pupils according to the specifications laid down. This demands good tools, specialized machinery, continuous measurement of production to see if it is according to specifications, the elimination of waste in manufacture, and a large variety in the output.[28]

In this cult of efficiency, all sorts of techniques were applied to the process of rationalizing selection and control; but it was testing, first used on a large scale by the military in World War I, which became the great link among institutions and the universal embodiment of the common faith. As early as 1919, one management journal asserted that "authorities on psychology are now in agreement that through the use of psychological tests the degree of intelligence of an individual may be accurately determined";[29] and by the mid-thirties such tests had become pervasive. Testing, used in factories, schools, hospitals, and clinics, became the universal rationale for intervention; it could predict and measure not only success on the job, but incipient delinquency, mental illness, and other forms of deviance. It could convert a whole set of more primitive attitudes into psychology; turn the fears generated by immigration, industrialization, and urbanization into numbers; and justify the practices which they generated in the name of medicine and science.

Through the tests, the practitioners created wholly new categories of deficiency, deviance, and disease which had never existed in the real world and which lack even the imprecise meaning of "intelligence": institutional abstractions like "hospital adjustment," anticipatory crimes like "dangerousness" and "delinquency proneness," mythological ailments like "minimal brain dysfunction"—all of them based on concepts of psychological or  social abnormality, which, as one industrial psychologist observed, "are purely impressionistic and cannot be tested from the scientific point of view."[30] Since none of them is real—since they only have meaning in terms of cultural preference and social bias, and in terms of the test that purports to measure them—none can possibly have a "scientific" or medical remedy. Yet the tests are given as if there were remedies; are used, indeed, to justify all sorts of intervention and "preventive treatment," to support clinics and laboratories and whole new professions, and to create wholly new systems of social service and pseudo-medicine. "The American people," said psychologist Karl U. Smith of the University of Wisconsin, have been fooled into believing that a few simple-minded true-false or multiple choice questions can be used to forecast the careers of their children in school and in the university, and to predict their own careers in work because of two influences: fear of the pseudoquantitative mental-medical mumbo jumbo of the psychiatrist and clinical psychologist, and the misleading propaganda of organized psychology in claiming that guesswork and statistical shotgun procedures have medical and scientific significance. . . . Testing is non-scientific double-talk . . . to classify, label, select and pressure people in terms of dubious standards and fuzzy concepts of traits and human abnormality.[31]

Yet Taylorism, for all its consequences in breaking down skills, in making the individual subject to control, and in fostering the ideology of efficiency and technological management, was only part of the great outburst of faith in behavioral science—the search for order—which took place in the first decades of the twentieth century and which continues to shape it today. Taylor's ethnocentric description of Schmidt as a stupid "little Pennsylvania Dutchman" reinforced his image of the man as an outsider fit for manipulation. At the same time, it also reflected the racism and class bias which ran, and to some extent still run, through many of the "sciences" of behavior and which, in turn, were deeply influenced by the genetic findings of Gregor Mendel, the social problems associated with immigration, and the Progressive politics of the years preceding the first World War. If one could breed better plants and cattle through genetic control, why not better human beings? If one could organize the factory as an efficient, technologically controlled environment, why not the office, the public school, or for that matter, the whole society? If one could promote public health through sanitation or the pasteurization of milk, why was it not possible to use similar methods to promote mental health and "social hygiene"? In America, the age of Taylor was also the age of Freud; of Luther Burbank; of the eugenics of Francis Galton; of the theories of Cesare Lombroso, the

Italian criminologist who believed all born criminals could be identified by certain physical characteristics; of "race betterment"; and of belief in a science of behavior that could be as rigorous and positive as anything in physics or chemistry.[32]

There was no single strategy: the race betterment people themselves were divided between those advocating sterilization or "segregation" of people they regarded as genetically unfit (generally estimated to be about 10 percent of the population) and those who believed the deviant could be treated or reformed, between genetic determinists and Progressive idealists. Yet there was a consistent spirit: agreement that the disproportionate numbers of foreign-born inmates in insane asylums indicated serious problems in immigration screening; a general fear of impending race "degeneration" through disease, "mongrelization," or other poor eugenic practices; a widespread belief that immorality, crime, low intelligence, and mental disease were often related—that "feeble-minded" girls, for instance, were all potential prostitutes—and an overarching faith that through science the problems had been, or could be, properly identified and remedied.[33]

From their beginnings, the movements overlapped. Scientific management, intelligence testing, applied psychology, mental hygiene, and eugenics became fashionable together and were often espoused by the same people. The American pioneers of testing—Henry H. Goddard, Lewis M. Terman, and Edward L. Thorndike—were all involved in the eugenics movement of the twenties and thirties, were all fearful that the descendants of what they regarded as inferior genetic stock—particularly Southern and Eastern Europeans—would take over the country, and were all believers in some version of Goddard's idea that the 4 million Americans of "superior intelligence" had to control the country and keep "the masses" from trying to "take matters into their own hands." "One sure service (about the only one) which the vicious and inferior can perform," said Thorndike in 1939, "is to prevent their genes from survival."[34] To help the cause,

Terman became a leading member of the California Human Betterment Foundation, which was credited with 6,200 eugenic sterilizations in the 1920s. And as late as 1966, in the midst of the Civil Rights movement, Henry E. Garrett, former president of the American Psychological Association and professor at Columbia, argued that "you can no more mix the two races and maintain standards of White civilization than you can add 80 (the average IQ of Negroes) and 100 (the average IQ of Whites), divide the two and get 100. . . . It is that 10 percent differential that spells the difference between a spire and a mud hut . . . between a cultured society and savagery." The tests proved that there were racial and ethnic differences in ability and intelligence (and therefore in "character"), and made scientific what had always been known about deviance. In industry it was the Schmidts, the Wobblies, the Bolsheviks, and the labor agitators; outside it was "the feeble-minded, insane, criminalistic (including the delinquent and wayward), epileptic, inebriate, diseased, blind, deaf, deformed and dependent (including orphans, ne'er-do-wells, the homeless, tramps and paupers)." In *Practical Psychology for Business Executives* (1922), Goddard told managers that "the intelligent group must do the planning and organizing for the mass. . . . Our whole attitude toward the lower grades of intelligence . . . must be based upon an intelligent understanding of the mental capacity of each individual."[35] The tests proved why it was necessary to control or reshape them, sterilize or deport them.

# V

Much of it was borrowed—testing from Paris, psychodynamics from Vienna, eugenics from London, criminology from Rome—and much of it logically could only lead to the conclusion that no intervention other than exclusion, segregation, or sterilization would make any real difference. What could be done with the "born criminal" who, in Lombroso's view, was probably an atavistic throwback to a more primitive human type; or with the lunatic child of a family of mental defectives; or with an individual who, according to the tests of science, was simply endowed with low intelligence? Testers like Goddard and Terman were prepared to follow the logic into eugenics; and by the end of the twenties, Congress, in passing restrictive immigration laws, and nearly half the states, in passing sterilization laws, had followed it too. Yet from the very beginning, America began to twist the logic, to look for ways to get around it, and to press upon the science of behavior the traditional faith in the transforming power of the New Jerusalem. If America could turn poverty into affluence, ignorance into enlightenment, and immigrants into citizens, why could it not convert deviance into conformity and illness into health? If the parent was hopeless, perhaps the child could be saved; and if it was too late for hardened criminals, there was still time to intervene with delinquents, incorrigibles, and truants. Since there were no officially recognized social classes, and since national theology professed unlimited opportunity for every person no matter how low his station, the formal mandate for reform and intervention was theoretically unlimited. Science and medicine were showing the way; they might even enable America to repeal the laws of genetics. "There is a hopeful future dawning for all classes of delinquents, degenerates and deficients, however handicapped by heredity, environment, accident or disease," said Dr. Stephen Smith, the president of the First National Conference on Race Betterment:

> The science of biology and physiology, which reveals to medical art the minute structure and function of the ultimate elements of the vital organs and thus makes it exact in practice to the great saving of human life, is penetrating further and further into the hitherto mysterious mass of apparently homogenous matter, the brain, and astonishing the world with its wonderful revelations. Here it has found the very

springs of human existence—the centers of consciousness, thought, action—the home of the soul, the ego, the man.

In these discoveries we find the basic principles of race betterment . . . and all our efforts to improve the individual and through him the race must center in the normal development and physiological action of the ultimate elements of the brain, the organ of the mind. . . . The great problem . . . is the betterment of all defectives as we find them in every grade of society. Considering the remarkable sensitiveness of the nerve cells of the brain to impressions born within and without the body, it is evident that the measures which may be employed to rouse the cells to activity and restore their normal functioning capacity are innumerable, and their effectiveness will depend upon the intelligence, patience and perseverance of the responsible caretaker.[36]

It was possible to have it both ways; if the test or the diagnosis could be used, on the one hand, to demonstrate the futility of therapy, education, or reform, it could—and would—be used on the other to show that even apparently hopeless cases, "however handicapped by heredity, environment, accident or disease," simply required earlier intervention and more of it. America had never acknowledged tragedy, frailty, or misery as immutable human conditions; there were only "problems," and problems were subject to correction. It was hardly surprising, therefore, that in a peculiarly domesticated form, Freud took in America as he did nowhere else; or that, as a historian of psychiatry wrote a generation ago, "this country is second to none in the application of psychopathological principles to medical and social problems."[37] Civilization and its discontents were ignored, but the psychoanalytic and therapeutic messages were heard. Psychoanalysis was know thyself, and know thyself was the first step to self-improvement. By the mid-thirties, every social worker in America had had some psychiatric training (most of it Freudian), and almost every major city had its child-guidance clinics to bridge "the gap," as two of its advocates said in 1934, "between a period when delinquency, dependency, and mental disease were attacked single handed by separate professional groups, and a future in which mental health may be as well guarded at danger points by an integrated social program as physical health begins to be."[38]

With the exception of scientific management in industry, the movements that grew out of the Progressive Era were richer in hope and ideology than they were in technique. There was sterilization, as specified in the Indiana law, of "confirmed criminals, idiots, imbeciles and rapists"; there was fever treatment for paresis, the syphilis-caused "general paralysis of the insane"; and by the late thirties, the beginnings of electroshock and lobotomy; but for the most part, "treatment," generally limited to schools, prisons, and mental hospitals, relied largely on physical restraint, counseling, and punishment. Yet the faith in effective remedies was sustained—probably had to be sustained in the absence of the formal class structures and the historic sense of limits and tragedy which dampened expectations in other societies and which helped keep people in their place. Tests in factories, schools, and clinics, and the military screening of recruits in two world wars, "proved" not only that there was a science of behavior that could define, diagnose, and explain social and mental problems, but also that a large proportion of Americans were mentally sick, intellectually feeble, and socially inadequate, and therefore required attention. Early in the twenties, the testers, sifting through the scores of recruits from World War I came to the logically dubious conclusion that, as one writer said, "the average mental age of Americans is only about fourteen"; and after the end of World War II, William C. Menninger, who had been the army's chief psychiatrist, reported the equally startling finding that of some 15 million men examined for induction, 1,875,000 were unfit for neuropsychiatric reasons.[39]

The process was—and is—tautological: the faith in effective remedies justifies the diagnosis and the test; the test justifies the faith and, at the same time, obviates some of the more invidious labels of race, class, and culture. (The child is segregated in school not because of his race but because of his IQ score; the nuisance on the street is locked up not because he looks peculiar and talks to Jesus but because he is a schizophrenic who needs treatment.) But since there are no effective educational or medical remedies, there is only incarceration, segregation, maintenance, and control (which are often promoted as therapy but which, in practice, are not so different from the remedies proposed by the eugenicists). The test, which had been promoted as a diagnostic instrument, thus became not a preliminary to treatment but an instrument of mystification which teaches the losers that they are disqualified or incarcerated on "objective" criteria and which reinforces the authority of the tester as the possessor of special knowledge and powers. The test is given as if there were a remedy and then used to justify categories of exclusion where there is none. In industry, the techniques of behavior control are theoretically limited by the productive and managerial objectives of the enterprise. In the realm of social service, where the individual is supposed to be the beneficiary, there are no theoretical limits, few scientific tests of success, and often not the vaguest way of validating the means employed; the only limits are budgetary and legal.

The new technologies, and particularly data processing and drugs, mitigate those limits. While it may be legally difficult to lock someone up indefinitely against his will and expensive to submit him to an extensive course of psychotherapy, drugs are relatively cheap and require no formal institutionalization. There are still no cures, but the ideology is now liberated from many of its economic and legal constraints; it thus becomes easy to join the ideals of "service" and "therapy"—the arrogant claim that it's all for the client's own good—to the expansionist ambitions of biocratic institutions and practitioners, and easy to carry testing, screening, and intervention into areas where it could never have existed before. In 1970, Leopold Bellak, a New York psychiatrist, wrote:

> Income taxes were once considered basic violations of personal freedom, and fluoridation of water was held to be a subversive plot. If a Clean Meat Bill and a Truth in Lending Act were finally enacted, why should a "Sound Mind Bill" [requiring universal screening and treatment for mental illness] be far behind?[40]

In industry, where the beneficiary is the manager and the criterion is profit, the process is more or less finite. In social service, where the beneficiary is supposed to be the individual or a "society" which has no bottom line, it is unlimited.

In the behaviorist view, the whole culture is a factory, a madhouse, and a prison. If the object of scientific management was to divest the worker of his craft, to de-skill him, and thereby make him controllable on the job, the effect, if not the object, of the broader social applications of behavioral science has been to create and justify new categories of disability and dependence that make the individual subject to manipulation in the world outside. Both teach the client or the worker that his manipulators have special knowledge to which he has no access; that, indeed, the nature of that knowledge is so complex or esoteric that he will never be able to possess it himself; and both have become part of a relentless economic and social process which creates ever more and ever larger classes of people who are formally certified for "service" and intervention: welfare cases and family-service cases, child abusers and "potential" abusers, including those who fail to give their children "adequate clothing and education"; drug addicts and potential drug addicts; martini-drinking executives and post-menopausal housewives; "predelinquents" and pre-orgasmic women; the "developmentally disabled" and the "learning disabled"; residents of nursing homes and public housing; children of divorce and relatives of the recently deceased; the violence prone and the potentially dangerous; infants "at risk" and carriers of sickle-cell trait; the hyperactive and the sexually dysfunctional; the anxious and the depressed; the old and the young; the poor and the black. Some of those categories are merely those of age or sex or economic status; some are pseudoscientific labels of mystification for annoying behavior (e. g., "hyperactivity" or "social maladjustment"), and some, despite their lack of validation or even of meaning, are represented as "indicators" or predictors of future deviance justifying preventive intervention. There are studies which "prove" that certain abnormal brain-wave patterns are predictive of violence; that hyperactive children become criminals; that males with an extra Y chromosome become psychopathic killers; that depressed and anxious parents become child abusers.[41] The list is enormous, and the varieties almost endless. Yet many of those who are on it share a place beyond the discipline and control of the automated economic system, beyond the traditional machinery of the criminal justice system, and beyond the ordinary ministrations of organic medicine. More generally they are members of a vast and still growing number of economically superfluous or socially nonconformist or aesthetically offensive people who, in Jacques Ellul's "completely technicized world . . . will have no place at all."[42] Every year, thousands more are defined into those categories; there are no longer automatic exemptions for the middle class.

In his elegant critique of Skinner's "science," Noam Chomsky argued persuasively that beyond common sense, there is no "science of behavior," that Skinner "confuses science with terminology."

> The system of Skinnerian translation is quite readily available to anyone and can indeed be employed with no knowledge of the theory of operant conditioning and its results, and with no information, beyond normal observation, of the circumstances in which behavior takes place or the nature of the behavior itself.[43]

That argument can be extended to a great many of the tests, screens, and "therapies" now being used on the growing list of people officially certified for "service" and intervention. Nearly all fail to cure, or in many cases even to define, the problem with which they are ostensibly concerned: alcoholism, delinquency, depression, minimal brain dysfunction, impulsivity, child abuse, social maladjustment, sociopathy, and scores of other recently medicalized forms of social deviance. Yet while, as Chomsky said, "there exists no behavioral science incorporating nontrivial, empirically supported propositions that apply to human affairs or support behavioral technology," there are technologies—chemical, surgical, electronic; and while there are few cures, there is growing maintenance and control in the systems which offer or impose them.[44] The technologies enable these systems to convert historically crude techniques into professionally smooth, specific, and "humane" methods—to replace incarceration with drug maintenance, corporal punishment with "behavior mod," and the rhetoric of crime and morals with the language of medicine—making acceptable in a new form what would have been regarded as cruel or intolerable in the old, and making it possible to extend intervention to millions of people who had never been "served" before. It has become commonplace for police or prosecutors to take cases which lack evidence for criminal conviction and deliver them over to mental-health authorities for "emergency intervention" or civil commitment, and in turn for mental-health authorities confronted (at least in some states) with the increasing difficulty of committing patients to enroll them in outpatient therapy consisting largely, if not entirely, of powerful and dangerous tranquilizers. The man who threatens his wife with a knife or loudly prophesies the second coming in a fashionable shopping area is more likely to end up on Thorazine than in jail, a change which may or may not be desirable but which nonetheless has enormous implications not only for his health but for his perception of authority and responsibility.

In the Skinnerian ideal, the initial reinforcers of operant conditioning—the gold stars, for example, which are given to children as token rewards for completing an exercise—are supposed eventually to be faded out and replaced by the intrinsic rewards of the work or the good behavior. "The policeman," said Skinner, "is there always and the paymaster is there always. They are constantly intervening in people's lives; they remain there. The control exercised by a teacher or a therapist is only temporary."[45] Yet it has been the policeman, the paymaster, and their surrogates and alter egos—the people who are there always—who have used the new technologies the most extensively.

Behavior control, in all its forms, is the veil of power. It rarely depends on its specific ability to deliver what it promises its subjects, and certainly not on its capacity to solve officially certified "social problems" (which, in any case, are usually defined in such a way as to ensure durability and justify the growth industries of intervention). It depends, rather, on pre-existing power; its function is to mystify and legitimize; its effect is sedation. In its contemporary forms it combines the empiricism of modern technology with updated versions of an ancient demonology—drugs to exorcize spirits, polygraphs as lie detectors, medical labels as explanations of deviance, tests and questionnaires as inquisitors, credit as loyal devotion to faith. It makes it increasingly difficult to determine who is doing what to whom, to learn who the enemy is, or, indeed, to know if there really is an "enemy." Ideology obviates conspiracy and technology conceals it. "When I was a kid," said an old AFL-CIO official in San Francisco, "my father told me I would have only one enemy, and that was my employer." But increasingly the employer has become an automated technological system and not a boss; a banker; a computer and a credit card; the police and government; a set of data banks, each of them operating by an incomprehensible inner logic that appears as immutable and "natural" as nature itself. The more "natural" it becomes, the more difficult it is to resist.

# TWO

# The Madness Network

# I

The centerpiece—as ideal, as policy, as propaganda—is "mental health." In less than a generation, what had been a hopeful vision seeking a benefactor, a home, and a method became an institution; and what had been a marginal movement became a $15-billion industry employing a half million people and touching every corner of American life. Virtually every little city now has its psychiatrists, its clinical psychologists, its school psychologists, its psychiatric social workers, its mental-health association; and in almost every crossroads village there are people with their bottles of tranquilizers. Altogether some 1,100 "free-standing" psychiatric outpatient clinics; 300 general hospitals with psychiatric outpatient services; 80 veterans hospitals with psychiatric outpatient clinics; 500 federally funded community mental-health centers; tens of thousands of nursing homes, board and care facilities, halfway houses, behavior clinics, child-guidance clinics, child-abuse, alcohol, and suicide prevention clinics; and perhaps most important, the great army of internists, pediatricians, psychiatrists, gynecologists, and general practitioners dispensing those drugs and writing those prescriptions. What had been a relatively small, obscure enterprise confined, on the one hand, to closed institutions, and on the other, to the psychoanalytically based practice of a small number of psychiatrists serving a small number of affluent clients has turned into an enormous establishment treating—depending on the definition of "treatment"—anywhere from 7 to 40 million people a year, and diagnosing millions of others. In 1977 there were more mental-health workers in America than there were policemen.[1]

The benefactor is government; the method is drugs, most of them developed and introduced in the past twenty-five years: minor tranquilizers like Librium and Valium; major tranquilizers like Thorazine, Stelazine, and Mellaril; antidepressants like Elavil and Tofranil; and antimanics like lithium carbonate, the wonder drug of current fashion. According to the conventional professional wisdom, those drugs have revolutionized psychiatry. They have made it possible to treat more people outside institutions, to reduce the length of hospitalization and the populations of mental hospitals, to prevent mental illness, and to offer hope to those sufferers for whom, as one psychiatrist said, "surcease by death offered the only lasting respite" in the past.[2] But that judgment is both too extravagant and too modest—extravagant in suggesting that the drugs cure mental illness and that the number of people in institutions is being reduced; modest in what it implies about the social and political effects of those drugs, about their consequences in medicalizing complaints and forms of deviance which had never been regarded as mental illness before, and about their impact in fostering the idea that at least one American in five can profit from psychiatric attention and the medication which usually accompanies it. Most important, perhaps, they have transformed the "lesson" of therapy from one that teaches responsibility—"you do what you want to do"—to one that teaches the individual that he is the unresponsible victim of his neurons and his chemistry.

In the past generation those drugs—now used by some 40 million people in this country—have become, for better or worse, the most powerful and extensive technology of mood and behavior control ever employed in a democratic society.

Most of them were unknown until the early fifties (Thorazine was introduced in 1954, Miltown in 1955), but by 1975 American physicians were writing 240 million pharmacy prescriptions annually for psychotropic medication for people who were not hospitalized—roughly one for every man, woman, and child in the country—enough pills all told to sustain a $1.5-billion industry and to keep every American fully medicated for a month.[3] The arsenal includes:

1. the "major tranquilizers," particularly the class of drugs known as the phenothiazines—Thorazine (chlorpromazine), Stelazine (trifluoperazine), Mellaril (thioridazine), Serentil (mesoridazine), Compazine (prochlorperazine), Trilafon (perphenazine), and Prolixin and Permitil (fluphenazine)—but also including derivatives of other chemical compounds, such as Haldol (haloperidol). These drugs, sometimes called antipsychotics, are among the most powerful central nervous system preparations ever developed. In 1975, they were prescribed 35 million times to people outside of hospitals, and enough pills were sold to keep nearly 2 million persons medicated full-time.

2. the antidepressants—Elavil (amitriptyline), Tofranil (imipramine), and Sinequan (doxepin)—which are given to "regressed, melancholic, apathetic, lethargic and depressed" individuals; and the "psychostimulants," sometimes listed under the antidepressants, which include the amphetamines and amphetamine-type preparations like Ritalin (methylphenidate) and Cylert (magnesium pemoline). In 1975, they were prescribed 20 million times.

3. the sedatives and hypnotics, including barbiturates. In 1975, they were prescribed 45 million times: 23 million prescriptions were filled for nonbarbiturate sedatives; 22 million for barbiturates.

4. the minor tranquilizers—sometimes called antianxiety agents—including Valium (diazepam), Librium (chlordiazepoxide), and Miltown and Equanil (meprobamate). In 1975, they were prescribed roughly 100 million times to an

estimated 30 million people; and Valium, with sales estimated at nearly $500 million, was far and away the most widely used drug in the country.

In addition to the major categories, the pharmacopeia includes dozens of combination drugs, particularly combinations of antipsychotics and antidepressants, as well as anticonvulsants, antimanics, and anti-parkinson drugs, which are used in attempts, often futile and dangerous, to control the common and frequently severe side effects of the major tranquilizers. Tardive dyskinesia, a wholly new and often irreversible central nervous system disease characterized by persistent involuntary movements, has been produced by the antipsychotics.

There is no agreement on precisely what any of these drugs do, how they act, how much should be prescribed, or for what, or to whom, or on their long-term effects, or, indeed, on how they should be described and classified. What is certain is that they are being prescribed to more and more people in increasingly large doses for increasingly vague ailments whose only common denominator is some problem in mood or behavior. Equally important, the typical dispenser of those drugs is no longer the Park Avenue psychiatrist (if, indeed, he ever was) but a disproportionate number of internists and gynecologists and general practitioners (who prescribe more psychotropics to each of their "emotional" cases than do psychiatrists) as well as those thousands of people who work for state and local government agencies, for community mental-health centers, "crisis clinics," nursing homes, public hospital outpatient clinics, and other institutions created and supported with public funds. The clients represent a disproportionately high number of the lower middle class, the poor, the near-poor, the old, and the black —people who pay for those drugs through Medicaid or Medicare and who sometimes have little choice about taking them, even if they don't accept the physician's judgment about what is good for them.[4]

In the advertisements that lace the medical and psychiatric journals, the typical patient is generally pictured as a distraught, hysterical woman, the doctor as a man; but in recent years, one manufacturer has conjured up a new class of deviant, whose typical representative, as pictured in a two-page advertisement in the *Archives of General Psychiatry* (May 1974), is a swarthy, dark-skinned, thick-lipped, leather-jacketed young man, fist clenched, who appears under the phrase "Assaultive and Belligerent?" "Cooperation," reads the message on the facing page, "often begins with Haldol (haloperidol). . . . Acts promptly to control aggressive, assaultive behavior." The basic message and the practices, however, are always the same no matter how the culprit is represented: the nuisances, the deviants, the nonconforming, and the nonfunctioning are almost surely victims of an ailment, a "personality disorder," a chemical imbalance, which makes it possible—indeed, makes it necessary—for someone else to manage them with psychotherapy and drugs. In those cases where there is doubt about the ailment, as there usually is, the effects of the drug itself may help define it: if the drug works, the problem must be the ailment for which the drug was indicated; if it doesn't, try something else, or try several drugs at once, or increase the dosage until the patient is stupefied. In almost every instance, the drug is not a technology controlled by the client but a management device that will be helpful to relatives, the doctor, the institution, the community, and society. Unlike the common commercial for over-the-counter drugs promoting self-medication, the "ethical" (prescription) psychotropics are almost always sold and used as means to "treat" someone else.

# II

It is a highly complicated story. To understand it at all, one has to forget the clichés about the dizzy housewife swallowing pills to deal with her anxieties and her boredom. There

are, of course, many such people: of the 61 million Valium
prescriptions written in 1975, two-thirds were for women
(although even among them, a disproportionate number
were working-class people).[5] But Valium, despite its prevalence, is a relatively unimportant drug in the arsenal, and the
people who take it are a relatively small part of an intricate
pattern involving organized psychiatry; the drug companies;
state and local agencies; the mental-health movement; the
medical schools; and a federal government which actively
fosters "mental health" through extensive subsidies and
propaganda and which, more than any other element, has
been responsible for the phenomenal growth of the psychiatric establishment. Just before World War II, there were
barely 3,000 psychiatrists in America; in 1950, largely as a
result of their military medical training and War Department policy fostering psychiatric intervention, there were
7,500; in 1976 there were roughly 30,000, of whom nearly all
were trained with the support of NIMH grants earmarked
for that purpose.[6] The federal government alone supports
twice as many psychiatrists today as there were in the entire
country on the eve of World War II. In the same period,
there was corresponding growth in related mental-health
professions—psychologists, technicians, nurses, orderlies,
social workers—many of them also inducted into the system
and trained with federal money—and along with them, a
proliferation of community mental-health centers, clinics,
and other county, state, and federally funded establishments.

Although those institutions (along with the drugs) are
frequently credited with the reduction of the institutionalized population, the government's data suggest something
quite different. In 1955, there were some 550,000 resident
patients in mental hospitals; twenty years later, that number
had declined to under 300,000. In the same period, however,
vast increases in the resident population of nursing homes
and halfway houses more than compensated for the decline
—many people were simply reclassified from mentally ill to
old and dumped in another institution—and the number of

psychiatric "treatment episodes" in hospitals, clinics, and mental-health centers (each episode is defined as one admission to a course of treatment) tripled from 1.6 million to more than 5.4 million, a figure which, in the estimate of NIMH statisticians, translates to 4.5 million individuals a year (the rest are repeaters).[7] In addition, millions of others were being diagnosed and treated outside the formal institutions of mental health, particularly in schools, family-service agencies, and nonpsychiatric clinics and hospitals. Those people tend to fall into the lower ranges of the social and economic spectrum (the affluent, currently perhaps 1.5 million people a year, continue to be served by private psychiatrists whose services are not counted in these figures), and increasingly they are the ones who are getting the heavy drugs. Even if one counts office visits to private psychiatrists, more than half the outpatient treatment in America, and nearly 90 percent of the inpatient treatment, is delivered by public clinics and hospitals.[8]

The mental-health movement might have remained a relatively small phenomenon without a series of fortuitous developments: the rediscovery of the brutality of mental hospitals by conscientious objectors, many of them Quakers, who had been assigned there in lieu of military service in World War II; the well-publicized data on the number of men rejected or discharged from military service for neuropsychiatric reasons; the apparent success of "early intensive treatment" of psychotics in the military; and in the fifties, the introduction of the new psychotropic drugs. The war, according to a historian sympathetic to the mental-health movement, revealed the severe shortage of adequately trained personnel, "lack of sound knowledge on the etiology of mental illness, lack of adequate methods for dealing with large numbers of psychiatric cases, and lack . . . of understanding of the role of psychiatry in the prevention and treatment of mental illness"; but it also demonstrated that individual motivation and high group morale were important prophylactics against psychiatric casualties, that combat troops could be best treated for emotional problems close to the scene of action, that group psychotherapy and the convalescent hospital were important treatment modalities. Army experience had, in addition, an unexpectedly high recovery rate for psychotic patients. . . . Early intensive treatment in the Army resulted in the discharge of seven of every ten patients admitted to hospital. The war had also proven the great value of the ancillary disciplines in the treatment of mental illness—psychologists, psychiatric nurses and social workers.[9]

It later turned out that that high recovery rate was due primarily to the fact that even by the hazy definition of what constitutes a psychotic, most of those so labeled by the military psychiatrists were, at worst, "short-term psychotics," men who broke down under the stress of combat and who automatically "recovered" in another environment, and that the most effective "treatment" was no treatment at all: that if a man was treated as "ill" and shipped to a psychiatric hospital, he was more likely to stay "ill" than if he were merely sent to the rear for rest and recuperation. Moreover, the rejection figures themselves were open to question; other armies with different standards and lower rejection rates were no more troubled by psychotic soldiers than the American forces. But what General Menninger called "the lessons from military psychiatry for civilian psychiatry" were carefully taught. "If these young men were representative of the Nation," asked Robert H. Felix, who headed the Division of Mental Hygiene at the end of war and who became the first director of NIMH, "what would be the absolute figures for the mental and nervous impairments of the entire population?"

At least one study [Felix recalled later] projected the figure of one American in ten who needed psychiatric help of some kind; treatment facilities were in woefully short supply, state hospitals were overcrowded and understaffed; private treatment was long and expensive and beyond the reach of most Americans; and our therapeutic armamentarium was limited.[10]

In 1946 Felix, supported by testimony from the chief psychiatrists of the army and navy and by General Lewis Hershey, director of the Selective Service System, sold Congress the bill which became the National Mental Health Act and which created NIMH. The act, which provided fellowships and grants-in-aid for psychiatric training, aid to the states in establishing clinics and treatment centers, and funds for research into the causes, diagnosis, and treatment of neuropsychiatric disorders, made the federal government the country's most important sponsor of mental-health research and training, and its most important promoter of the idea of mental health. A year before the act was passed, Vannevar Bush, director of the Office of Scientific Research and Development, had reported to President Franklin D. Roosevelt that "approximately 7 million persons in the United States [are] mentally ill, and their care costs the public over $175,-000,000 a year." By the mid-sixties, the budget of NIMH alone was almost double that.[11]

# III

The crowning ornament of the federal program is the Community Mental Health Centers Act. Passed in the fall of 1963, shortly before the assassination of John F. Kennedy, and administered by NIMH, it was (and is) promoted as not only creating the great alternative to the inhumane conditions of hospitalization but as providing the basis of preventive care at the community level. People could be treated in their communities, they could often live at home, and they would no longer have to be locked up in the notorious back wards of state institutions. Such a policy was obviously at-

tractive not only to the patients but to state legislatures
confronted with the rapidly increasing costs of maintaining
those institutions. Ultimately, in the expectations of the plan-
ners at NIMH, there were to be 1,000 or 1,500 or 1,800
federally supported Community Mental Health Centers
(CMHC's) around the country, each providing diagnostic
and referral services, inpatient and outpatient therapy, counseling for everything from family fights to "acute psychotic
breakdowns," and "consultation and education" for other
agencies and for the community in general. "I propose,"
Kennedy said,

> a national mental-health program to assist in the inaugura-
> tion of a wholly new emphasis and approach to care for the
> mentally ill. This approach relies primarily upon the new
> knowledge and new drugs acquired and developed in recent
> years which make it possible for most of the mentally ill to
> be successfully and quickly treated.[12]

The key to the program was drugs, its objective was prevention, and its hope was to reach those 20 or 30 or 40 million
people who needed help. The federal government was going
to treat everyone.

No one, of course, was (or is) clear about what prevention
was, how it was supposed to work, or precisely what was to
be prevented. In the vision of its most ardent professional
advocates, it included the detection of mental illness among
ordinary people who hadn't the faintest suspicion that they
were suffering from anything other than "the normal upsets
of life crises" and who simply appeared in a center for advice
about a marital problem, "career adjustment problems," or
any number of other routine matters. In *Principles of Preventive Psychiatry,* Dr. Gerald Caplan of Harvard, one of the
great advocates of early intervention and a leading enthusiast
for the federal program, argued that

> clients do not initially have to define themselves, or be defined
> by others, as being potentially mentally disordered. Not only
> is this an effective face-saving maneuver for those clients who

are diagnosed as cases of mental disorder, but it brings under psychiatric surveillance a large group of other people suffering from difficulties in adjustment which, although not currently diagnosable as psychiatric abnormalities, may be transitional states which are the earliest stages of mental disorder.[13]

Caplan's book, which included a foreword by NIMH director Robert H. Felix lauding it not only as "a primer for the community mental-health worker" but as "a Bible," was written to coincide with the beginning of the CMHC program. But Caplan was hardly alone in his enthusiasm. There was Leopold Bellak, professor of psychiatry at New York University, who likened mental health to public health in its need for required legislation "to protect the community against emotional contamination." There was Harold Visotsky, commissioner of mental health for the state of Illinois, who believed that "a benignly aggressive approach should be made to reach out and seek these people rather than sit and wait for them" to come in. And there was Bertram S. Brown, then director of NIMH, who estimated in congressional testimony that as many as 40 million Americans—one of five—needed psychiatric care.[14]

Beyond the estimates there was an even grander vision: "community mental health" would not merely treat people but whole communities; it would, if possible, take on "the mayors and the people concerned about the cities . . . as clients"; it would treat the society itself and not merely its individual citizens. "We must remember," said the president of the American Psychiatric Association in 1963, "that the support we have received is based on an expectation that sooner or later we will be able to find answers to many social problems. . . . We are being handed the opportunity and we cannot afford to hand it to others or to put it down."[15]

In practice, however, there was never any clarity on what the centers were supposed to do, how they were to be controlled, or what model of service they were supposed to follow. From the beginning, there had been a struggle between those who regarded the centers as a wholly new category of social intervention dealing with community and environmental problems and those who saw them merely as another set of clinics run by psychiatrists. In some instances, the "center" has become merely a device whereby the private hospital can secure federal aid for the construction of new facilities; in others, it is a way to balance a budget; and in still others, the center is largely a referral service that sends clients to the private psychiatrists and psychologists who participate in its program. There have been battles between psychiatrists and other mental-health workers, between the professionals and the community, and between CMHC's and county authorities operating other public psychiatric clinics. Nonetheless, the program itself has given mental health a status it never had before: it created institutions which, while they deliver the same kinds of therapy as other clinics, are often more modern, brighter, and cleaner; free from the original sin associated with the benighted state asylums; less crowded and bureaucratized than other local clinics; and more heavily engaged, under their mandate of "consultation and education," in carrying the message of mental health to schools, PTA's, service clubs, the police, women's clubs, and any other organization willing to listen. The CMHC has made mental health respectable.

By 1969, three years after the first federally funded centers opened their doors, NIMH was ready to celebrate. "This program," said NIMH Director Stanley Yolles in an appearance before a congressional committee, "has really gone across with the people of the United States. Largely because of the impetus of community mental-health centers we have seen a startling reduction of patients in mental hospitals in the United States." It was an argument which would become the staple of NIMH policy and which would be followed in press releases, pamphlets, and other pronouncements from that time on. "We had 557,000 in mental hospitals in 1957," said NIMH Director Bertram S. Brown in 1972. "We are down to 308,000 in 1971. That is the kind of progress you can see." By the mid-seventies, with 500 federally funded centers serving more than 1 million people, some NIMH officials were willing to recognize that the picture wasn't quite as simple as they had claimed—that some other elements might be partly responsible for the declining population of mental hospitals—but they still adhered to the position that, as one of them said in 1976, "we're breaking the back of the asylum system."[16]

On closer inspection, however, the biocrats at NIMH had it backwards. The resident population of mental hospitals had been declining for almost a decade before the federal program got under way—partly as a consequence of economic pressure, partly because new state laws were making it somewhat harder to commit people indiscriminately, and partly (if not largely) because the new drugs introduced in the fifties—the "chemical straitjackets"—made it possible to control patients outside closed institutions. It was the drugs, and particularly the phenothiazine-type tranquilizers and the antidepressants, which made the CMHC program feasible, and it was the drugs which gave it its most powerful technology.

The defenders of those drugs like to argue that whatever its other effects, medication improved the lives of those who had heretofore been locked up in those back wards and who were sometimes tied to their beds to keep them from injuring themselves or hurting others (practices which, according to many studies, were related more directly to the fear of the keepers than to the behavior of their clients). What the druggers do not emphasize is that by the mid-seventies, enough phenothiazines and antidepressants were being prescribed outside hospitals to keep some 3 or 4 million people medicated full-time—roughly ten times the number who, according to the druggers' own arguments, are so crazy that they would have to be locked up in hospitals if there were no drugs. In addition, many more are given drugs in those clinics which are not counted in the prescription totals.[17]

NIMH, which collects and publishes great quantities of

statistics, claims to have no data on the percentage of those 5.4 million psychiatric treatment episodes that involve drugs —does not even have them for the million or so outpatients who are served by the 500 CMHC's for which it provides funding. One can learn that in 1971 (the latest year for which such figures are available), the average number of episodes of outpatient care in each CMHC was 2,230, and that each of them included an average of 4.4 "individual," 0.6 "group," and 0.5 "family" treatment sessions. One can learn the age, sex, race, and diagnosis of each patient, the number of nurses and psychiatrists and social workers who "care" for them—everything, indeed, except how many are drugged, how much they are drugged, and with what they are drugged. Since NIMH is constantly trying to "evaluate" those programs, and since the only psychiatric technology for which any substantial statistical validation has been claimed is medication, one would have to assume that the omission is a consequence of policy, not negligence. NIMH officials assert that the information is unimportant, that someone is already collecting it, that there are plans to collect it, and that in any case (as one of them said), "the CMHC's have such low psychiatric staffing that there aren't enough psychiatrists to give a lot of drugs."

There are indications, however, that the percentage of outpatients in public clinics receiving drugs is extremely high. At the Westside Community Mental Health Center in San Francisco, a coalition of clinics and other facilities considered among the most progressive and enlightened in the country, more than half the outpatients get drugs; across San Francisco Bay, in Richmond, an anti-drug psychiatrist who was appointed to head the local mental-health clinic in 1977 discovered that more than 80 percent of his patients were on drugs; in a public "crisis clinic" operated by Alameda County in Oakland, more than 60 percent get drugs, and some get nothing but drugs; in a Baltimore clinic, half the patients diagnosed as nonpsychotic who come in for more than three visits get drugs (among those diagnosed as psychotic, nearly all get drugs); and in a coalition of some twenty "independently operated" clinics associated with the Los Angeles county mental-health system, enough money is budgeted for medication to dispense a bottle of pills to almost every client each time he or she visits the clinic.[18] Blacks are drugged more often and with more powerful drugs than whites; the poor, more often than the middle class. In a study in Detroit, a group of researchers concluded that

> the psychotherapeutic patients [those who were not drugged] were significantly higher in social class than the [62 percent who were] drug patients. . . . The patients who received individual psychotherapy are judged as having higher communication and ego strength, suitability for treatment, physical attractiveness and more similarity to the therapist than the patients who receive drug therapy.[19]

Studies conducted in clinics in California came to similar conclusions. "More than half of all the clients at the Clinic," said one, "receive some form of medication. White men and women are the least likely to get drug therapy and black men and women the most likely." Typically, from case reports:

> Ms. J. is a 39-year-old Black woman, whose diagnosis was deferred. The worker said she gave her a month's supply of phenothiazines because "she does seem to need it." The patient is described as "cheerful, looking well and feeling fine but has pressured speech and trembling knees."

> Mr. G. is a 32-year-old Black man diagnosed as drug dependent. He came in because of difficulty sleeping and feeling things closing in. He has a history of using a wide variety of drugs. The worker wrote, "His parents [who came in with him] are as vague as patient in . . . describing reason for such extensive drug use and such a purposeless life. Patient explains very little about himself spontaneously, tries to answer questions but seems not to have the vocabulary to do so very thoroughly. The parents wanted hospitalization today to keep him away from drugs. I refused it. We must assume patient will use Thorazine for sleep only—parents may hope for more magic from it."

> Mr. M. is a 22-year-old Black man diagnosed as paranoid

schizophrenic. He came in because he is anxious and tense about his wedding in two weeks to a girl who is six months pregnant. . . . The worker wrote, "His hearing voices was the beginning of a relapse of schizophrenia either under the stress of his impending marriage or because he had not taken any medications for the last half year or so." She gave him a two months' supply of a phenothiazine and told him to come back when the supply ran out.[20]

Consistently, the poor are drugged with major tranquilizers at a rate more than double that of the general population and, in some areas, at a rate nearly four times that of other citizens. Nationwide in 1975, physicians wrote nine prescriptions for Thorazine, Stelazine, and Mellaril—the most common phenothiazines—for every hundred people. The U. S. Department of Health, Education and Welfare maintains no comparable data for its indigent Medicaid clients—detailed data on consumption of legal drugs in this country is harder to obtain than information on illegal drugs—but in one group of six states for which some information is available (two in the Northeast, three in the South, one in the West), Medicaid paid for twenty-one such prescriptions for every hundred Medicaid-eligible people.[21] In Illinois, the rate is roughly thirty such prescriptions for every hundred Medicaid-eligible people; and in California, which keeps what are probably the most detailed and extensive records of any state, physicians wrote thirty-two major phenothiazine prescriptions for every hundred people eligible for its Medi-Cal system. All told, in the year ending June 1975, California doctors prescribed enough major tranquilizers to keep more than 70,000 poor people drugged around the clock and enough psychoactive drugs of all kinds to provide each of the state's 2.3 million Medi-Cal-eligible men, women, and children with 110 pills or other "dosage units" of medication.[22] Those figures do not include the millions of pills dispensed directly by mental-health clinics (which charge them against their operating budgets and which rarely know—or admit they know—how much medication they use) or those dispensed or forced upon inmates in the state's prisons and mental hospitals.

Invariably, black and minority clients also tend to get the more serious diagnoses, a pattern which corresponds to a generation of professional folklore (more on this in Chapter Three) that the poor and the black are crazier—in degree and in number—than the rest of the population: "Their problems," said a therapist in an Oakland clinic, "tend more often to be psychotic and difficult to treat. They're not motivated to help themselves. The concept is you go to a doctor and he fixes you. Not you fix yourself."[23] That concept, of course, is precisely the concept which the drug industry advertises and which the mental-health industry fosters.

"The best evidence," said Frank M. Ochberg, head of the NIMH Division of Community Mental Health Service Programs, "is to compare today's situation with the asylums of twenty years ago. Because of it, two million people are getting care where there used to be nothing." The figures are somewhat debatable: federally funded CMHC's do not handle 2 million people—the number is closer to 1 million—yet they have undoubtedly played a major part in the vast expansion of "mental-health" intervention to millions of individuals who were once left to "fix yourself." (Another 2.5 million are treated in other public clinics.) The "evidence," however, is hardly reassuring. In the years between 1950 and 1970, while the population increased from 150 million to 210 million, the number of institutionalized Americans rose by precisely the same proportions (from 1.5 million to 2.1 million); and while the number of persons incarcerated in state and county mental hospitals declined, the population of homes for the aged and dependent tripled from just under 300,000 to more than 900,000.[24] (By 1975, it exceeded 1 million.) In what is probably the best available analysis of that "evidence," Andrea Sallychild of the California State Health Department concluded that while "movement from mental hospitals to homes for the aged and dependent . . . is purely inferential," the figures provide strong indications that "a large proportion of 'back ward' residents who were removed from hospitals [and, we may assume, are now not going there initially] were older people" who were placed in nursing homes, where the maintenance is cheaper, the care is inferior, and where tranquilizers are the basic instruments of client management.[25] The evidence suggests that CMHC's and the other growing institutions of the madness establishment—state and locally funded clinics, counseling centers, and related mental-health organizations—are not replacing closed institutions but augmenting and complementing them, and that they have, as some of the visionaries of "preventive psychiatry" had hoped, found a large and wholly new clientele. Roughly half the clients of the CMHC's, according to NIMH official Lucy Ozarin, do not suffer from "classic" psychiatric symptoms.

Once again, it is the drugs which have made this expansion possible. The fact that, as Ochberg said, the centers "have such low psychiatric staffing" leads not to the conclusion that they couldn't be doing much drugging but to its very opposite: it is common knowledge (demonstrated again and again in studies) that for a physician the fastest "turnaround" in the office, the ritual that signifies the formal conclusion of the visit, is the writing of the prescription. The less time available and the more short-handed the staff, the higher the ratio of drugs to other forms of "treatment." Talk takes time, counseling requires energy and concern, but writing a scrip (or taking a pre-printed slip provided by the pharmaceutical manufacturer or a sample package of pills) and handing it to the client takes only a few seconds.[26] The effects of cultural, social, and racial bias—the bias against clients who lack "higher communications skills and ego strength [or] physical attractiveness"—the fact that the poor are more likely to be social and economic nuisances to their relatives and to other elements of the social-service system, and the fact that the heavy drugs are the fastest way of making them docile, tractable, and manageable make it almost inevitable that for the poor, the near-poor, the old, and the black, the mental-health system is primarily a drug system.

The pattern appears to be pervasive not only in clinics, public facilities and other institutions but in the the offices of private physicians serving patients covered by Medicaid, Medicare, and other forms of fixed payment. Predictably, the heaviest drugging outside mental institutions (where everyone is drugged) takes place in old-age nursing homes, where, according to a study by the U. S. Senate Special Subcommittee on Aging, the average patient's drug bill comes to $300 a year—$60 for tranquilizers alone—and where the two leading drugs, Thorazine and Mellaril, alone account for an average of three to four prescriptions per inmate per year.[27] (The nursing-home staff, says the ad in the trade journal, "benefits from this far-reaching effect of Mellaril since they find their work load greatly lightened as patient demands are replaced by a spirit of self-help and self-interest. . . . In difficult-to-manage patients the most obvious changes include a calmer, more cooperative attitude . . . and fewer demands for special attention.") Predictably also, the heaviest prescribers of drugs are not psychiatrists but general practitioners, internists, gynecologists, and the other "primary care" physicians, who are sometimes regarded as the first and most important providers of mental-health treatment. Roughly a third of all office visits to psychiatrists involve a drug prescription as part of the treatment; more than two-thirds of all office visits to nonpsychiatrists with "a principal diagnosis of mental disorder" result in a drug prescription. Those figures may be misleading, since most prescriptions are presumably large enough to last beyond the next visit and since a patient is more likely to make repeated visits to a psychiatrist for "mental disorders" than he is to a general practitioner. But they indicate that the network of mental health extends far beyond the 6 or 7 million people who are formally enrolled in the system in any given year.

Of all the prescription drugs sold in the United States, the federal government pays for nearly a third; of all drugs dispensed to the poor, the federal government pays for nearly everything.[28] Officials at the Department of Health, Education and Welfare who have wanted to study excessive expenditures for drugs through Medicaid have been discouraged by superiors who point out that since the government's drug bill represents only a small fraction of total Medicaid costs, even a substantial cut in drug prescribing would have a small effect on the bottom line—might, in fact, have a reverse effect in creating more demand on physicians, clinics, and hospitals; in holding the line, medication is the accountant's friend. In one guise or another—trainer of psychiatrists, backer of research, promoter through NIMH of the benefits of psychoactive medication, patron of "community mental health," provider of Medicaid—Uncle Sam is far and away the biggest drug pusher of them all.

# THREE

# The Book
# of Labels

# I

The rationale for the expanding network of psychiatric intervention is the "mental illnesses," "mental disorders," and "emotional disturbances" which are supposed to afflict some 40 million Americans and which, according to the official *Diagnostic and Statistical Manual of Mental Disorders* (*DSM*) of the American Psychiatric Association, includes some 150 ailments ranging from "schizophrenia" (fifteen types) to "adjustment reaction of adult life," "social maladjustment," "marital maladjustment," "dyssocial behavior," and "runaway reaction," one of several "behavior disorders of childhood and adolescence." Among the definitions:

308.3  Runaway reaction of childhood (or adolescence)

Individuals with this disorder characteristically escape from threatening situations by running away from home for a day or more without permission. Typically they are immature and timid, and feel rejected at home, inadequate and friendless. They often steal furtively.

308.5  Group delinquent reaction of childhood (or adolescence)

Individuals with this disorder have acquired the values, behavior and skills of a delinquent peer group or gang to whom they are loyal and with whom they characteristically steal, skip school and stay out late at night. The condition is more common in boys than girls. When group delinquency occurs with girls it usually involves sexual delinquency, although shoplifting is also common.[1]

Not surprisingly, there is no professional agreement on what most of those labels mean nor, in many cases, on whether they have any meaning at all. There is no medical definition of psychosis (described in *DSM* merely as the affliction of those whose "mental functioning is sufficiently impaired to interfere grossly with their capacity to meet the ordinary demands of life") or neurosis; no psychiatric definition of "syndrome," "symptom," or "symptom complex." Two-thirds of the APA's diagnostic categories have no demonstrable organic base; by consensus, and often by formal vote, the psychiatric establishment creates new categories on demand and discards old ones as they become socially embarrassing or culturally obsolescent. (Among the more famous rejects of the nineteenth century was "drapetomania" —the malady of slaves who made persistent attempts to escape; among the more notorious recent examples is "homosexuality," discarded in 1973 by formal vote of the APA.) Even such pillars of psychiatry as Karl Menninger have called many of the official APA categories "sheer verbal Mickey Mouse."[2] Not surprisingly, psychiatric diagnoses are frequently vulnerable to parody, cartoon humor, and to the challenge of common sense. Many psychiatrists really do talk the way they do in films and plays. The following is from the transcript of a recent case in the District of Columbia; the attorney is interrogating the psychiatrist:

Q. Doctor, is it your testimony that mental illness is basically anything that can be labeled in a psychological sense; for example, is alcoholism a mental illness?

A. It could be.

Q. Sir, are you familiar with the *Diagnostic and Statistical Manual for Mental Disorders?*

A. Yes.

Q. The so-called *DSM-II*. Could you tell us, sir, what is that basically?

A. It is a statistical manual which is published by the American Psychiatric Association and within it are described the various mental and emotional disorders which commonly come to the attention of mental-health professionals, and which may vary in the degree of severity.

. . . . .

Q. With regard to the other diagnoses that are in this case, for example passive aggressive personality . . . you say that is a mental illness?

A. It is. That has been defined as a mental illness. I believe you will find passive aggressive personality, aggressive type, in *DSM-I*. I'm not 100 percent sure that it is in *DSM-II*.

Q. And what does that come under, sir?

A. I think I am correct in my assertion that it used to be between aggressive and passive.

Q. Does that come under a sub-grouping or is that part of a generalized scheme of diagnostic headings?

A. It's under a sub-grouping of personality disorders and certain other non-psychotic mental disorders.

Q. Could you read the introductory paragraph that talks about what diseases or difficulties or disorders of maladapted behaviors are described?

A. Yes . . . "This group of disorders is characterized by deeply ingrained maladaptive patterns of behavior that are perceptibly different in quality from psychotic or neurotic symptoms. Generally these are lifelong patterns, often recognizable by the time of adolescence or earlier. Sometimes the pattern is determined primarily by malfunctioning of the brain, but such cases should be classified under one of the non-psychotic organic brain syndromes rather than here."

Q. Now is it true, sir . . . there is a significant difference between a schizophrenic diagnosis and a personality diagnosis?

A. My answer is yes. . . . You can have a psychotic thought disorder and in addition to that have a typical way of dealing with life problems which could be characterized by any of the personality disorders that are listed here. . . .

Q. Let me narrow it down to personality disorders, which is the diagnosis in this case, passive aggressive personality. Is there any language in here that defines that as a mental illness?

A. The term illness does not appear in the introductory paragraph.

Q. How about in non-psychotic brain syndrome, that is, in this case?

A. The specific term "illness" does not appear here either.

Q. Isn't it true that mental illness is not even a psychological or psychiatric term?

A. I think I would prefer the term "mental disorder."

Q. Can you define "mental illness," sir?

A. Yes. A mental illness is a disorder of function which significantly impairs a person's ability to function effectively in the social world.

. . . . .

Q. Do you subscribe, sir, to the theory that almost everybody in the world is mentally ill to some degree and needs therapy of some kind?[3]

The sport is easy, but the consequences are serious. As long as the psychiatrist's basic technique was talk (or incarceration), the labels were merely the familiar trinkets of mystification—the scientizing of the classic stigma of madness—but once they become indications for supposedly specific drugs, including many highly powerful drugs, they assume new significance. It was the drugs which rescued psychiatry from its medical limbo and gave it new status as "science." It was the drugs which gave it its most efficient technology. It is the drugs which, in the majority of cases, have become the first line of "treatment." Yet the indications for those drugs remain bound to cultural and social definitions, relics of other ages, part mythology, part literature, part law, part superstition, part medicine, part common sense, part "Mickey Mouse." The psychiatrist is still a moral agent of culture, but he can now pretend to be something else.

There is no need here for an extended discussion of Thomas S. Szasz's famous proposition that "mental illness is a myth" which has no organic base; that it "undermines the principles of personal responsibility, the ground on which all free political institutions rest"; that madness is essentially an ethical, moral, legal, or political issue, not a medical one; and that psychiatry as currently practiced is an institution of social and political control serving inquisitorial functions. "Since heresy could be destroyed only by destroying heretics," Szasz writes in *The Manufacture of Madness,* "and mental illness can be controlled only by controlling people alleged to be mentally ill, both social movements involve curtailing the liberties, or taking the lives, of the stigmatized members of the group."[4] It is true, as Szasz wrote in *The Myth of Mental Illness,* that

> modern psychiatry—and the identification of new psychiatric diseases—began not by identifying such diseases by means of the established methods of pathology, but by creating a new criterion of what constitutes disease: to the established criterion of detectable alteration of *bodily structure* was now added the fresh criterion of alteration of *bodily function;* and, as the former was detected by observing the patient's body, so the latter was detected by observing his behavior. This is how and why conversion hysteria became the prototype of this new class of diseases—appropriately named "mental" to distinguish them from those that are "organic," and appropriately called also "functional" in contrast to those that are "structural." Thus, whereas in modern medicine new diseases were *discovered,* in modern psychiatry they were *invented.* Paresis was *proved* to be a disease; hysteria was *declared* to be one.[5]

The difficulty with the argument is not in proving Szasz right or wrong, but in getting around the everyday evidence of "madness" which is not criminal (or not yet criminal) but which, in the view of those around it, appears sufficiently destructive or dangerous to require outside intervention. It was not psychiatry that locked up the lunatic or taunted the village idiot; all psychiatry did was to give each of them a scientific label. Currently, a whole army of researchers is at work trying to find the organic causes of functional "disease" —the chemical imbalances, the faulty neurotransmitters— responsible for "schizophrenia" or "depression" or "mania." They may or may not find them; but even if they do, the discovery—which would undercut Szasz's distinction between the "structural" and the "functional"—will not alter the fact that it was social, political, or cultural criteria which defined the deviance in the first place. Possibly if one searched long enough, one could also find the chemical or organic correlates of anger or amusement or an interest in theater, but that does not necessarily make any of them an illness. Similarly, one can argue, as Ivan Illich does, that even in the case of conventional physical illness,

> people would rebel against [industrial society] if medicine did not explain their biological disorientation as a defect in their health, rather than as a defect in the way of life which is imposed on them or which they impose on themselves. The assurance of personal political innocence that a diagnosis offers the patient serves as a hygienic mask that justifies further subjection. . . .[6]

Szasz's case is too clean and categorical: if he were to lose the structural-functional argument (say, on depression) to some future biochemist of the brain, that would hardly change the fact that the definition of depression as a disease is culturally based; at the same time, he has already lost part of his case to those political and social forces which, while they may be abetted by the mental-health establishment, would go on merrily even without it. Psychiatry began by medicalizing the behavior of people who had already been locked up or ostracized. What "mental health" is doing now is to medicalize nearly all behavior.

By whatever name, "madness" always served a social function. The special significance of its current form is that while it loses some of its classic stigma, it becomes increasingly prevalent and fashionable, spawning more and more marginal ailments and anticipatory symptoms (which may later be escalated into "syndromes" and "disorders"); and that there is growing acceptance of Karl Menninger's proposition that "all people have mental illness of different degrees at different times, and sometimes some are much worse, or better." Historically, madness was usually a yes-or-no proposition—the individual was either a lunatic (or a heretic), or he wasn't. He was either in or out of an institution; he was one of us or one of them. Nowadays we are all supposed to be a little bit crazy.

# II

The contemporary American classification of mental illness has a curious origin. It was not the consequence of science —the definition of discrete diseases, the discovery of specific organic malfunctions, the isolation of a virus—but of the military's need in World War II to fill neat bureaucratic forms, to develop a system, subsequently institutionalized by the APA in *DSM*, that would reduce what was patently unscientific and unsystematic—labels, theories, diagnoses, jargon—to something sufficiently precise for manuals and standard operating procedure in large organizations (and something which, for the same reason, would later be adaptable for insurance forms, hospital records, statistical summaries, and other bureaucratic purposes). It was as a consequence of that system and the screening procedures which it served—much of it the work of Dr. (then Brigadier General) William C. Menninger—that nearly 2 million of the 15 million men examined for induction into the military in World War II were rejected for neuropsychiatric reasons—some 40 percent of all rejections for all causes.[7] It was those criteria which produced the psychiatric "lessons" of the war—many of which later turned out to be myths and misapprehensions —and which, in turn, persuaded people like Menninger that millions of people required attention and treatment, and which stimulated the psychiatric evangelism of the decades that followed. "The bitterly learned lessons of the war years," wrote a psychiatrist-reviewer of Menninger's book *Psychiatry in a Troubled World,* "the startling and unexpected revelations of the mental health and weakness of our citizenry in a delicately balanced world must bear fruit in the postwar life of our nation if we are to remain healthy, strong and preserve our way of life."[8] Since Menninger developed it in World War II, the original classification system has gone through three official APA revisions, each of which added more categories and sub-types (which is why William's brother Karl objected to the new "Mickey Mouse"), but the basic classifications have remained consistent.

Even for the severe "hard" ailments—the various forms of depression and schizophrenia, that "sacred symbol," in Szasz's words, "of psychiatry"—there is little agreement on symptoms and definitions. In general, the "depressive disorders" are said to reflect inappropriate feelings and mood, while schizophrenia is regarded as distortion of thought; but those distinctions and their many refinements haven't managed to obviate the fact that blacks are more likely to be labeled "psychotic" or "schizophrenic" than whites with similar symptoms, or that what American psychiatrists call schizophrenia their British counterparts are almost as likely to call personality disorder, depression, or mania. According to a World Health Organization report summarizing extensive international studies:

> The prevailing concept of schizophrenia is much broader in the USA than in Britain, embracing substantial parts of what British psychiatrists would regard as depressive illness, neurotic illness, or personality disorder and almost the whole of what they regard as mania. Thus a considerable amount of

literature on both sides of the Atlantic concerned with epidemiology, genetics, family psychopathology, drug treatment and rehabilitation needs to be reconsidered. . . .[9]

The literature, needless to say, is vast. In schizophrenia: genetic studies; biochemical studies; intercultural studies; drug studies; neurological studies; attempts to define, specify, and categorize; attempts to prove that schizophrenia is, in fact, an organic disease which can be inherited and runs in families; attempts to locate the electrochemical processes in the brain related to mental illness; attempts to demonstrate that schizophrenia exists in every culture and society or (conversely) that it does not—some $5 million a year in NIMH-supported research on schizophrenia alone—all of these efforts leading to the conclusion (in one NIMH report) that "the diagnosis of schizophrenia is based on signs and symptoms which may bear little relationship to biological abnormalities or even to clinically significant entities." Its symptoms, according to the same summary, include "an inability to use language effectively and logically, disturbed patterns of learning and performance, decreased motivation or apathy in many situations, distorted sensory acuity and perceptions, and disturbed conceptual processes." Even that summary, however, left the writers, two of them psychiatrists, with a sense of inadequacy that finally forced them to declare that "in schizophrenia, the person *is* the disorder," a logical construct that can only lead to the conclusion that the best way to eliminate the disorder is to eliminate the person.[10]

The currently prevalent view is that certain people labeled as schizophrenics suffer from a chemical or neurological malfunction—the person who hears voices, the person with the loaded shotgun at the door to fight off the Martians or the Communists who are coming to get him; but there is no certainty whether schizophrenia is one disease or many, or, indeed, whether it is a disease at all. As originally formulated by Emil Kraepelin in 1883, "dementia praecox" was thought to produce an inexorable course of personality disintegration, while manic-depressive psychosis was marked by cycles of mood and by periods of exacerbation and improvement. In 1911 Eugen Bleuler changed the name to schizophrenia after he observed that deterioration was not inevitable and when he concluded that the distinguishing characteristic of the ailment was a splitting of the patient's psychological life. Since then, the definition has been modified, amplified, and qualified; subcategories have been added and others eliminated; and psychiatrists are constantly meeting in further efforts to develop a "standardized symptomatological approach"; but there is still no evidence that there is any single ailment that can be called schizophrenia. "Kraepelin and Bleuler," said William T. Carpenter, Jr., the director of Schizophrenia Research Programs at Albert Einstein Medical College,

> made landmark contributions in defining the diagnostic class we now call schizophrenia, but progress in nosology since 1911 has been relatively modest. We continue to identify patients as schizophrenic based primarily on signs and symptoms, but even when well-defined and stringent criteria are used, we have a heterogeneous patient population in terms of genetics, biochemistry, psychology, environment, treatment, course and outcome.[11]

Those "landmark" contributions are themselves open to question, since the list of symptoms developed by the patriarchs are (in the words of the World Health Organization Report) "so insusceptible of definition [that] its boundaries could be varied within wide limits by those making the diagnosis." Schizophrenia is a label for "several overlapping symptom clusters" and not for any organically or chemically identifiable malfunction.

Yet even if one assumes that there is a real ailment called schizophrenia, the label itself is used for so many forms of behavior—including, in 1964, Barry Goldwater's politics—that it now serves as "the residue of residues," the category that's left when nothing else will do. Soviet psychiatrists diagnose "sluggish" or "creeping schizophrenia," which is characterized by "unsociability, sluggishness, loss of interest in life, inadequate thoughts and actions, stubbornness and inflexibility of convictions, suspiciousness, etc." Many American psychiatrists diagnose "borderline" cases. Both seem to be used when symptoms are "barely" or "only slightly" manifest among people who had "no severe or continuous experiences [of mental illness]." As diagnostic categories such as hysteria and depression have become, in the words of sociologist Thomas J. Scheff, "conventionalized names for residual rule breaking, a need seems to have developed for a still more generalized diagnostic category. . . . Schizophrenia is an appelation, or 'label,' which may be easily applied to those residual rule breakers whose deviant behavior is difficult to classify." A schizophrenic, said Szasz, "is a person who is not a child and who is not functioning as an adult."[12]

In the case of the "depressive disorders," the situation is equally confused. There is general agreement in the psychiatric establishment that such ailments are either bipolar (manic depressive) or unipolar, that they are either "situational" (i. e., the client is depressed because he has had a depressing experience) or "endogenous" (he is depressed without anyone knowing why). Depending on the survey, between 4 million and 30 million Americans suffer "significant depressive symptoms" every year. Among the more vocal psychiatric evangelists, physicians like Nathan S. Kline assert that "certainly 7,000,000 and possibly 15,000,000 are in need of . . . treatment [for depression] but are not receiving it" and Dr. Ronald R. Fieve, the country's most vocal proponent of lithium maintenance, puts the estimate at between "18 and 20 million Americans suffering from depression."[13] Like schizophrenia, however, depression has so far eluded diligent attempts to prove an organic or chemical base—some demonstrable and specific malfunction which would make it a medical "illness" and not merely a label for moods or forms of behavior that trouble the individual, his relatives (more commonly her relatives), or the authorities; like schizophrenia, it responds to no "cure" which, without continuing drug maintenance (and often even with it), can be regarded as final and permanent. Here again, the literature is ample with theories and speculations—findings that depressed patients regard themselves as losers, that "the excitatory systems of the nervous system are overactive [or] that the inhibitory systems are overactive"; theories that depression may be caused by glandular malfunctions, that it may sometimes be inherited (particularly by women), that it is usually characterized by light, fragmented "shallow" sleep, that it may be related to drug and alcohol abuse, violence, and racism—all of them leading to the conclusion (as summarized in another NIMH report) that "little agreement exists today as to diagnosis, epidemiology, causes, and effective therapy; only that depression is ubiquitous and universal, and that it appears to be part of the human condition, ranging from a normal mood state to severe illness. . . . Locating the critical line that separates health from illness is very difficult."[14]

Amid all this uncertainty, however, there are clues which the psychiatric and medical industries have largely ignored. Among all the major psychiatric ailments, the only category in which women represent a highly disproportionate number of the "patients"—outnumbering men by roughly two to one —is in the "depressive disorders." Roughly twice as many women as men are hospitalized for depression, twice as many women as men get electroshock treatments, and, it appears, twice as many women as men are treated as outpatients, many of them between the ages of 35 and 50.[15] According to the conventional medical wisdom, that phenomenon is the obvious result of chemical and biological changes associated with menopause, and it has generated what by now has become the scandalous and dangerous practice of indiscriminately administering estrogens—22 million prescriptions in 1975—or other hormones or drugs. (In 1971, for example, an article in the *British Medical Journal* asserted that 50 percent of menopausal women require treatment, and that "estrogen therapy in conjunction with other therapeutic measures is suggested."[16]) What may be more scandalous is the fact that while medical literature is full of references to the "menopausal syndrome" as a cause not only of certain physical problems but, more significantly, of irritability, anxiety, and depression, there are virtually no systematic studies— none current, none in the past—which have ever delved into the "syndrome" or examined the question of whether it even exists. In one of the few recent reviews of the literature (published, significantly, in the *Journal of Biosocial Science* and not in a medical journal), the authors conclude that "menopausal symptomatology, its origin and treatment, is repeatedly described with no empirical basis other than 'experience.' "

> "Clinical experience" has assumed unparalleled legitimacy as a basis of knowledge and practice, regardless of its lack of objectivity and substantiation through further, adequately controlled studies. This reliance of physicians on subjective "experience" is particularly evident with regard to the menopause. Discussions of symptomatology and treatment recommendations, usually with no clear empirical basis, form the bulk of the medical literature on this subject.[17]

With the rise of the women's movement in the late sixties, sociologists and journalists began to mount attacks on the conventional gynecological wisdom, and particularly on the dominance of men and male attitudes in the profession. Few of these attacks, however, turned to the issue of depression or menopause—it was, after all, a young women's movement —and even among those which did, the best known, Phyllis Chesler's *Women and Madness,* failed to challenge the premise that while depression and other forms of mental illness are produced by a male-dominated society, they were real illnesses nonetheless.[18] Put another way, the same statistics combined with the same paucity of hard medical evidence are far more conclusive as an illustration of a cultural process and of social control than they are suggestive of illness. Pauline Bart, a medical sociologist at the University of Illinois, has collected considerable data to indicate that depression typically is an affliction of women who have lost their roles as mothers and housewives, and that the highest incidence among women occurs among "housewives with maternal role loss who have overprotective or overinvolved relationships with their children."[19] Many women, as Chesler points out, really feel ill, and are, in that sense, "volunteers." Many others—through suggestion, coaxing, or coercion—are recruits. (As late as the second half of the nineteenth century, an Illinois law provided that "married women . . . may be entered or detained in the hospital at the request of the husband or the guardian . . . without the evidence of insanity required in other cases.") Frequently, the line between "voluntary" illness and coerced treatment—like the line that "separates health from illness"—is impossible to establish. When people become socially or economically superfluous (or when they feel they have), one available role is "illness"; when women become socially superfluous, the medical culture offers "menopausal syndrome" and depression.

# III

In 1972, a Stanford University psychologist named David L. Rosenhan and seven others, none of them with any psychiatric problems, past or present, got themselves admitted to a group of private and public mental hospitals on the East and West Coasts, among them some of the most reputable in America. Except for Rosenhan himself, whose presence as a "pseudopatient" was known to the administrator and chief psychologist of his hospital, none of the individuals—a graduate student, a painter, a housewife, a pediatrician, and several psychologists—were known to hospital staffs. Using a false identity, each pseudopatient "arrived at the admissions office [of the hospital] complaining that he had been hearing voices [which] were often unclear, but as far as he could tell they said 'empty,' 'hollow' and 'thud.' "

> The choice of these symptoms [Rosenhan reported] was occasioned by their apparent similarity to existential symptoms. Such symptoms are alleged to arise from painful concerns about the perceived meaninglessness of one's life. It is as if the hallucinating person were saying, "My life is empty and hollow." The choice of these symptoms was also determined by the *absence* of a single report of existential psychosis in the literature.[20]

Other than falsifying their identities and "presenting symptoms," the pseudopatients told their life histories as they actually occurred—relationships with parents and children, with spouses and with people at work and in school, which "if anything . . . strongly biased the subsequent results in favor of detecting sanity, since none of their histories or current behaviors were seriously pathological in any way." Once admitted to a psychiatric ward, moreover, the "pseudopatients ceased simulating *any* symptoms of abnormality." They behaved normally and told the staff that they felt fine. The only thing which surprised them—and which made some of them nervous—was that they were admitted so easily; many of them feared that they would quickly be found out as frauds. None ever was.

During the course of hospitalization—ranging from seven to fifty-two days—they engaged other patients in conversation, took extensive notes, secretly at first, then, when it was clear that no one seemed to take notice, quite openly, and accepted medication as dispensed but did not swallow it. All told, the eight were administered nearly 2,100 pills of psychoactive drugs, particularly Elavil, Thorazine, Compazine, and Stelazine. With one exception, all were admitted with a diagnosis of schizophrenia (one with a diagnosis of "manic-depressive psychosis") and discharged as schizophrenics "in remission." ("If the patient was to be discharged," Rosenhan observed, "he must naturally be 'in remission'; but he was not sane, nor, in the institution's view, had he ever been sane.") Among them was a man who, in Rosenhan's summary,

> had had a close relationship with his mother but was rather remote from his father during his early childhood. During adolescence and beyond, however, his father became a close friend, while his relationship with his mother cooled. His present relationship with his wife was characteristically close and warm. Apart from occasional angry exchanges, friction was minimal. The children had rarely been spanked.

In the hospital records, that history was interpreted as follows:

> This white 39-year-old male . . . manifests a long history of considerable ambivalence in close relationships, which begins in early childhood. A warm relationship with his mother cools during his adolescence. A distant relationship to his father is described as becoming very intense. Affective stability is absent. His attempts to control emotionality with his wife and children are punctuated by angry outbursts and, in the case of the children, spankings. And while he says he has several good friends, one senses considerable ambivalence embedded in those relationships also.[21]

Although the pseudopatients were rarely questioned about their flagrant note taking, the nursing records for three of them incorporated such things as "patient engages in writing behavior," thereby again translating the ordinary into the pathological, a practice that was accompanied (and obviously abetted) by the consistent failure of staff members to take any notice of patients as individuals.

Rosenhan carried his experiment one step further. He informed the staff of a research and teaching hospital that at some time during the following three months, one or more pseudopatients would try to gain admission and, in effect, challenged the staff to find them out:

> Judgments were obtained on 193 patients who were admitted for psychiatric treatment. All staff who had sustained contact with or primary responsibility for the patient—attendants, nurses, psychiatrists, physicians, and psychologists—were asked to make judgments. Forty-one patients were alleged, with high confidence, to be pseudopatients by at least one member of the staff. Twenty-three were considered suspect by at least one psychiatrist. Nineteen were suspected by one psychiatrist *and* one other staff member. Actually, no genuine pseudopatient (at least from my group) presented himself during this period.[22]

The point here is not merely the ease with which a person can get himself hospitalized (or committed by others), but the facile way labels are applied; the extent to which they distort all subsequent perceptions of the individual, including, eventually, the individual's perception of himself; and the difficulty, if not the impossibility, of escaping the label and its stigma once they are attached. Although many of the "real" patients on the wards suspected that the pseudopatients were journalists or professors "checking up on the hospital," the staff consistently regarded everything the patients did—no matter how motivated or stimulated—as manifestations of disease. "Once the impression has been formed that the patient is schizophrenic, the expectation is that he will continue to be schizophrenic," Rosenhan notes. "When a sufficient amount of time has passed during which the patient has done nothing bizarre, he is considered to be in remission and available for discharge, with the unconfirmed expectation that he will behave as a schizophrenic again." Any diagnostic process, Rosenhan observed, "that lends itself so readily to massive errors of this sort cannot be a very reliable one."[23]

The labels are tokens of exchange, converting what is vague, impressionistic, anecdotal, and unscientific into an

appearance of diagnostic precision, converting peculiar behavior into medication, "thud" into Thorazine, and deviance
into incarceration. Equally important, those same labels—
despite their lack of precision, if not their total lack of meaning—have, in conjunction with related screens and tests,
become part of the rationale and foundation for community
mental-health and other programs, and for the broad social
theories on which they are based. Ever since (and perhaps
before) the Massachusetts Commission on Lunacy concluded (in 1854) that "insanity is . . . a part and parcel of
poverty," the conventional professional wisdom has included
the belief that among those millions of untreated cases, the
sickest were the poor and the black, among whom (as everyone knew) there was a higher incidence of mental illness than
in any other group. "During its years of savagery," explained
a writer in the *Psychoanalytic Review* in 1913, "the [colored]
race had learned no lessons in emotional control, and what
they had attained during their few generations of slavery left
them unstable. For this reason we find deterioration in the
emotional sphere most often an early and a persistent manifestation."[24] By the mid-twenties, there no longer remained
much doubt in the mental-health movement that, as one
senior state official put it in *Mental Hygiene,* "dementia
praecox is more frequent in some European races than others
[*i.e.,* among Southern and Eastern Europeans]," that it was
more prevalent among the foreign-born, and that it was more
common among Negroes than among whites. The writer,
Horatio M. Pollock, had no real data to support his racial
distinctions; what he had for the nation as a whole—all of
it based on the populations of mental hospitals—indicated
exactly the opposite, but he attributed that to the exclusion
of blacks from mental hospitals in the South.[25] Beginning in
the late thirties, however, and particularly after the publication in 1958—four years before the introduction of the Community Mental Health Centers Act—of an influential study
conducted in New Haven, Connecticut, by August B. Hollingshead and Fred C. Redlich, interest shifted from race to

class differences, and even more vexing, to "the role of heredity versus social environment in the etiology of these disorders"—whether (in the simplest terms) the poor were crazy
because they were poor, or whether they were poor because
they were crazy. The general figures for the prevalence of
mental illness varied, depending on the study, from slightly
over 1 percent to 64 percent of the whole population, though,
significantly, the percentage reported in studies published
after 1950 was, on the average, several times as high as that
reported before 1950.[26] The most ambitious of those efforts,
the so-called Midtown Manhattan Study (1962), concluded
that nearly a fourth of some 1,700 New York City residents
surveyed through detailed questions and interviews later
analyzed by psychiatrists suffered from psychological disorders, and that in the lowest stratum, the number of those
afflicted was close to 50 percent. Similar findings were reported in comparisons between blacks and whites. In one
survey, published in 1957, the authors concluded that "four-
fifths of the families in the lower social strata contained at
least one mentally ill member."[27]

What's surprising about those findings is not that the
prevalence of disorder is so high or the class differences so
great but that given the criteria, they are so small. After
extensive analysis of the Midtown data, researchers from the
Midtown project, and others, concluded that twenty-two
items on the Midtown interview questionnaire "could be
scored to provide a close approximation of the evaluations
made from the entire interview by the psychiatrists on the
study." Among the twenty-two items:

> Are you the worrying type—you know, a worrier?
> You sometimes can't help wondering if anything is worth-
> while anymore.
> Do you feel somewhat apart or alone even among friends?
> You have personal worries that get you down physically,
> that is, make you physically ill.
> You are bothered by acid or sour stomach several times a
> week.

Are you ever bothered by nervousness, that is, by being irritable, fidgety, or tense?[28]

Many of those same items had been (and still are) standard on psychiatric screens—among them the army's World War II Neuropsychiatric Screening Adjunct—and have been "validated" against professional psychiatric evaluations, including the famous wartime diagnoses of combat-shaken troops as "mentally ill," who turned out to be "three-day schizophrenics." In the case of the Midtown study, the scholars concluded that *four* affirmative answers to any of the twenty-two items would provide "a close approximation" to psychiatric diagnoses of psychological disorders. It was hardly surprising, therefore, that subsequent researchers were puzzled by the finding that a group of predischarge (mental) ward patients "had an average symptom score lower than the scores of two nonpatient groups consisting of college students and a cross-section of the community," a problem some of them tried to ascribe, significantly enough, to "conscious or unconscious resistance [among those surveyed] to admitting characteristics they judged to be undesirable."[29] Few of the researchers, however, had the temerity to suggest that however complex their statistical routines and validations, such a possibility, which would probably make the less sophisticated look sicker, was strong enough to make the whole exercise absurd. In what has probably been the most extensive review of the field, Bruce P. Dohrenwend and Barbara D. Dohrenwend of Columbia University observed that "the determinations of psychological disorder made in community studies . . . can no longer be accepted at face value." Their own field work with the crude questions of the 22-item scale made it clear that there were no simple correlations along ethnic or economic lines. (In their findings, the healthiest people were Jews earning under $3,000 a year, the sickest were Puerto Ricans making over $7,500.) Nonetheless, the Dohrenwends blithely concluded that "despite unreliable measures, higher rates of psychological disorder are consistently found in the lowest social class."[30]

Compared to studies demonstrating that blacks are sicker than whites, however, the evidence for social-class differences is positively scientific. "It is clear," according to one of the most quoted surveys, "that Negroes have a higher incidence [of mental disorder] than whites." What is not clear are the criteria on which those judgments are based: the most common standard is the population of mental hospitals, a transparently unreliable index, since even if commitment procedures were, in fact, based on real disorders (which they are not), and even if they were unbiased (which they are not), whites, because they are more affluent, still have many more options and resources for the treatment of "mental disorder" than do blacks. The few studies which have examined the commitment process all seem to conclude (as one of them said) that "persons of lower socioeconomic background are more rapidly and less carefully institutionalized than their more affluent and better-educated fellow citizens." The studies also make clear that when they have similar "symptoms," blacks are more likely to get the severe diagnoses, whites the more benign. One extensive survey conducted in Baltimore indicated that while the per-capita rate of institutionalization in state hospitals was nearly twice as high for blacks, when all cases of "mental disorder" were counted and the community surveyed in a careful sampling procedure, the prevalence rate for whites was 12 per thousand, that for blacks 7 per thousand. What all the studies seem to prove is that the poor and the black have more social and economic problems than whites—hardly news—and between the lines they seem to suggest, as one study concluded, that "the most efficacious way to alleviate the burdens of lower-class social position is not by therapy . . . but by changing the social conditions to which lower class people are subject." Most of the studies, however, do not say that: their effect is to justify precisely the reverse.[31]

At the fringes, almost every complaint qualifies as a manifestation of psychiatric disorder, and almost every week new criteria and new ailments are proposed. As early as 1916, in their classic study sponsored by the National Committee for Mental Hygiene and the Eugenics Record Office, A. J. Rosanoff and his colleagues conjured up "parapsychiatric conditions" as measures of mental health—"school retardation, truancy, unruliness, sexual immorality, criminal tendency, vagrancy, welfare recipiency, inebriety, drug habits and domestic maladjustment"—and in a survey of "mental health needs" in a rural Ohio county in 1955, the researchers included rejections for military service, "school maladjustment," juvenile delinquency, adult crime, and divorce.[32]

By the early seventies, such criteria, rather than having been discarded as quaint, had been expanded, sanctioned with NIMH research grants, incorporated in studies to demonstrate "the consistent relationship between low social class and high prevalence rates," and reported with full scientific regalia in the *American Journal of Orthopsychiatry* and the *Archives of General Psychiatry*. The researcher in this case was Dr. Milton Mazer, director of the Martha's Vineyard (Massachusetts) Mental Health Center, whose list of "parapsychiatric events" included

> fines, probation, jail, juvenile delinquency, marital dissolution [separate support, desertion, or divorce], premarital pregnancy, single-car accident, chronic alcoholism, acute public alcoholism [jailed until sober], suicide attempts, suicides, high school disciplinary problems [defined by Mazer as "those major infractions of the published school code recorded in the high school principal's file"] and high school underachievement.[33]

Despite those sweeping categories, and despite the extensive violations of privacy and confidentiality which the study involved, Mazer found that only 22 percent of the resident population of his island suffered a psychiatric or parapsychiatric event during a five-year period, surely a testimonial to the public sobriety, marital stability, and sexual restraint of the islanders, and to the good behavior and decorum of their high school students. Nonetheless, Mazer concluded (in 1974) that "the human wastage in pain suffered, in creativity stifled, and in joy lost, is almost beyond comprehension." For, in addition to those suffering from the various problems in his catalogue, "the largest group are those who remain invisible, suffering quietly, but gradually corroding the lives of those with whom they live. For psychiatric disorder behaves like a communicable disease with a long incubation period." He is not clear at this point whether he has just introduced another group—those whose lives are being corroded by those who suffer quietly—or whether he has merely been swamped by his own rhetoric. "Disorder in parents," he goes on to say, "is associated with high rates of disorder in their children, and disorder in one spouse often results in social isolation and eventually disorder in the other —statements which suggest that the quiet sufferers are the victims of disorder rather than its causes. To an evangelist like Mazer, however, it doesn't make all that much difference, since, in the final analysis, the inexorable process of psychiatric contamination is going to infest the entire population one way or another. "It is probable," he said, "that much psychiatric disorder in a community produces sociocultural disintegration of that community and the resulting disintegration further increases the rates of disorder." Those who work in mental health are like "the man surrounded by snakes. He has neither the time nor the composure to make a plan. The best he can do is to keep on killing snakes in the hope that he will kill the last one before he himself collapses."[34]

# FOUR

# The Sympathetic Ear

## I

The Peninsula Community Mental Health Center in Burlingame, California, is a bright, modern, reasonable place run by bright, modern, reasonable people—a national model, in the view of NIMH, of what a community mental-health center should be. Housed in the glass-and-concrete and carpeted facilities of the Peninsula Hospital some fifteen miles south of San Francisco, the center offers everything NIMH regulations require: inpatient services, outpatient services, partial hospitalization (day treatment), 24-hour emergency services, and consultation and education (C and E) for other organizations and individuals in its "catchment area." The living spaces for inpatients more closely resemble the rooms and lounges of the Holiday Inn down the road—color television, comfortable chairs, potted plants—than they do the conventional mental hospital with its fading pastel walls, locked doors, and barred windows. Unlike most mental-health clinics, moreover, this one provides most of its outpatient treatment—primarily counseling, psychotherapy, and drugs—in the private offices of some sixty psychiatrists and psychologists outside the hospital; the majority of its clients rarely, if ever, see the inside of the hospital. Emergencies are handled by members of the inpatient staff. Other cases are referred directly to one of the extramural staff members; for those patients, the center is a clearing house and a referral service rather than a clinic. Once a week the staff meets to review active cases, and to try to prevent individual therapists from prolonging treatment unnecessarily and from fostering the classic patient-doctor dependency, which can turn the acute into the chronic. The federal government pays for roughly a third of its $700,000 budget; the state and county pay for another third; and Medi-Cal, Medicare, private insurance, and individual clients pay for the rest.

Yet, beneath the façade of modernity and sweet reason, the Peninsula CMHC, like most such facilities, is a place with a limited budget where, in the words of its director, Dr. Donald E. Newman, "you have to work hard not to get choked to death." It has to cope, on the one hand, with people who were originally coerced into state mental hospitals and who, for economic reasons, are now being pushed out, and, on the other, with the growing number who have been invited or coaxed or pressured into the system by C and E and by the ideology of community mental health itself. Every time a staff member visits a local school or other community agency, Newman explained, "the referral rate jumps"; because the center exists, "a lot of chronic problems are coming out of the woodwork." At the same time, he complains that the community lacks the social structures, the neighborhood organizations, and the residential facilities—halfway houses, sheltered homes, and all the rest—that might provide support for those discharged mental patients or that might keep people from becoming mental patients in the first place. In talking up mental health, members of Newman's staff have helped organize some community groups to provide, for example, recreational companions to retarded children; but such efforts haven't begun to solve the problem. Mental hospitals were—and still are—institutions for people whom nobody wanted, places for the dead storage of human beings; now those people are being discharged into communities where local clinics and community mental-health centers are supposed to take care of them but where, in many cases, they are still unwanted. In addition, for many more who have never been hospitalized, and probably never will be, the problem is not even remotely medical: the housewife who is or feels abused; the child who can't function in school; the retired man with no friends and no place to go; the newly arrived Samoans and Filipinos who have no resources or community organization; and the hundreds of people for whom there is no suitable housing, no jobs, no friends. "I'll treat anybody," Newman said, "but I can't take them home with me."

It's hard not to be sympathetic. People who have been institutionalized for years are sent "home" or to nursing or "board-and-care" homes, where the neglect and brutality are often worse than in the hospitals where they were treated. In some areas, private entrepreneurs are contracting with counties to house "patients"—either after, or in lieu of, hospitalization—in low-budget facilities, which have become decentralized back wards and which, while they offer no more in the way of care, are even less visible than the state hospitals they replace and, therefore, less subject to inspection, investigation, and reform. More commonly, county mental-health clinics and local day-treatment facilities are charged with the responsibility for caring for those released mental patients; in theory, they offer counseling, talking therapy, and help finding accommodations and employment. In most instances, however, "rehabilitation" is founded on the self-confirming proposition that most of the clients are "chronic" cases who have to be maintained, usually on drugs, for no more than it costs to keep them from becoming nuisances to the rest of the community.

Federal and state policy, founded on the illusion of a fast cure (most of the mentally ill, John Kennedy said, can be "successfully and quickly treated"), created what was essentially an outpatient system to handle among others, people who had been hospitalized in the first place because they had nowhere to go. But since there rarely is such a cure for the quasi-medical problems of "mental illness," let alone the social problems which helped cause it, the system rarely works as intended. "The traditional verbal psycho-therapeutic modes of intervention," said a clinic director, "which seemed adequate when community mental-health programs focused on the less chronic patient and depended on state hospitalization for the treatment of chronic patients, are no longer adequate."[1] As a consequence, deinstitutionali-zation, theoretically a prime objective of federal and state mental-health programs, has become notorious for its lack of coordination, its human and economic contradictions, and its routine abuse of clients. "Many persons," according to a 1976 General Accounting Office report, "have been released from state institutions only to be reinstitutionalized often inappropriately in nursing or rest homes which may provide medication or medical treatment but lack resources to han-dle developmental or mental health problems. Many others have found their way to boarding homes where there are no services at all."[2] They are shuffled from agency to agency, program to program, while the practitioners complain about the thousands of people in the "revolving doors" who are released only to be readmitted to a hospital or a clinic a few months later. They are pushed into hospitals, then pushed out into local clinics or into the community, and then pushed back into hospitals. Hospital stays are shorter, and therefore the number of inmates is smaller; but the number of people treated in mental hospitals or in psychiatric wards of other hospitals every year is as large as it ever was.

Wherever they go they are drugged—the courts and the professionals make drugs and continued "therapy" a condi-tion of formal release from institutional treatment. The ad-mission—the confession—that one is or has been ill is a measure of the chances for recovery; the willing ingestion of medication is a measure of the recovery itself, a test of the individual's ability to function. In the language of a typical county report, "the rehabilitation unit provides medications for the chronically mentally ill who are dependent on medication for satisfactory adjustment to the community. This population is typically characterized by well-established histories of inability to manage without medication."[3]

What no one asks is whether they should be in the system at all. *Cases:* Until he injured his back in the spring of 1972, Jack Parker was a promising prospect as a defensive back for a professional football team. Thereafter he worked at odd jobs and lived on disability payments while trying to get back in shape. At least twice he was involved in loud and ugly arguments with his father, who called the police; and twice the police delivered him to a mental-health clinic, which sent him to a state hospital for evaluation. In the spring of 1976, Parker visited his parents and had another argument with his father in which he shouted, "I'll kill you." Again the father called the police, and again Parker was sent to the state hospital. Now Parker, represented by a lawyer from the County Public Defender's Office, was before a judge of the California Superior Court pleading for his release. Under the law, he had to be "dangerous" to himself or others, or "gravely disabled," to be institutionalized for more than seventeen days. In the face of a social worker's affidavit indicating that Parker had, in fact, never been physically violent toward his parents—that it was the father who "almost deliberately . . . attempted to make Jack blow up"—the county prosecutor, in his effort to keep Parker in the hospital (he had, of course, never been charged with any crime), tried to show that he was spending his money unwisely—that he had quickly run through funds he had obtained from the sale of a car—and was therefore "gravely disabled." Supporting his argument was an affidavit from a hospital psychiatrist who stated that Parker

> makes dependency demands upon his parents and when they are not fulfilled, becomes angry and threatening toward his family. Patient clears when hospitalized but soon regresses when released. He stops his medication, becomes confused

and disorganized, develops paranoid delusions and loses impulse control.

In the ensuing interrogation by the judge—the whole proceeding lasted six minutes—it became apparent that Parker was a big spender and something of a brawler who, in his own words, "can't just walk away from a fight," and who, when he had money, was "everybody's friend." But what interested the judge was Parker's "ability to take his medicine." He ordered Parker returned to the hospital: "If you demonstrate to me that you can function adequately, that you take your medicine, then I'll reconsider."[4] A few months later, in another economy move, Parker was released and sent to a local "rehab" center.[4]

Joan Smith, an unemployed schoolteacher, had been sent to the personnel office of a San Francisco hospital where, she was told, there might be a job. Once she got there,

> a young man cheerfully suggested that after I filled out the application I go talk to a psychologist [who] spoke to me briefly, called a psychiatrist and attendant and the next thing I knew I was being held for three days of observation . . . because they decided I was dangerous to myself or others. I was given medication, told my underwear was not clean and put under guard. . . . I was then told they wanted to keep me 18 days. One psychiatrist commented on how fast I revived from the initial shock of this incarceration. After the guard was removed the second day I could go to the bathroom alone. . . . After two days of begging they decided to release me but they didn't have enough in their funds to cover this involuntary hold so before they released me they took my check for $225 for two days in the hospital. My therapy consisted of uppers to which my muscles reacted adversely, so they added a counteractive. [The doctor] made me promise like a five-year-old that I would continue buying the pills and consult a psychiatrist and/or participate in a group therapy program.[5]

When, in the spring of 1971, he was fired from his job as a bag machine operator, Matt Collins had worked for Union

Camp Corporation in Savannah, Georgia, for nearly seventeen years. During the months before he was discharged,
Collins had filed five grievances and two charges of unfair
labor practices against the company, more than any other of
the 3,700 union-represented employees at the local plant;
management considered all of these complaints "baseless."
As a consequence, he was ordered to see a company doctor
—it was a condition of continued employment—who informed the company that "this 34-year-old white male has
paranoia with a systemic series of reasonings which lead to
ideas of persecution, ideas of reference, and it is apparent
that he will go to any end to attempt to press his own point
to his advantage. . . . I think his problem is entirely psychiatric." The company physician sent him to Dr. A. H. Center,
a local psychiatrist, who concluded that

> the whole climate of the patient's thinking is along paranoid
> lines, and I feel that he is showing a paranoid type of psycho-
> sis. Although he may not show the complete incoherence and
> disorganization of the deteriorated schizophrenic, yet I feel
> that he is paranoid schizophrenic with ideas of reference, and
> is in need of therapy and hospitalization. I feel that as a result
> of his condition he would not likely make an adequate adjust-
> ment on his job, and will continue to harass and threaten the
> company with further grievances and legal action.[6]

Collins was placed on medical leave, hospitalized for a
week, sent back to Dr. Center for treatment, placed in group
therapy, and diagnosed by Dr. Center again. The first time,
Collins had been labeled as "schizophrenic reaction, paranoid type"; the second time, his ailment was simply a "paranoid condition." Management informed him that he could
not return to work until "a doctor who is a diplomate of the
American Board of Psychiatry and Neurology" certified that
he was well. Two other doctors subsequently told the company that Collins was able to return to work and that, as one
of them said, "this patient certainly falls within the limits of
normal." The company, however, refused to reinstate him

because, management said, the doctors were not diplomates
of the American Board. In the interim, Collins was elected
vice-president of the local union of the Paper Mill Workers,
and vice-president of one of its special departments. He also
continued to press his seven complaints: one of them was
resolved in his favor when the company agreed to pay the
rate sought in the grievance; a second, based on the first, was
withdrawn when the company settled; a third was decided in
his favor by an arbitrator; and a fourth, based on the denial
of a credit-union loan, which resulted from false company-
furnished information that Collins was only a temporary
employee, was settled when the company formally conceded
that Collins was not a temporary employee. A year after he
was fired, a labor arbitrator ordered Collins reinstated to his
job with back pay, finding, among other things, that "in light
of the foregoing, it is difficult to conclude that these . . .
grievances were 'frivolous or malicious.' " The arbitrator
pointed out that there was "no evidence whatever" that Collins was ever violent, that he threatened violence, or that he
"was even disrespectful in his attitude and relationship toward his superiors or his fellow employees."[7]

The stories are commonplace. In Chicago, the police arrest a man named Robert Friedman for trying to panhandle
a dime in a bus station. Friedman had supported himself
most of his life and had never been in trouble; but when the
cops discovered that he was carrying nearly $25,000 in cash,
all of it his own, he was immediately sent to a psychiatric
ward for observation, and heavily drugged with tranquilizers. Five days later, acting on the recommendation of a
Cuban-born psychiatrist, who spoke only in broken English
and who labeled Friedman "schizophrenic," a judge committed Friedman to a mental hospital to protect him from
people who, the judge said, might be after his cash. Friedman
begged the judge to release him and order the money returned. Until he was laid off a few months before, he had
worked steadily as a clerk-stenographer; the rent on his
apartment was paid; he had been convicted of no crime; he

even promised to stop panhandeling and put his money back in a bank. A devout Jew, what he most wanted was to go to Israel and, eventually, to get married. The judge committed him because "letting you go would mean you would be unable to take care of yourself."

Friedman would never be a free man again, nor would he ever again see his money. When he died fourteen months later, more than half of it was gone. The State of Illinois had taken $800 a month for his treatment—largely drugs administered against his will; legal fees took another $5,000. (Those fees did not go to his own attorney, a law professor named Edward Benett, who donated his services, but to a lawyer hired by relatives who wanted to have Friedman committed.) More important, the drugging and brutality of the hospitalization had turned Friedman into a pathetic shell who defecated on himself, ran naked around the hospital corridors, and could no longer understand what was happening to him. When he learned of Friedman's condition, even the judge who committed him was shocked; he allowed Friedman to be released to a nursing home, but by then he could no longer function. When he died a few months later, the official cause of death was listed as cardiac arrest brought on by pneumonia. He was forty-four.

In New York City, a 58-year-old woman living in a welfare hotel becomes a nuisance to other residents: because of a physical problem, she uses the toilet too much; because she is a Christian Scientist, she refuses medical assistance; because she weighs 190 pounds, she rarely eats. After she begins sending letters of complaint to city authorities, the police and the men with the straitjackets arrive and haul her off to a mental hospital with a note from the Welfare Department that "she has been sending letters to the Mayor's Committee demanding a room with a bath, but despite attempts by the department to help her move, she has been unable to leave the hotel room or clean herself up so that she could be acceptable in a public hotel"—a Catch–22 problem, which was itself exacerbated, if not created, by the fact that other residents tried to keep her from using the bathroom. In the hospital, she tries to refuse medication—"I'm not sick," she insists. "I don't need any pill"—and is given the drugs intramuscularly by injection. Four months later, after continuous medication—no ailment had ever been diagnosed—she is released to live under what her attorney calls "the constant apprehension that she would be carted off to the hospital for the slightest misstep."

In Oakland, California, an applicant for public housing becomes involved in a screaming match with the clerk handling his case. The clerk calls the police; and the police take him to a "crisis center," where he is immediately put on drugs, held for three days, and released on condition that he continue his medication. In the year in which he is admitted, the crisis center daily reports that "37 percent of [a certain class of patients] tried suicide. For some these threats occurred just prior to admission; for others, the suicidal threats or gestures were noted while on the ward, but not prior to admission." (There is no indication that the writer suspected any irony or intended any joke.) The county mental-health system to which that clinic belongs commits some 4,000 people a year to closed institutions on an involuntary basis; of these 4,000, nearly 1,000 walked into their local clinic voluntarily.[8]

# II

Given the unlimited number of syndromes, symptoms, reactions, and disorders in the professional catalogue—psychiatric events, parapsychiatric events, maladjustments—and given the fact that most mental-health services are now delivered on an outpatient basis and involve neither the legal formalities nor the expense of incarceration, there is almost no "symptom" which by definition is unsuitable for the system and its ministrations. Yet in practice the mandate goes further, extending to virtually anything troubling anyone for which no other remedy is readily available. "Clients," said the annual report of a California clinic serving Asians, "have been provided counseling services which include translation, immigration issues, legal questions, cultural conflict problems, disorientation anxieties, and family problems." "Much emphasis," said the report of another, "is placed upon assisting individuals in negotiating their relationship with systems upon which they must rely for employment, training, education, legal aid and social services." In still another clinic, mental health includes "positive parent" training in the proper management of children; in a fourth, it includes a toy-lending library; and in a fifth, it comprises, among other things, sex counseling to "pre-orgasmic women." Nearly 60 percent of all treatment episodes in outpatient clinics involve problems which fall outside the major categories of mental illness in the diagnostic manual—problems, that is, which do not include a diagnosis of retardation, organic brain syndromes, schizophrenia, depressive disorder, drug disorder, alcohol disorder or other psychosis.[9] Nonetheless, at least half—and probably more—of all cases treated in those clinics include drugs as part of the treatment.

What all the centers have in common is "outreach"—the C and E, or the C, E, and I (consultation, education, and information)—of the local clinic. As defined in the federal program, C and E was to be the mandatory component which would alert the community and its officials to mental-health issues; which would look for "populations at risk," particularly those who just had a traumatic event in their lives; and which would satisfy the demands of the psychiatric evangelists who saw the snakes all around them. Psychiatrist Leopold Bellak, for example, advocated "a network of metropolis-wide or county-wide central registries [where] the social, emotional, and medical histories of every citizen who had come to attention in any way because of emotional difficulties would be tabulated by computer" and who, when they encountered "difficulties," could be offered "guidance and treatment." Since such proposals are sometimes modeled on public health and the control of contagious disease, the "offer" of treatment might, in fact, have to be mandatory. "Has a patient suffering from pulmonary tuberculosis a right to spit in public places?" asked psychiatrist Lawrence Kubie. "Has the patient with a sick mind a right to spread filth and violence?" Serious members of the profession have advocated psychiatric screening of candidates for public office, judicial positions, and civil-servant posts; in 1964, 1,200 members of the American Psychiatric Association declared Barry M. Goldwater "psychologically unfit to serve as President of the United States" (one of them declared the senator was probably a "schizophrenic, paranoid type"); and in 1971, the president of the American Psychological Association, Kenneth B. Clark, proposed in his presidential address that there be research in medication for public officials and candidates for office that would "assure their use of power affirmatively [to achieve] an internally imposed disarmament."[10] Most commonly, however, the population "at risk" is defined as people who are already in the medical or social-service systems, or those easily accessible to it: schoolchildren and their parents, pregnant women, old people in nursing homes, poor people, and various ethnic and racial minorities. "Being poor, disabled, a school dropout, unskilled, elderly or a child," said the *Alameda (California) County Plan for Mental Health Services,* "represents a now infamous cluster of significant variables."[11]

As a formal program operated by local centers, outreach rarely amounts to much. Most community mental-health organizations are already so busy, so sparsely staffed, and in some instances, so poorly administered that they are barely able to manage the clients who walk (or are dragged) through their doors. There is simply no time or money for the agency to do its own screening or find its own clients. Nor, for the most part, is it necessary. Those unlimited definitions of "disorder" have combined with administrative convenience to eliminate the distinction between the intramural and extramural activities of mental health. In many jurisdictions, the police have learned that it is easier and faster to dispose of cases by hauling them to the clinic than to jail or to court—the drunks, the junkies, the exhibitionists, the screamers, the people involved in family fights, the sidewalk nuisances—and in many communities, the other agencies of social service, welfare, schools, and housing refer their difficult clients for counseling, "evaluation," or "treatment." Richard A. Cloward and Frances Fox Piven, a team of Columbia University sociologists, reported on the case of a mother and three children who were burned out of their apartment in the Bronx.

> The mother desperately sought housing for several weeks, but could find nothing that welfare officials would approve and for which they would advance a security deposit. She then went to the public housing authority. When she was shunted aside, she began to scream and refused to leave the office until something was done to insure housing for her and her children. The police were called, with the result that she was placed in a mental hospital and her children sent for placement. The mother was promptly diagnosed as "schizophrenic —paranoid type," was medicated, and was involuntarily detained for several months. . . .

In another case, Cloward and Piven quote one of their students:

> Mrs. K. came to this country a few years ago from Puerto Rico. She was separated from her husband. She just had her second baby, and was trying to arrange for a friend to baby sit so she could return to work. The babies were often ill, and that required numerous visits to clinics [which] were also costly, and she had little money. Although Mrs. K. had previously worked double shifts she had used up her money during the pregnancy and she had been advised by the social worker to apply for public assistance, but no one had given her any help in dealing with the application process.
> Anyway, Mrs. K. didn't get the assistance, and she came

to the social service department of the hospital where I am in training. She was very upset; she always cried and appeared extremely nervous. She was then diagnosed by the team as . . . a "depressive neurotic" and therapy was recommended. . . .[12]

The cases are commonplace. The institution of social service converts what are essentially problems of money, housing, or education into "mental illness," and the mental-health system converts them into drugs. Those cases have no common denominator except, perhaps, for the client's unwillingness to accept bureaucratic decisions quietly, nor do the agencies have any hard data on how many such clients they have. Typically, mental-health organizations will report that between 10 and 20 percent of their clients were referred by other agencies; but those figures do not include the thousands of people who are persuaded by a welfare department, the police, or a social worker to seek treatment voluntarily and who are listed as "self-referrals"; the process of conversion which justifies mental-health intervention also functions to conceal the real source of the problem, and the most serious of those problems is lack of resources.

Informally, mental health has the outreach of an octopus —liaisons with schools, welfare agencies, private physicians, police, the courts—all of it backed by extensive advertising and public relations for crisis clinics, hot lines, alcoholism programs, and counseling centers. It is hard to find a school in which the guidance counselor, the principal, or the psychologist hasn't been "educated" by a community mental-health outrider to identify children with "emotional" problems and refer them for treatment; it is even harder to watch a night of television without seeing a public-service announcement for a local crisis center, a drug-treatment program, a suicide hot line, or a parent counseling class. "The message," said Peter Breggin, a Washington psychiatrist, "is bring in your sick relative, bring in your alcoholic."

Agencies that profess to provide schooling, housing, or

recreation become witting, covert extensions of mental health; and problems that had once been defined as matters of education, poverty, or character become diseases and syndromes. "The schools," said Joseph R. Perpich, who worked as a psychiatrist for the District of Columbia schools in the early seventies, "continually sought psychiatric evaluation for the problem child."

> Instead of fashioning a program to meet the child's needs and instead of trying to eliminate the conditions creating the child's problems, they preferred psychiatric treatment. If, in trying some other approach, I refused to give a psychiatric label to the child's problems he was referred to the juvenile court. Once again he was referred to a psychiatrist, but this time the court's interests dominated. If the child was placed on probation, the scenario was repeated, with the probation department's interests dominating. The child became a product of each institution's assembly line. . . . [13]

In Evanston, Illinois (suburban Chicago), the mental-health organization assigns a staff member to the local office of the Illinois State Employment Service to identify job seekers with a "mental-health problem" through "clues" which include "big gaps in the work history, inability to hold a job, aggressiveness and crying"; to "diagnose" their disorders; and to refer them to treatment. (The program was started because "when counselors suggested that perhaps a client needed mental health rather than vocational counseling, trouble often resulted.") In New York City, a community facility which represents itself as a recreation center providing day care gets itself licensed as a community mental-health facility so that it can collect Medicaid funds, and begins to diagnose the children to comply with Medicaid requirements; the clients—parents and children—are not informed of either the change or the fact that the kids are being diagnosed. In Denver, a "crisis intervention team" accompanies the county medical examiner to the homes of people who have suddenly died to offer preventive mental-health services to the surviving relatives. In San Jose, California, police answering calls to handle domestic disturbances—usually family fights—call in a team of mental-health counselors to take over once the dishes stop flying. And almost everywhere, schoolchildren are screened and tested for developmental and psychological problems; family histories are taken; and clients—parents and children—are referred or coerced into treatment.[14]

On paper, nearly all outpatients are volunteers, but the patterns of evaluation and treatment which follow that voluntary enrollment are so diverse that no generalization is possible. In places like the Peninsula CMHC, the process is almost identical with private therapy; it is therefore as good or bad as the private doctor to whom the patient is sent. In others, if the situation is not an obvious emergency—if the cops, for example, don't bring the client in—there may be a waiting period for an appointment. Typically, when a person shows up at a crisis center (for "crisis," read "routine problem"; real crises are handled by "emergency clinics"), he is sent to a "therapist," generally a psychiatric social worker, who interviews the client, jots down his observations in quasi-clinical shorthand ("45 yr old W/M, oriented, depressed, disheveled . . . "), and records personal data—marital status, financial status, education, history of mental illness—and, in many clinics, a list of "presenting symptoms," a "schedule of recent experience," a "global assessment," or a "client episode summary," which rate such things as "anxiety," "inappropriate affect, appearance, or behavior," "sexual problems," "housekeeper role—admission of doing a poor job as a housekeeper, no pleasure or satisfaction in any aspect of household duties," "social isolation—lack of friends," and scores of others. Usually the therapist will also record a diagnosis in the *DSM* code ("psychotic depressive reaction: 290.0"; "marital maladjustment: 316.0"), discuss a "plan of treatment" with the client—individual sessions, group sessions, medication—and schedule the next appointment.[15]

It is all done with the greatest clinical sympathy—a combination of concern, sober interest, and detachment—yet from the beginning, the client's life begins to recede behind those charts, rating forms, and assessments: first the problem is medicalized and then it is bureaucratized. The file may be two inches thick with anecdotal observations, descriptions of the patient's appearance, diagnostic workups, medication records, financial statements, and other data, without giving a real sense of the personal and social problems—or the strengths—behind them. *Cases:* Forty-year-old Jose Ramirez, recently separated from his wife, comes to a local clinic complaining that he is having trouble "getting her out of his mind." According to his chart, he is "depressed and suicidal, and has few social resources," and his treatment consists of five individual sessions and medication with antidepressant drugs. The background report records the fact that Ramirez was one of three survivors in a unit of several hundred men who were killed in Korea, and that Ramirez himself has worked twelve hours a day, seven days a week, for twenty years to maintain a small business; but these are not discussed in therapy or in the psychiatrist's notes. The psychiatrist says Ramirez "wants a marriage and a wife to play into."[16]

Edna McGuire is a 42-year-old white Catholic, twice divorced, who had been hospitalized a half dozen times, generally after making obvious but ineffective suicidal gestures in the presence of her "boy friend." Once she tried to poison herself with iodine; another time she took an overdose of the tranquilizers prescribed by the clinic to treat her "chronic undifferentiated schizophrenia"; and once she was picked up by the police after she tried to beat up her landlady. Although she completed high school, she has no skills, has never held a job, and is afraid to go out looking for one. Every page of her record suggests, but never makes explicit, the fact that she has absolutely no self-confidence, and that through most of her life everywhere she went she was trained to be dependent—on a husband, on welfare, on drugs, on a clinic. Discharged from the hospital, she is enrolled in a local outpatient clinic, where she sees a therapist once a month or once every two months and where, on each visit, she gets another set of refill prescriptions for her antipsychotic tranquilizers, her antidepressants, and for the anti-parkinson drug that is supposed to control the side effects of the tranquilizer. The clinician's notes for each visit in her "progress record" generally consist of one- or two-line entries: "Doing ok—needs appt." "Doing well—saw son after two yrs—Thinks she has diabetes—will call for appt." "In for meds—getting nervous again." "Worried about everything but life has never been better." "Worried about the people where she lives." "In for pills—doing ok. Afraid of violence in neighborhood." At each visit, the psychiatrist records "meds refilled" or "meds." In three years, she consumes nearly 8,000 pills; there is no medical examination, no attempt to help change her life! A few years earlier, after one of her suicide attempts had landed her in the hospital, the physician who prescribed most of those drugs outlined his "plan" for treatment: "Medicate," he ordered, "and hope for the best." In 1975, she is discharged from the clinic; in 1976, she is back asking for more medication. A psychologist gives her a prescription from a pad of presigned slips left for such purposes by a doctor. Later, the doctor signs the medication entry on McGuire's record.[17]

The advocates of community mental health claim that the thousands of clinics and programs established in the past twenty years have created not only an alternative to formal incarceration—either in jail or in a hospital—but that they represent an extensive system of "primary prevention" or "preventive intervention" which catches problems early, keeps them from worsening, and prevents the contamination from spreading. The first of those claims is undeniable: in most areas, local clinics have created new, tempting, and relatively cheap alternative means of intervention. The second is debatable. The few inadequate studies which have attempted to gauge the success of "primary intervention" indicate that it makes little or no difference. In a report on the Denver "crisis intervention" teams, for example, a team of psychiatrists concluded that "results did not support the hypothesis that such services decrease the risk of psychiatric illness, disturbed family functioning, or increased social cost to the families." The only difference, they reported, between the "treated" group of relatives of people who had died suddenly and a similar control group of untreated people was that the untreated group exhibited "significantly less concern than the treated group over their socioeconomic and social well-being six months after the death."[18] In general, programs of early intervention appear to have the same record of success as psychotherapy in general: roughly a third of the patients get better, a third get worse, and a third stay the same. The rate of spontaneous remission, according to British psychologist H. J. Eysenck, is higher than the rate of cure. "We are generally asked," said psychiatrist B. L. Bloom, "to evaluate the outcome of an undefined program having unspecified objectives on an often vaguely delineated recipient group whose level or variety of pathology is virtually impossible to assess, either before or after their exposure to the program."[19]

Most preventative psychiatry programs never bother with evaluation or even with definition. "It seems," said a psychiatrist at Albany Medical College, "that we are trying to saturate the environment with 'therapy' as though we were randomly filling the skies with massive amounts of flak without knowing whether the 'weapons' have any value or if the 'enemy' is even within range." Neither the practitioners nor the federal government, which helps support their work, seem to care about such issues; in the avalanche of official statistics, virtually nothing can be used to gauge the failure or success of the programs. "When one is among the devotees of specialized preventive interventions [suicide preventive interventions, suicide prevention, crisis intervention, premarital counseling, etc.]," said an editor of the *American Journal of Orthopsychiatry* more than a decade ago, "pressing the issue of evaluation receives about the same reception as questioning the long-range value of baptism during a christening."[20] Nothing has changed since those words were written.

What some clinics do provide as evidence of their success, other than those statistics on hospitalization, are surveys and anecdotes—before-and-after stories—about happy clients. Every therapist can cite instances of people who, after a few sessions, were less anxious, less guilty, and less depressed; and some agencies collect client reports indicating that a majority are "satisfied" or "very satisfied" with the services they received. Those reports appear to indicate that for those people who have been treated—those who didn't defect from the clinic and who were willing to answer the questionnaire —mental health (*i. e.,* the government) is providing, often for the first time, someone who will listen, a sympathetic ear, a sense of care. The level of that sympathy clearly depends on the personality and experience of the therapist, but its existence is undeniable. To call it pacification is too crude; call it diversion, the creation of a new concern for the client, a new relationship, an occupation in which the patient gets something new—an ailment, a syndrome, a problem—to think about and work on, even, for people like Edna McGuire, a whole career. If people like Newman are correct, the most important thing community mental health provides is not mental health but community.

# III

At the pinnacle are the closed institutions—mental hospitals, homes for the retarded, prisons for "defective delinquents" —and the half-closed institutions, which are supposed to represent one of the humane alternatives to total incarceration. The story of those closed establishments—the drugging, the brutality, the depersonalization, the filth—is by now so familiar that it is hardly worth restating. What is important here is that the closed institution, with its population of professedly severe cases, gives the whole system its credibility. It legitimizes the definitions and categories of madness, the anticipatory symptoms, the maladjustments; it legitimizes the clinics and the programs of prevention; and it legitimizes the drugs and the other "treatments" which are supposed to help avert disorder and illness. The closed institution thus becomes a symbol not only for those who are or have been in it, not only for the millions of others who are enmeshed somewhere in the formal programs of the mental-health system, but for virtually every person in the society.

Two generations ago, the prison was commonly represented (to children, for example, and more generally in the moral didactics of popular literature) as the end of the line for the social transgressor; since the fifties, and particularly in the last decade, the mental hospital has achieved equal, if not superior, symbolic importance. If one is of the middle class, he may be fairly certain that he can avoid jail; but there is no similar certainty that he can avoid a "nervous breakdown" or any of the other forms of madness so insistently advertised by the profession, the lay mental-health organizations, and the federal government. The individual is taught that it is not within his control: some day he may wake up to find . . . some day they may come to fetch him. To avert it, it would be well if, as advertised by a mental-health center in Tacoma, Washington, he would undergo a periodic "stress checkup," which, it is hoped, will become "as much of a reality one day . . . as dental and physical exams are today." (Such an idea is also being studied by the Kaiser-Permanent Medical Care System, the largest prepaid medical program in the country.) To avert a "nervous breakdown," it might also be a good idea, as proposed by the director of a mental-health institute in Wisconsin, if the society established "sane asylums" where the "worried well" could rest and recuperate before they reach a breaking point. To avert it, it might be advisable to take a tranquilizer for that "psychic tension" or check into a lithium clinic or get some estrogen tablets for that "middle-age depression."[21]

In the past decade, thanks to the efforts of civil-liberties lawyers, the Network Against Psychiatric Assault, and organizations like the Mental Health Law Project, as well as to the parsimony of state legislatures, the criteria of admission and commitment to closed mental institutions have become somewhat more stringent and the inducement to "community treatment" considerably greater. It is harder, in most states, to lock someone up against his will than it was a generation ago. ("Psychiatrists used to be proud to commit people to institutions," said Szasz in a moment of euphoria. "Now you'll find few who'll sign commitment papers."[22]) Yet, as late as 1973, the last year for which such figures are available, there were some 1.7 million inpatient "psychiatric treatment episodes" in mental hospitals and psychiatric wards of general hospitals, of which, according to the best estimates, at least half involved "involuntary" or "nonprotesting" patients.

In most states, it is still the law—and the practice—that a person may be involuntarily confined for temporary or emergency care (anywhere from one to thirty days) on the statement of any person (fourteen states); of a relative, guardian, spouse, or friend (seven states); or of a public official (thirty-two states or other jurisdictions). For longer commitments, the criteria include dangerousness to self or others, "need for treatment," and the client's "welfare" or the welfare of "others." In California, regarded as a highly progressive state with a model law, a person initially confined for three days on the authority of a mental-health professional designated by the county may be held for an additional fourteen days if the staff of the facility in which he has been confined feels he needs it. Thereafter, he is entitled to judicial review. If the court finds the patient suicidal, he can be held an additional two weeks; if he is found dangerous to others, he can be held for an additional ninety days; if he is found gravely disabled, a "conservator" (guardian) is appointed and the patient can be held indefinitely, subject to periodic review.[23]

In practice, however, the formal criteria are often meaningless; and the judicial hearing is usually a quick and cozy exercise in which the patient is addressed by his first name, judges and attorneys shuffle and pass papers about his condition that the patient never sees, the certifying psychiatrist appears only in the form of an affidavit, and public defenders who use every legal recourse in representing kidnappers and killers make their own decisions about their client's sanity and arrange his fate accordingly. "What they all want to avoid," said a lawyer in a California public defender's office who had been assigned to the "nut run," "is a jury trial. The county counsels really get pissed if you press them. . . . Of course I'll fight like hell in a serious criminal case, but this is different." In a study of psychiatric screening and commitment procedures conducted in the Midwest in the early sixties, the researchers found that the average length of the examination on which the psychiatric recommendation was based was 10.2 minutes, and the average duration of the judicial hearing was 1.6 minutes. "It's not remunerative," an examining psychiatrist told them. "I'm taking a hell of a cut. I can't spend forty-five minutes with a patient. I don't have the time; it doesn't pay." The screening, the researchers concluded, "is usually perfunctory, and in the crucial screening examination by the court-appointed psychiatrists, there is a presumption of illness."

In the intervening years, some state commitment laws have been tightened with additional procedural safeguards, including, in a few states, the right to a hearing before a jury (a highly significant addition, since a decent lawyer can usually make the psychiatrist look like the defendant); but most hearings involve no jury and are often colored by a patient so heavily drugged that he is barely able to speak. Many people in the profession, of course, are convinced that patients who ask to be released or who insist on their rights are —almost for that reason alone—sicker than their fellow inmates. One recent study of visitors to a "Patients' Rights Office" in a mental hospital, for example, concluded that such visitors "suffered from more pathology than the typical patient in their respective units."[24]

Yet, even if commitment procedures were less perfunctory, they would still lack any reasonable criteria on which decisions could be based: What is "gravely disabled?" What's the meaning of "dangerous to self or others," and how can it be established? How does a judge or jury determine what's best for the patient's "welfare," and what, in any case, gives them the right to do so? It has been demonstrated again and again that there is no accurate way to predict "dangerousness" (or even, indeed, to define it); that mental patients and former mental patients, despite headlines suggesting the contrary, are involved in fewer crimes than the general population; and that the vast majority of people who were incarcerated as "dangerous to others" and who are released against the wishes of their keepers (usually by blanket court order) do not get involved in criminal or violent activities.[25] Even in the few studies which claim "diagnostic reliability" for certain criteria—the most common (all obvious) are a history of childhood bed-wetting, fire-setting, violence toward animals, and parental deprivation—the majority of those persons released, despite a diagnosis of dangerousness, commit no offenses that bring them back into the system. In a project carried out by Massachusetts psychiatrist Harry L. Kozol, of 304 men arrested for sex crimes who were diagnosed by a psychiatric team and recommended for release, 9 percent were subsequently re-arrested for a similar crime; of thirty-one "sexually dangerous men" not recommended for release but released anyway, 39 percent became recidivists; of eighteen similarly diagnosed and subject to an average of two and a half years of "therapy" in a closed institution, 28 percent became recidivists. Those figures led Kozol to claim a high rate of effectiveness in prediction, if not in treatment.[26] Yet it also means, in the words of Alan A. Stone of Harvard, one of the most respected American scholars on the complex relationship of psychiatry and the law, that

> they had 61 percent false positives [people predicted as dangerous who were not] despite the fact that the patients invariably had already committed dangerous sex crimes before being admitted, and despite the fact that they had 60 days to examine the patients; and these predictions under these circumstances were made by five mental-health clinicians who had long experience with dangerous persons. Contrast that with the usual situation of one examining psychiatrist after a 1-hour or less interview of an alleged mental patient who has not yet committed a dangerous act, attempting to make this same sort of prediction as required by statute.[27]

Even people like Kozol concede that "no one can predict dangerous behavior in an individual with no history of dangerous acting out," a situation which, one would assume, is covered by ordinary criminal justice proceedings and does not require resort to the vague standards of civil commitment. Most studies, moreover, come to even more negative conclusions. In one survey of 14,000 patients released from New York state hospitals, the researchers found that the ex-patients had an arrest record of 6.9 per thousand, while the crime rate for the general population during the same period was 99.7 per thousand; and in a study of a group of "dangerous" inmates transferred under court order from correctional hospitals to civil hospitals or released outright, "the group transferred against psychiatric advice fared considerably better in civil hospitals and in the community than had been expected, was released at a higher rate than the [psychiatrically] approved transfers, and had only slightly more criminal activity after release."[28] What such studies often find is that the psychiatrist functions "as a conservative agent of social control" who would rather lock up a dozen people who are not likely to be dangerous than to be charged with the responsibility for releasing one who subsequently commits a crime; that psychiatrists therefore "overpredict dangerousness . . . by a factor between ten and a hundred times the actual incidence of dangerous behavior"; that race, age, and criminal record are the prime criteria in predicting dangerousness; and that laymen are just as successful in their predictions as professionals. "It can be stated flatly," said Stone, "that neither objective actuarial tables nor psychiatric intuition, diagnosis, and psychological testing can claim predictive success when dealing with the traditional population of mental hospitals."[29]

It is the very vagueness of the criteria that makes them so useful for social control, that gives the psychiatrist so much arbitrary power, and that makes the system's extensive interventions possible. With the exception of the juvenile justice system, no other social institution has the legal authority to confine individuals who have been convicted of no crime and who want no treatment; no other system gives such enormous authority to a professional group; no other system operates with a legally sanctioned mandate that it can incarcerate people indefinitely for their own good, the "welfare" of others, or for the purpose of preventive detention. The defenders of the mandate sometimes argue that a mentally incompetent person is in roughly the same condition as an unconscious accident victim who needs emergency treatment; the ailment itself makes it impossible for him to give informed consent, and his "real interests" must therefore be inferred and expressed by someone else. Even if one accepts the analogy, it has clear limitations in time, if not in substance; even if there were accurate means of prediction, there are no cures. "As the term of a civil commitment lengthens," wrote Robert A. Burt, professor of law in psychiatry at the University of Michigan, "its claim to a therapeutic purpose loses all plausibility. Community protection becomes its predominant, if not exclusive, purpose, and civil commitment becomes the functional equivalent of criminal commitment."[30]

But there is no reason to accept the analogy. The two situations are different. In the one case, there is an organically definable condition which makes consent, at least for the moment, impossible; in the other, there is often active resistance: the patient says "no" but is subject to treatment anyway, while his keepers conjure up a shadow person, a hypothetical individual in his "right mind," who really wants their intervention. At the same time, community protection may become anything from fear of dangerousness to a cosmetic dislike of nuisances, difficult relatives, ugly people, or uncooperative clients. Without standards, observed a judge in Washington, " 'dangerous to others' . . . could readily become a term of art describing anyone who we would, all things considered, prefer not to encounter on the streets."[31]

The importance of such fears—rarely discussed even among the most rabid opponents of civil commitment—is that in the past decade, the lines and distinctions between the various elements of the mental-health system have eroded, and that "mental health" has been extended to individuals who have never been inside a closed institution or even an outpatient clinic. Thus, while civil-liberties lawyers and organized groups of patients and ex-patients mount their attacks on the standards of incarceration, on the shabby and coercive conditions inside mental hospitals, and on the dangerous treatments these institutions impose, millions of other individuals are subject to the same treatments and to similar control simply because those institutions exist. "It's a hydraulic system," said Alan M. Dershowitz, a civil-liberties lawyer at Harvard. "Once a person is in the system he almost never gets out."[32] As standards and definitions change, people who would once have gone to prison are sent to mental institutions, and people who would once have gone to mental institutions are sent to nursing homes. In Florida recently, the legislature narrowly defeated a proposal to convert part of the G. P. Wood (Mental) Hospital, now unused, into a jail; and in Wisconsin, the mental-health director who proposed the creation of "sane asylums," suggested that vacant mental hospitals could be used for that purpose.

It is legislative policy and budgets, not medical science, which dictate how deviants are defined and handled. If there is more money for mental health and less for welfare, more poor people will be labeled as mentally ill; if there is money to educate retarded children in the school budget, retarded children will be found; if budgets of mental hospitals are cut, more people will be taken to clinics or to jail. Such shifts make it patently obvious that the concern is control, not treatment. At the same time, however, that hydraulic system continues to expand. In the 1840s, Dorothea Dix pleaded with the Massachusetts legislature to authorize the construction of asylums to get "the helpless, forgotten, insane, and idiotic men and women" out of the prisons and almshouses. A generation later, having succeeded, she discovered that the reforms she inspired had produced a whole new class of deviants; and that while the prisons remained full, the equally crowded asylums offered little that was better for those "wretched" beings than what they had had before. It was the prisons and the almshouses which gave the new system its credibility and, indeed, its entire reason for existence. Similarly, the asylum is now giving credibility to still another system and to the control and treatment of millions who had never been defined as deviants before.

More than a century after Dorothea Dix made her plea in Massachusetts, another hopeful reformer, Chief Judge David L. Bazelon, of the U.S. Circuit Court of Appeals for the District of Columbia, suffered a similar disillusionment. Bazelon had written some of the landmark opinions dealing with mental health, among them the 1954 Durham decision, which permitted psychiatrists great latitude in court to explain antisocial conduct in their own language, and thus, it was hoped, to bring psychodynamic insights to a criminal process whose moral overtones had, until then, been limited only by the question of whether a criminal defendant could tell right from wrong. By the early seventies, however, the psychiatrists had become witch doctors, and Bazelon was

disenchanted. "If you play Wizard," he told the American
Psychiatric Association in 1970, "then you let the rest of us
escape the hard confrontation that might bring about
change."

> Society is looking to you for the pill that will allow us to
> continue our pleasures without confronting the consequences.
> You can refuse to lend yourselves to that fruitless and danger-
> ous quest. If we are going to lock up our old people, or our
> ugly people, or anyone else, we should do it without leaning
> on you.
>
> It may be possible to build the community mental health
> center into the institution on which the community relies for
> solutions to its problems, and make all the solutions seem
> to turn on psychiatric decisions. But that route troubles
> me. . . .
>
> In the current clamor for law and order I see that our
> behavioral experts are willing to diagnose a wider and wider
> spectrum of so-called misfits as "dangerous." The effect is to
> implement a system of preventive detention and to ignore
> civil liberties. . . .[33]

What Bazelon was describing was the shell of the grand
vision. The system does, in its own ironic way, have the
"mayors and the people concerned about cities" as its clients;
but what they are getting (and what, in most cases, they ask
for) is not psychiatric guidance in environmental manipulation—assuming such a thing were even possible—but that
which psychiatry has always provided when it served the
state: the control and management of social deviants. (Soviet
psychiatrists have a theory, expressed in a monograph entitled *The Theory and Practice of Forensic-Psychiatric Diagnosis,* that "any illegal act, by virtue of its illegality alone,
merits psychiatric analysis [because] under socialist conditions there are no social causes for criminal acts."[34]) In the
system's willingness, as Bazelon said, to "diagnose a wider
and wider spectrum of so-called misfits," in its persistent
blurring of the lines between institutional and community
treatment, and in its intrusion into the lives of more and

more people the mental-health system has become a form of control impinging on the whole society. By defining deviance as illness and deviants as cases, it teaches everyone that its standards of normative behavior rest not on moral authority, cultural tradition, or political fiat, but on a "science" from which there is no appeal and against which there can be no rebellion.

—— FIVE ——

# The Chemistry
# of Liberation

## I

Drugs make the system feasible; drugs give it its extensive extramural capabilities. Without them there is only institutionalization and talking psychotherapy, which are prohibitively expensive, and electroshock and psychosurgery, which even their defenders believe should be used only in serious or "intractable" cases. With drugs virtually anyone can be brought within the orbit of "mental health," including millions of people who have never met a psychiatrist or anyone else formally associated with the madness network. The psychoactive drugs (unlike antibiotics, for example) never cure anything; at best they constitute a technology of maintenance which may enable the therapist or the institution to control or reduce hallucinations, bizarre behavior, or other "symptoms," and thus manage the client while talking psychotherapy does its work or until the conditions producing the anxiety, psychic tension, or stress are gone. The difficulty with the theory, as most of the controlled studies indicate, is that psychotherapy alone, or psychotherapy in combination with drugs, is no more effective than drugs alone; and that there are no cures, aside from "spontaneous remission," for most of the vaguely defined ailments classified as "mental disorder" or "mental illness." Therapy, as measured by effect, thus almost always means maintenance, and maintenance almost always means drugs.[1]

No one is certain how most psychotropic drugs work, why they work (when they work), or even how the major classes of drugs differ one from the other; nor is there any chance of agreement until the conditions which those drugs are supposed to mitigate are more precisely defined. There is, after all, no reliable way to judge the effects of antipsychotic phenothiazines (Thorazine, Stelazine, Mellaril) on schizophrenia if the "schizophrenia" is really "depression"; nor is there a way to measure the value of antidepressants on a "situational" depression produced by a depressing experience. Here, as in many similar controversies, science tends to follow politics. Most members of the psychopharmacology establishment insist that many drugs are highly specific, that the minor tranquilizers are ineffective in reducing hallucinations or other "distortions of thought" associated with schizophrenia and that, conversely, the antipsychotics have little impact on anxiety,[2] a dubious belief that seems to derive from the "traditional conception," as one writer put it, "of drug specificity exemplified by Paul Ehrlich's notion of the 'magic bullet' wherein a given chemical agent is believed to seek out a specific target in the organism."[3]

Many radical psychiatrists, on the other hand (as well as others who see most forms of mental illness in political or economic terms), contend that the phenothiazines are like all other tranquilizers, only more powerful and dangerous, that they simply suppress certain physical energizing systems in the body, that none of them has any specific effect on physiological functions, and that the apparent impact of antipsychotics on delusions or hallucinations is simply the consequence of suppression. In this view, the "specific" effect is a myth created by the doctors. Downers are downers.

Either way, it is clear that all psychotropic drugs have an enormous range of side effects—the antipsychotics, said one review of drug research, "can influence the function of almost every organ system in the body"; that many can be used to sedate, stupefy, or "snow" patients (and often are); and that, as medical sociologist Henry Lennard has pointed out, a drug's side effects may eventually be escalated and promoted as its prime effect.

> Drugs are sometimes relabled when their "side effects" prove to be more interesting than their main effect. The history of psychoactive drugs is replete with such examples. Phenothiazine was initially used as a urinary antiseptic and chlorpromazine [Thorazine] was then used to induce artificial hibernation to facilitate anesthesia during surgery, an action Henri Laborit [the French physician who used the drug for such purposes] termed "pharmacological lobotomy." Only later were its psychoactive properties identified as its main attributes. The discovery of the "specific" effects of lithium, amphetamines . . . and others have similar properties.[4]

Anyone who has ever taken Thorazine or has seen patients do what is sometimes called the Thorazine shuffle can understand why many people become "drug defectors" and what the textbook euphemisms really mean when they say that "the patient experiences a state of indifference or apathy, with a drowsy feeling and motor retardation." Typically, from a young woman:

> My tongue was so fuzzy, so thick, I could barely speak. Always I needed water and even with it my loose tongue often could not shape the words. It was so hard to think, the effort was so great; more often than not I would fall into a stupor of not caring or I would go to sleep. . . . I could not focus my blurred eyes to read and I always fell asleep at a film. People's voices came through filtered, strange. They could not penetrate my Thorazine fog; and I could not escape my drug prison.
>
> Yet to detail the physical suffering caused by these drugs is to touch only on one aspect of the pain they cause. Psychologically and emotionally they are devastating. They cause sensations—drowsiness, disorientation, shakiness, dry mouth, blurred vision, inability to concentrate—that would be enough to unnerve the strongest among us. . . . It is common practice among psychiatrists *not* to inform their patients that the disturbing things they are experiencing are

drug induced. . . . My hands would shake as I held a coffee cup, my legs would beat a wild tattoo on the floor, and sometimes I would fall asleep in the middle of a conversation. I *knew* I was deteriorating, going slowly, surely insane. No one thought it necessary to advise me otherwise. "But why do you *think* people are looking at you strangely?" Dr. Sternfeld would ask. Why indeed?

From a young man:

> After 10 days or so, the effects of the Prolixin began building up in my system and my body started going through pure hell. It's very hard to describe the effects of this drug and others like it, that's why we use strange words like "zombie." But in my case the experience became sheer torture. Different muscles began twitching. My mouth was like very dry cotton no matter how much water I drank. My tongue became all swollen up. My entire body felt like it was being twisted up in contortions inside by some unseen wringer. . . . But most disturbing of all was that I feared that all these excruciating experiences were in my mind, or caused by my mind—a sign of my supposed sickness. . . .[5]

The issue of specificity is further confounded by fundamental disagreement about the differences between drugs. One textbook, published in 1968, for example, asserts that the properties of antidepressants like Elavil and Tofranil—now among the most frequently used—"are quite similar to those of the antipsychotic tranquilizers"; and as late as the fall of 1975, a writer in the field observed that pharmacologically the antidepressants "behave like weak phenothiazine-like neuroleptics."[6] Some antidepressants were first synthesized as possible substitutes, or analogues, for the tranquilizers and were only later reported useful in treating endogenous depression. In the past five years, however, most psychiatrists and psychopharmacologists have begun discussing the two classes of drugs as if they were totally different in structure, chemical composition, and function: the antidepressants for depression ("mood disorders"), the antipsychotics for schizophrenia ("thought disorders"). There are similar disagreements about the two basic classes of tranquilizers: should the minor tranquilizers (Miltown, Valium, Librium) be classified with the "sedatives and hypnotics," should they be treated as a totally separate category ("antianxiety") with unique properties and effects, or should be listed with the major tranquilizers?

The issue is significant because the labels themselves help create an illusion of medical specificity and scientific precision where there may be little of either. If the drugs are specific, then there may be justification for the claim that they are "medicine"; if they are not specific—if they are indistinguishable from each other—then the person prescribing them is using them primarily as instruments of pacification and control.

Probably the most confounding element of all is the fact —on which there is nearly universal agreement—that in practice, the drugs are almost never used with any specificity; that a substantial number of patients are overdosed; that many physicians—psychiatrists as well as internists, gynecologists, and pediatricians—prescribe psychoactive drugs indiscriminately, redundantly (polypharmacy), and paradoxically (e. g., a tranquilizer and a stimulant); that they are fearful of reducing dosage or eliminating drugs altogether; that drugs are often, if not usually, prescribed without a physical examination despite package warnings listing extensive dangers and cautions; that dosage often depends on the clinician's personal fear, cultural and racial bias, or the requirements of institutional management rather than medical judgment; that drugs are used increasingly for marginal or nonexistent ailments (even by the loose definitions of existing practice); that side effects produced by the drugs are frequently written off as "symptoms" of the diseases for which they have been prescribed; that the long-term effects of the phenothiazines often include an irreversible form of neurological damage—tardive dyskinesia—which was unknown to medicine before the drugs were introduced; and that over the long run, heavy use of the minor tranquilizers may be as addictive and dangerous as the conventional street drugs of abuse. While the federal government tries to crack down on heroin and cocaine, the U. S. Drug Enforcement Administration's own figures indicate that diazepam (Valium) is more often involved in drug-related deaths and other hospital and crisis-center emergencies than heroin, marijuana, or alcohol. In such a context—the context of practice—specificity is always an illusion.[7]

# II

Their history is almost as old as mankind—various snake-roots and hallucinogens have been used for centuries—and by the time of World War II, amphetamines and barbiturates, the classic uppers and downers, were standard items in the pharmacopeia of mood and behavior. Virtually every army in the world provided amphetamines to its troops, and particularly to its fliers, to keep them alert for long hours; and most physicians have used barbiturates as sedatives and sleeping pills for many years. None of the drugs known at the end of the war, however, were reliable in controlling the behavior of mental patients—many of whom were often chained or locked in padded cells—without, at the same time, sedating them into oblivion. (Both amphetamines and barbiturates were also highly addictive, but that was not to be recognized for many years.) The breakthrough came in the early fifties when a group of French physicians and pharmacologists searching (as one of them would say later) for a drug that might "produce the cold-bloodedness, 'indifference' or ataraxia extolled by the Stoics," stumbled on chlorpromazine (Thorazine), a drug synthesized in 1950, which "reproduced in warm-blooded animals conditions existing in cold-blooded or hibernating ones" and which was originally intended for use in surgery to slow heart rate, pulse, and other organic functions.[8] In 1951, it was tried on manic patients in a French military hospital, where the psychiatrists "found its effects interesting but not strong enough, and returned to electroshock therapy"; in 1952, it was tried on schizophrenics; and by 1954, physicians on both sides of the Atlantic were administering it to thousands of institutionalized patients with what its advocates, then and now, regarded as near-miraculous results. The description of the effects borders on the lyrical. Before, in the words of Frank J. Ayd, Jr., a Baltimore psychiatrist, publisher of the *International Drug Therapy Newsletter,* and perhaps the greatest American advocate of psychoactive drugs,

> nurses and attendants, ever in danger, spent their time protecting patients from harming themselves or others. They watched men and women who either refused to eat or gorged themselves. . . . Trained to be therapists, they functioned as guards and custodians in a hellish environment where despair prevailed and surcease by death offered the only lasting respite for their suffering charges. . . . For lack of more effective remedies, they secluded dangerously frenetic individuals behind thick doors in barred rooms stripped of all furniture and lacking toilet facilities. They restrained many others in cuffs and jackets or chained them to floors and walls. . . .

After:

> Beside the salutary decrease in patient population, a transformation has occurred in mental hospitals in the past two decades that defies description. Visit one today. You will be impressed by the serenity you observe and feel. You will sense the attitude of realistic optimism that predominates. Flowers, curtains, paintings, music, fresh air, comfortable tidy lounges make a pleasant environment for clean, tranquil patients being offered a myriad of therapies. . . . [9]

Whether or not Thorazine and the other major tranquilizers introduced in its wake actually produced the transformation Ayd recounts is debatable—most mental hospitals are not the sylvan places he describes, nor have straitjackets, manacles, and locked rooms vanished—but there is no question that for thousands of people, the drug made physical restraint unnecessary and that, beginning in 1955, the resident population of American mental institutions began to decline. With the introduction of Miltown (meprobamate) in that same year, the euphoria spread from the institutions to the world outside, and psychoactive medication entered its heroic age, a period when even sober medical journals reported that drugs like Miltown were judged "uniformly successful by all observers," and when the antianxiety effects of the minor tranquilizers and the antipsychotic effects of the phenothiazines suggested to a growing number of practitioners that drugs could be used to do almost everything. The enthusiasm—in popular literature, in the medical journals, and at professional conventions—was unbounded: the drugs (one or another, or all of them together) would cure mental illness, end anxiety, wipe out senility, eliminate stress and tension, and create possibilities for virtually unlimited enhancement of experience. As late as 1964, when it was already clear (according to one survey of the literature) that the claims for Miltown were based largely on "uncritical, unscientific reports," Frank M. Berger, the Wallace Laboratories scientist who synthesized meprobamate, was to declare in the *Journal of Neuropsychiatry* that "the drug most needed is the one that would liberate our minds from their primitive and outdated ways. Meprobamate may be the first substance of this type."[10]

Predictably, the profession and industry promised remedies not only for the formally established categories of mental illness but for a long list of complaints which had never been regarded as illnesses before, and each year, they have managed to find more maladies susceptible to drug management and invent them where they did not exist.

During the last two decades, the medical and psychiatric journals have been full of pictures of women with anxious faces and disheveled hair standing in front of stacks of dirty dishes or cowering behind prisonlike bars holding mops and brooms, and of men with angry expressions exclaiming, "Women are impossible," and, under them, the reassuring message of the drugger: "You can't set her free but you can help her feel less anxious." "In pre-menstrual tension, your prescription of Equanil can help ease his wife's anxiety, thus reducing her irritability and nervousness." "She has insomnia . . . so he's awake. Restless and irritable, she growls at her husband. How can this shrew be tamed?" Hoffmann-La Roche conjured up the anxious college student for whom "exposure to new friends and other influences may force her to reevaluate herself and her goals" and for whom Librium might be indicated; CIBA offered "environmental depression . . . often expressed as listlessness"; and Smith Kline and French offered readers of the *American Journal of Psychiatry* a choice between an African mask representing "the spirit of the underworld . . . basic tool of primitive psychiatry" and Thorazine, "basic tool of Western psychiatry" (apparently with no suspicion of irony). But perhaps the most inventive was Sandoz, which promoted Serentil, a major tranquilizer:

> For anxiety which comes from not fitting in—the newcomer in town who can't make friends and the organization man who can't adjust to altered status within his company, the woman who can't get along with her new daughter-in-law, the executive who can't accept retirement, these common adjustment problems of our society are frequently intolerable for the disordered personality who often responds with excessive anxiety. Serentil is suggested for this type of patient.[11]

The hero-drugs in this heroic age are the antidepressants and the antipsychotic phenothiazine tranquilizers—Thorazine, Stelazine, Mellaril—which, according to most studies, including large-scale "collaborative" investigations conducted by the Veterans Administration and NIMH, have played a major part in reducing the length of hospitalization or in preventing it altogether. In one study, the "relapse rate" for a group of "chronic female schizophrenic outpatients" treated with Thorazine was 13 percent, while that of a con-

trol group receiving a placebo was 56 percent. Other studies
have come up with figures of 35 and 80 percent respectively,
or with 19 and 31 percent, with an average difference between drug and placebo clients of some 40 percent. There are
comparable, though somewhat less conclusive, differences
for antidepressants. One review of reports published between
1965 and 1972 found that roughly two-thirds concluded that
antidepressants are "superior" to placebo, while a third did
not. (One of the most careful and extensive studies, however,
found little difference between the effects of antidepressants,
Thorazine, and placebo on depressed patients and concluded
that "at best, treatment differences accounted for only 10
percent of the predictable variance on any outcome measured."[12])

The difficulty with such conclusions is that even if one
takes their definitions at face value—if one assumes, for example, that "hospitalization" or "recidivism" is really an
indication of illness, that clinicians' evaluations of "severity"
measure real sickness, or that their tests and scales reflect
medical and not cultural criteria—the studies themselves
demonstrate that roughly half of the people who receive such
drugs don't need them and don't benefit from them. There
are indications, moreover, that "relapse following drug dis-
continuation can be reversed in the majority of cases by
prompt resumption of drug therapy"; that the people who
relapse on drugs are, for reasons unknown, in worse shape
than those who relapse on placebo; and that those who "survive" on drugs (i. e., do not relapse) have a more difficult
time in daily life than those receiving a placebo, a conclusion
which is hardly surprising considering the side effects of
those drugs.[13] In one of the few such reports to be published
in an establishment journal (American Journal of Psychiatry), a group of researchers under William T. Carpenter at
NIMH pointed out that "all too frequently the effects of
treatment on outcome are determined by measuring unitary
dimensions such as length of hospital stay" (in fact, only four
of thirty-one studies on maintenance drug therapy in schizo-

phrenia published before 1975 used criteria other than "symptom relapse" or "rehospitalization"). Using "social or work function" as well as the conventional criteria to determine the effects of treatment, Carpenter's team found that a group of "acute schizophrenics" treated with little or no medication fared as well or better than a similar group receiving what they called the "usual" treatment. "In an illness with so many paradoxes," they concluded, "we raise the possibility that antipsychotic medication may make some schizophrenic patients more vulnerable to future relapse."[14] And in a similar study using only hospitalization as a criterion, a group of researchers headed by California psychiatrist Maurice Rappaport found that of a group of eighty men diagnosed as "acute schizophrenics" who were assigned randomly to Thorazine or placebo treatments, those on placebo fared better in every category than those on Thorazine—roughly 28 percent of the placebo patients were rehospitalized within three years, whereas roughly 60 percent of the Thorazine patients were rehospitalized—results which led Rappaport to conclude (with considerable modesty) that "the study supports previous observations that there is a subgroup of schizophrenics who do well or better long term without the routine or continuous use of antipsychotic medication." In an interview Rappaport said that while the data might have justified more extravagant and sweeping conclusions, he intentionally toned them down to increase the chances that the study would be accepted for publication in a major psychiatric journal. It was not.[15]

The Rappaport and Carpenter studies are among the few that challenge the conventional wisdom about antipsychotics. Yet, as one careful survey pointed out,

> Even though the conclusions [of large-scale collaborative investigations] and other studies are supported by impeccable methodology and highly sophisticated studies, the questions still remain: How many patients benefit from drug therapy? How effective are those drugs? Reports on the subject are

extensive, complex, and often contradictory, but . . . investigations, with the patient's ability to remain in the community as a criterion of drug effectiveness, reveal that 60 to 70 percent of acute schizophrenics on no drugs are readmitted within one year. . . .

However, the difference between those patients treated with drugs and those not treated with drugs decreases over time. According to one study, the difference may be only on the order of 10 to 15 percent after several years. As for the quality of the patient's adjustment after he leaves the hospital, the results of drug therapy are even less encouraging: the majority of those who live in the community continue to be unproductive and are often a burden to their families.[16]

Beneath such questions lies a morass of conceptual and definitional problems. The use of "the patient's ability to remain in the community" as a criterion makes the arbitrary standards of hospitalization measures of medical effectiveness, converts tautology into science—he is sick because he is in the hospital—and thus legitimizes medication through practices now universally recognized to be unscientific and imprecise. "A malfunctioning brain," wrote George E. Crane, research director of a state hospital in Maryland,

is not the only cause of interpersonal and social difficulties for the schizophrenic patient. The deprivation and stresses of the poverty in which this person is forced to live . . . are also responsible for what is often called unacceptable behavior. . . . Hence drugs are prescribed to solve all types of management problems, and failure to achieve the desired results causes an escalation of dosage, changes of drugs, and polypharmacy.[17]

Given such practices—and they are commonplace—the studies themselves render control of socially or culturally defined forms of unacceptable behavior a major test of drug effectiveness. All over America sit those people—some three or four million—who are being "successfully" treated—nodding in rocking chairs; staring out of windows of nursing homes; shuffling into clinics for their monthly shot; listening to doctors or nurses or relatives warning them that if they don't behave, the medication will be increased, or to judges informing them that if they don't take their Mellaril, they'll have to be locked up. "People are propagandized into believing that they need drugs," said Berkeley psychiatrist David Richman in an interview, "or they're so afraid of going to the hospital, or of getting shock treatment, that they take them."

The shuffle is characteristic of antipsychotic medication, as are the involuntary extrapyramidal movements: the twitches, rigidity, and tremors. Among the possible adverse reactions listed by the manufacturer for Stelazine are "drowsiness, dizziness, skin reactions, rash, dry mouth, insomnia, amenorrhea, fatigue, muscular weakness, anorexia, blurred vision, motor restlessness, pseudo-parkinsonism, persistent tardive dyskinesia. . . ." For Thorazine: "drowsiness, fainting, dizziness, and, occasionally, a shock-like condition; pseudo-parkinsonism, motor restlessness, persistent tardive dyskinesia, psychotic symptoms, catatonic-like states, convulsive seizures, hyperglycemia, hypoglycemia, dry mouth, nasal congestion, constipation. . . ." For Elavil; "hypotension, hypertension, confusional states, disturbed concentration, disorientation, delusions, hallucinations, excitement, anxiety, restlessness, insomnia, nightmares, dry mouth, blurred vision, constipation. . . ." ("Of course the phenothiazines are downers," Richman said. "The muscles are rigidified—there's no threshold; it zonks them out; they're chemical restraints. I've seen people six weeks after their last shot of Prolixin and they're still rigid.") People on Thorazine—even those on low doses—score substantially lower on tests of attention and concentration than control groups who are not drugged. In the prosaic language of a medical textbook, "considerable evidence exists in humans indicative of drug-induced decreased efficiency."

> *Memory* [immediate recall] was impaired in both normal and in schizophrenic, psychoneurotic, and depressed patients undergoing drug therapy with diazepam, meprobamate, chlor-

promazine. . . . *Reasoning* ability [organizational and problem solving abilities] and capacity to abstract [judgment and learning of conceptual relationships] declined after meprobamate, chlordiazepoxide and chlorpromazine. The *mental speed* with which a simple task [arithmetic ability] was carried out was slowed by meprobamate, diazepam, or chlorpromazine. *Learning* [incorporation of new information or new relationships] was deleteriously affected in normals and in patients undergoing drug therapy: meprobamate, diazepam, trifluoperazine, and chlorpromazine have been shown to retard the learning process.[18]

The authors of this summary caution the reader "that such effects . . . are not an essential accompaniment to drug administration. . . . In most instances these effects occur only in some patients, in individuals with specific personality characteristics, only at specific dosages, or only at certain times during the course of extended drug use." In the classic studies of the effects of the major tranquilizers on concentration and attention, however, the average drug-induced deficit on low to moderate doses is 1.9 years, precisely the same as that found in people who have been lobotomized.[19]

The most significant of the side effects is the ailment called tardive dyskinesia, an apparently irreversible form of brain damage which affects (depending on the study) anywhere from 2 to 40 percent of those medicated with antipsychotics; the percentages tend to rise with the length and dosage of medication and, it is believed, with the age of the patient. First reported in Europe in the late fifties, it was originally described in one case as follows:

The tongue permanently projected forward and backward following a rapid rhythm; at times the projection is to the side, sometimes to the right, sometimes to the left; a torsion motion, or rotation on its axis complicates its incessant coming and going motion. The mouth is half open and lip movements accompany this continuous dyskinesia. The patient is slightly bothered by this, and her speech is slightly troubled, but remains comprehensible. . . . The act of speaking or of swallowing temporarily suspends these motions, which resume immediately afterwards. Asking the patient to execute a hand motion considerably accentuates the seriousness. . . . The lips participate in this dyskinesia in the form of stereotyped sucking motions, pursing, rolling and incessant champing in synergy with rhythmic contractions of the jaw. Sometimes, on the other hand, there is rhythmic opening of the mouth which facilitates protrusion of the tongue.[20]

Since that description was published, other studies have also reported "a peculiar gait with abduction of the arms," "continuous jerky movements of the upper and lower extremities, particularly of the fingers, ankles and toes," grimacing, overextension of the spine and neck, and other abnormal postures and movements. Unlike more routine "extrapyramidal" movements and contortions associated with antipsychotic medication, tardive dyskinesia often is not apparent until after medication has been stopped; unlike other extrapyramidal symptoms, which can sometimes be controlled with anti-parkinsonian drugs (which are themselves dangerous in long-term use), tardive dyskinesia appears to respond to no known form of treatment. It is permanent and irreversible.[21]

The problem of side effects is compounded by the inability or unwillingness of many practitioners to distinguish them from the symptoms of the disease for which the drugs were allegedly prescribed. In tardive dyskinesia, resumption of psychotropic medication sometimes masks the dyskinetic effects, and there are indications that many doctors will continue or reintroduce drugs to conceal the problems which the medication caused originally. "We believe," wrote George Gardos and Jonathan O. Cole, two Boston psychiatric leaders in the psychopharmacology establishment, "that at least some relapses, especially during the first four to six weeks after [medicine is withdrawn] are attributable to withdrawal emergent dyskinesia rather than to psychotic decompensation."[22] What that means is that yesterday's drug caused today's problem. Equally important, many of the other neurological side effects of psychoactive drugs are conveniently ascribed to the syndromes for which they were originally administered and are therefore reported as part of the disease and not as a consequence of the remedy. In one Scandinavian study, researchers concluded that more than a third of the elderly patients admitted to the psychogeriatric unit of a public hospital were suffering not from any mental illness but from "confusional states attributable to psychotropic medication." There is no way of knowing how many similar "confusional states" are ascribed to schizophrenia, organic brain damage, or other ailments, but most studies indicate that at least half of those who take antidepressants or antipsychotics suffer from one or more drug-induced problems—physical, psychological, or neurological. The temptation is always there, particularly in light of the fact that many therapists are unwilling to admit that in roughly a third of the cases, the drugs have no positive effect—even by their shaky criteria—and that in some they produce a "paradoxical disinhibition" which aggravates the symptoms. "Evidently," said Brian M. Learoyd, an Australian psychiatrist who reviewed such cases, "as a patient becomes progressively more excited, prescribed drugs were increased in number and dosage, ultimately leading to an uncontrollable subject necessitating admission to hospital. Complete withdrawal of all medication usually corrected the situation."[23]

Such caveats, however, hardly trouble most of the practitioners. They are luxuries for medical-journal articles, testimonials to professional caution. "Many physicians," wrote Crane in 1973, "are still unaware of [dyskinesia] or seem to be completely unconcerned about it. . . . Lack of clinical information cannot explain this ignorance of a major health problem—more than 100 papers reporting 2,000 cases of tardive dyskinesia have been published since 1957. The diagnosis offers no major difficulties. . . ." What Crane and others suggest is that the doctors have simply become too dependent on their drugs to face the possibility that the technology may be as dangerous as the ailments it is designed to control.

"The problem of tardive dyskinesia should be viewed as another example of large-scale and inefficient application of a potentially useful technical discovery without consideration for its long-term effects on the individual and his environment."[24]

# III

It is often difficult to distinguish the studies from the promotion, the doctors from the drug companies. In 1971, while American medical schools were spending a total of $977 million for all their educational activities, the Social Security Administration estimated that the pharmaceutical industry was spending roughly $1 billion to promote drugs, an average of nearly $5,000 per practicing physician. From the moment students enter medical school they are, in the words of a statement from an organization of Chicago medical students, "bombarded [by drug firms] with 'gifts' of stethoscopes, reflex hammers, pamphlets and books, culminating at graduation with engraved black bags to keep it all in. In the classroom drug companies reach students by providing films, slides, speakers, research grants, and even pharmacology teachers." "The Eli Lilly Company," reads the circular from the associate dean at Rush Medical College, "is again offering to all incoming medical students a free gift of a stethoscope, tuning fork, and percussion hammer"—and once the students begin practice, the gifts become more generous.[25] It is the drug companies and NIMH, whose community mental-health program rests on drugs, which support nearly all domestic psychotropic drug research; it is the drug companies which subsidize the medical journals in which that research is reported, the conventions where it is discussed, and the professional conferences where it is evaluated (and which are often conducted in great medical centers like

Puerto Rico, New Orleans, and Miami Beach). In testimony to a U. S. Senate subcommittee in 1974, psychiatrist Paul Lowinger "confessed" that

> I received money from Hoffmann-La Roche to attend the International Congress of Psychotherapy in England in 1964 and in 1965 I received money from Geigy to attend an American Psychiatric Association meeting in Hawaii. They were most interested in their sales of Librium and Tofranil respectively at the Lafayette Clinic [in Detroit] where I directed the outpatient service and trained medical students, psychiatric resident physicians and practicing physicians taking post graduate work in psychiatry. I was also engaged in research on Librium and Tofranil. . . . My social responsibility has improved since the mid-sixties, so I can now urge my colleagues who receive similar goodies to come forward. The acceptance of honoraria by physicians in administrative and drug testing positions is well known around the industry, the hospitals and the medical schools.[26]

The ethics and the practices haven't changed; and although Lowinger is one of the few to make such a public admission, thousands of doctors continue to be showered with everything from trinkets to trips. "The Society of Biological Psychiatry," says the convention program, "gratefully acknowledges the grant support given to its 1976 scientific meetings by Endo Laboratories, Inc., E. R. Squibb and Sons, Inc., Hoffmann-La Roche, Inc., McNeil Laboratories, Inc., Merck Sharp and Dohme, Parke-Davis and Company, Smith Kline and French Laboratories [and] Searle Laboratories."

It is a cozy relationship. Most of the major figures in drug research serve as consultants to drug firms and, at the same time, to NIMH and the Food and Drug Administration, which licenses the drugs. They review each other's grant proposals, sit on the same committees, work on the same studies, write for each other's journals, attend the same meetings, and go to the same parties. NIMH employees collaborate with drug-company consultants in mental-health research; NIMH consultants appear before FDA review committees on behalf of drug companies; editors of journals heavily supported by drug-company advertising serve on "impartial" FDA committees reviewing the safety and efficiency of medication produced by their advertisers.

In the case of Cylert, a controversial pediatric stimulant now being marketed by Abbott Laboratories of North Chicago, Illinois, the FDA named Chicago psychiatrist Daniel X. Freedman to head a review committee. Freedman, who recently served as a vice-president of the American Psychiatric Association, is editor of the monthly *Archives of General Psychiatry,* a journal laced with drug-company advertising, and which, in the first year that Cylert was on the market, published at least twenty-eight pages of advertising for the new product. When representatives of the company appeared in Washington to press their argument for a license, they brought with them Donald F. Klein, a prolific drug researcher at Long Island Jewish-Hillside Medical Center who was, at the same time, a consultant in neuropharmacology to the FDA, a member of the Clinical Psychopharmacology Research Review Committee of NIMH, and a paid consultant to Abbott; and Paul Wender, another Abbott consultant, then serving as a half-time employee of NIMH.[27] "I felt like an outsider," said Mary C. Howell, a pediatrician who served briefly on the FDA Psychopharmacology Advisory Committee. "They're not dishonest by their own standards, but they all have their in-jokes, they went to the same schools, they go to the same meetings, and they do the same kind of research." There is simply no money to support research to prove that drugs don't work, or that they are dangerous, or that they are ill-used. When Howell suggested that the FDA require a package insert for psychoactive drugs warning that "long-term use in the absence of adjunctive measures . . . is rarely in the best interests of the patient's mental health," the proposal was referred to a subcommittee (to which she was not named) that killed it.

The evidence for or against drugs is further skewed by the

companies' penchant simply to conceal unfavorable results, to hide reports of dangerous side effects, and to present available evidence in its most favorable terms. In 1965, for example, Lowinger, at the time an associate professor of psychiatry at Wayne State University in Detroit and head of outpatient services at the Lafayette Clinic, discovered accidentally that although his findings that the drug Dornwal produced "serious toxic effects on the blood" had been sent to the manufacturer, they had not been reported to the FDA as required by law. Subsequently, Lowinger followed up on twenty-seven new drug studies in which he had been involved between 1954 and 1966 (among them many of the psychoactive drugs now on the market, including Librium, Stelazine, and Equanil) and for which he had reported problems of safety. Although the FDA first refused to release the information because "it would be inappropriate to divulge the names of firms who have failed to submit certain clinical data," Lowinger managed to procure it through the aid of two U. S. Senators and discovered that of the nineteen firms for which he had conducted studies, twelve had submitted no reports, while two others had submitted reports on some studies but not on others. "Drug safety problems which were unreported," Lowinger later testified, "included dizziness, drowsiness, mood depression, anxiety, insomnia, blurred vision, loss of anal sphincter control, ringing in the ears, headaches, itching, dermatitis, weakness, fatigue, nausea, diarrhea, abdominal distress, constipation, and a possible case of hepatitis." In 1966, before he decided to pursue his own inquiries, Lowinger had written a letter to *Science,* "asking how often pharmaceutical houses conducting new drug investigations failed to report the results of their studies to the FDA. I received no answer from my colleagues in medical science, the pharmaceutical industry or the government."[28] If there is an establishment anywhere, there is one in psychopharmacology.

Among the persistent themes characterizing the drugs is that they are liberating potions, preparations that will calm

(Compazine, Serentil), lift (Elavil), mellow (Mellaril), or free (Librium) the patient from his demons. Thus, even a highly respected (and highly prolific) researcher like Leo E. Hollister, a Veterans Administration psychiatrist, seeks to clarify confusion in drug labeling and functions by proposing the theme of liberation:

> The unfortunate introduction of the epithet "tranquilizer" created much misunderstanding about the value of psychotherapeutic drugs. Many, opposed on ideological grounds to all drug therapy of emotional disorders, construed these drugs as "chemical straitjackets." Much evidence to the contrary has developed . . . so that these drugs may more properly be called "liberating," when properly used. Although many other names have since been suggested, the "anti-" system has much to recommend it, because it indicates the uses of the various types of drugs. Thus we speak of antianxiety drugs, antidepressives, antipsychotics, and antimanic agents.[29]

The consistent theme of drug literature and advertising suggests that the drugs do not free the patient from his demons, his anxieties, and his psychoses as much as they free the physician, the institution, and the society from the patient himself. In the ads, the physician (male) often appears as anxious as the patient (generally female); for him, as one of them says, "the buck stops here"—he is "the last resort." "Elavil," says another, "once daily at bedtime to help improve patient compliance." "Prolixin," says a third, "can save time, it can save money, and it can even save people." Who is being freed from what in that Haldol advertisement depicting the "assaultive and belligerent" dark-skinned young man standing there with his fist clenched?

# IV

In practice the drugs are consistently used as a means of control. The clients walk in or are coaxed in or are dragged in: the 65-year-old woman who has been an embarrassment to her suburban children and who thinks the injection is for her back pains; the alcoholic who has to take his Valium or his Antabuse because he has to be in "treatment" in order to collect his federal disability benefits; the girl who was pulled off the railing on the bridge; the probationer from the mental hospital who must appear every three weeks for his shot of Prolixin; the housewife who refuses to cook her husband's breakfast any more and believes she is suffering from a nervous breakdown.

Roughly 90 percent of those diagnosed as "schizophrenic" are drugged automatically; virtually everyone who is hospitalized is drugged; virtually everyone who comes in (or is brought in) to an emergency clinic is drugged; any person considered homicidal or suicidal is drugged; mentally retarded children are drugged; prisoners are drugged; and a growing number of people—now certainly numbering in the millions and including highly disproportionate numbers of the poor and black—are drugged preemptively to prevent "relapse," "recidivism," or generally bad behavior.[30] "While I was getting the shots," said a former patient, "the doctor asked me if I had thought about what he had said about my rebelling. He asked it in a tone of voice as if to say, 'Have you learned your lesson yet, Miss Brewer?'" "When the [patients] refused medication, refused to cooperate in other ways, threatened to break rules or did break them," said another, "it was common to inject three or four times their normal dose of tranquilizer . . . to render the patient comatose and make it clear to him who's boss." The stories are substantiated by reports that (as described in a study of practices at the Massachusetts Mental Health Center in the sixties) "some physicians impatiently 'snow' patients with massive doses to render them powerless, controllable, and asleep," and by increasing experimentation with drugs and hormones to control the "aggression" of prisoners, mental patients, retarded children, juvenile delinquents, "hyperactive" children, sex deviates, persons with "personality disorders," alcoholics, drug abusers, epileptics, boys with "precocious puberty," and individuals presenting problems of "verbosity, hyperactivity, stubbornness, and generally obnoxious behavior."[31]

Because of the drugs, aggression itself is being transformed into a disease and the major tranquilizers (or other medication) credited, in the words of a report in the *Journal of Nervous and Mental Disease,* "with some kind of 'specific' effects on aggressive symptomatology" in people "without psychosis." At the California Medical Facility in Vacaville, for example, a group of twenty-seven prisoners was dosed with large quantities of lithium for periods ranging from three to eighteen months to reduce aggression (as measured, in part, by frequency of prison-rule infractions), and similar studies are now under way at the Cheshire (Connecticut) Correctional Facility and other institutions. At the Johns Hopkins University in Baltimore, teams of doctors have been experimenting with hormone treatments—described by one of them as "chemical castration"—in the control of sex offenders and "sex deviates" (including transvestites, homosexuals, and exhibitionists), while at the University of Maryland's School of Medicine, Russell B. Monroe, one of the most active researchers in the field, is treating "female adolescents" who have been locked up for "incorrigible behavior" with tranquilizers and anticonvulsants.[32] The accumulating results of those proliferating experiments have yielded virtually nothing to indicate that the drugs have any specific use in controlling aggression, which is not a disease in any event. "The state of the art," according to one survey of the field, "is poor, and much needs to be learned." The drugs have the same effect on aggression as they have on most of the other conditions for which they are used: they impair the individual's capacity to respond, his ability to act; and, if used in sufficient dosage, they either terrorize him into submission or reduce him to a zombie who can be neither aggressive, "schizophrenic," nor fully human. Nonetheless, people like Monroe assert that "there are substantial indications . . . that the pharmacological approach might be of significant help in reducing aggressive behavior from the social as well as the individual standpoint." Citing a study which purports to show that "50 percent of the aggressive acts committed by [ghetto adolescents] were done so by 6 percent of this population," Monroe asserts that "it is this group that deserves intensive study by the psychiatrist and the pharmacologist."[33]

In the business of therapy and control, the general practice is to increase dosage until something happens; or if one drug fails to do the job, to administer others, even though the additional drugs are either identical to those already being taken or are not indicated for the patient's diagnosis. In one study of practices at Veterans Administration hospitals, the U. S. General Accounting Office found that roughly 10 percent of some 6,000 patients surveyed were receiving drugs above the recommended maximum doses and that

> many were taking three or more psychotherapeutic drugs. One patient was taking eight different drugs—three antipsychotic, two antianxiety, one antidepressant, one sedative and one anti-parkinson. Three of these drugs were being given in dosages equal to the maximum recommended. Another patient was taking seven different drugs—three antipsychotic, two antianxiety, one sedative, and one anti-parkinson. Two of these drugs were being given in dosages above the maximum recommended.[34]

From a patient:

> I told them I don't want the drug to start with—they grabbed me and strapped me down—and gave me a forced intramuscular shot of Prolixin. . . . They gave me Artane to counteract

the Prolixin and they were giving me Sinequan, which is a kind of tranquilizer, to make me calm down, which over-calmed me, so rather than letting up on the medication, they then gave me Ritalin to pep me up.[35]

From a nursing-home employee:

This nurse would . . . deliberately increase the dosage of a sedative much higher than the prescription in order to quiet down patients, but then she would put on the chart that she had administered the required dosage. She would take seda-tives from the prescriptions of other patients to do this.[36]

From a pharmacologist:

Here is a patient who fits the typical description: he is initially diagnosed as senile so he is put on phenothiazine like Mellaril. A second drug, such as Elavil, is then added to his regimen perhaps because of depression. The patient has a little stom-ach problem, so Donnatal is added to take care of the stom-ach. In the meantime, drug-induced Parkinsonism occurs be-cause of the administration of Thorazine or Stelazine or Permitil or Prolixin. This necessitates the use of an anti-Parkinson drug, such as Artane. . . . It is no wonder that the patient has difficulty.[37]

Or, in an extreme case (from a clinical report):

A 34-year-old woman on admission was oriented, euphoric, agitated, hyperactive, talking to God, had pressured speech and flight of ideas. [Physical tests were normal.] Manic de-pressive psychosis was diagnosed and 2 days after admission, haloperidol (Haldol) was begun. . . . For the first two days of therapy, she was uncooperative, with inappropriate behavior, delusions and hallucinations. During the next two days her condition improved. Lithium carbonate was then added and the combined regimen was given for eight days. On the fifth day, she was confused, tremulous, weak, lethargic, had immo-bile facies, cogwheel rigidity. . . . Temperature was 100.6°F. Haloperidol was decreased and Cogentin [an anti-parkinson drug] was added. Temperature continued to rise, reaching 102.8°F by the eighth day. Haloperidol and Cogentin were discontinued. At this time she was prostrate, stuporous and restless with involuntary purposeless movements of all limbs and trunk, occuloyric crisis, and lead-pipe and cogwheel rigidity. . . . Temperature rose to 104.8°F.[38]

The report goes on to discuss further physical examinations and concludes with the observation that "results of repeated examinations over a ten-month period remained unchanged. She was conscious but with masklike facies, totally demented, incontinent, and did not respond to any commands or speak. . . . She could swallow when fed but was otherwise completely helpless." In a week she had been turned from a slightly crazy lady into a vegetable. After a report on the case was read at the 1973 World Neurological Congress attributing "severe neurotoxicity and irreversible brain damage" to the combination of haloperidol and lithium, another group of doctors "deliberately gave three patients lithium and haloperidol to test the . . . hypothesis."[39] All three developed similar symptoms.

The alternative to polypharmacy—what someone called psychopharmacological roulette—is escalation: the use of injectable, long-acting depot drugs to curb "defectors," and a growing penchant toward "meganeuroleptic therapy," one of the euphemisms for the administration of massive doses far exceeding the daily maximums recommended by the manufacturers, the American Medical Association, and the *Physician's Desk Reference.* "There are in and out of hospitals," said Dr. Frank J. Ayd, Jr., "at least one million patients who have responded partially or not at all to the neuroleptics prescribed for them. . . . These prisoners of psychosis are a formidable challenge to the therapeutic skills of the psychiatrist." Ayd, one of the most prolific professional advocates of psychotropic medication in America, goes on to say that

if the patient is not a drug defector, the failure to improve optimally may be due to an inadequate dose, even though the daily dose is high by ordinary standards. It is now evident that some chronic patients improve only when massive doses of a neuroleptic are administered. Such therapy is not employed as often as perhaps it should be. This is because many psychiatrists are fearful of possible adverse effects from meganeuroleptic therapy.[40]

It is hard to know what such statements mean, since many doctors already prescribe doses well above the recommended maximum (as in the Veterans Administration hospitals, for example), since the few controlled studies on dose differentials are highly inconclusive, and since, in the words of one report, "some schizophrenics not only do not require antipsychotic medication but in fact tend to get worse when given phenothiazines." Ayd's statement is significant, however, because it illustrates how even the theoretical distinction between therapy and control becomes obliterated. In the classic theory of treatment, drugs are supposed to be "adjunctive" to other therapy; however, once the patient is "snowed" into a stupor, as many are, there is no way for him to confront his problems, and the drug becomes counterproductive (except as a technique of management). "You try to teach people not to be dependent and not to become chronic," said Terry Kupers, a Los Angeles psychiatrist who works in a ghetto clinic.

You try to make the real world more appealing and thereby encourage them to give up their fantasy world. The drugs do work in small doses—they will stop hallucinations—but then you have to work with those people, to help them find the source of those voices. Once you start giving a megadose there's no hope for that. The trouble is that psychiatrists who have to see thirty patients in a morning can't do anything, and medication is automatic. If patients come in with any complaint, the doctor increases the medication. That's why you have them vegetating all over the place. We had a meeting with a drug company detail man [a salesman], and when I told him that he asked whether we'd like to have Dr. Ayd come in and talk to us.

By its very definition, specificity implies limits, but in practice there are few limits: long-term talking psychotherapy is a luxury few people can afford and which few publicly supported facilities have the resources to offer. What was adjunctive in theory becomes primary in practice. If all the psychiatrists listed on the rolls of federally funded community health centers devoted full time to their work in those centers (which most do not), and if they devoted all of that time to work with individual patients (which most do not), each would have an average of ten minutes for each patient visit. Since most of them spend substantial portions of their time writing reports, meeting with staff, attending conferences, and seeing private patients, the average is closer to five minutes, or perhaps even two or three. One-third of all patient visits to psychiatrists in private practice involve medication; one can barely imagine what the proportions are in public outpatient facilities, whose "main function," as George Crane said, is "to dispense drugs," and whose clients include enormous numbers of those—particularly the poor and black—who are always the most heavily drugged. Inevitably, therefore, the doctor becomes both a writer of prescriptions and, even if he has the best of intentions, an agent of control. "What the hell are you going to do?" asked Matthew P. Dumont, formerly associate commissioner of mental health in Massachusetts and now director of a small clinic outside Boston.

> Of course being crazy is a function of economic, social and political issues; a lot of people become crazy to oblige the system—it's their way of cooperating. But if you have a guy that's going to go home and beat up his kids, you give him a drug to try to keep him from doing it. Obviously, it's control —it's the nearest thing to putting Thorazine in the drinking water—but what else are you going to do?[41]

The ultimate weapons in the arsenal—the long-acting depot drugs—make the matter totally transparent. If one can inject the recalcitrant, the "intractable," and the difficult

with a tranquilizer every two or three or four weeks—or if
one can threaten them with it—there will be no need to put
Thorazine in the drinking water. The form of the drug—the
way it is administered—is in itself a means of control, a
statement the doctor makes to the patient. Given the effects
of the antipsychotic drugs, it should hardly be surprising that
many people refuse to take them, or that they forget them,
or that they slip them into the toilet when the keepers aren't
looking. Yet there have been scores of articles and studies
speculating on the reasons: rejection of the drugs, said a team
of British psychiatrists, was associated with paranoid delusions; rejection, said another report, was common among
hostile patients who used the drugs "as a convenient focal
point for their hostility and aggressive impulses"; rejection,
said a third, was a consequence of "intrapsychic conflict";
rejection, said a fourth, was the result of the patient's refusal
to admit that he is sick or, among some, "because patients
desire to be in complete control of their lives, and view the
drug as an external dominating agent or identify the drug
with irrational authority or dominating parents." What they
all agree on is that while many people take the drugs and
sometimes learn to depend on them for good behavior, nearly
half the people they study are reluctant to take them.[42]

Among the more conventional solutions has been to slip the
medication into the food of the incarcerated—Haldol, for
example, comes in the form of "an undetectable, tasteless
liquid concentrate for the patient . . . unwilling to swallow
tablets"—a practice which, one might assume, does won-
drous things for "paranoid delusions." But clearly such remedies are impossible for the 2 million outpatients who get
antipsychotic drugs at any given time. For them, in Ayd's
view, and in the view of many others, the future lies with the
depot drugs. In recent years, the side effects of those drugs—
which appear to be even more frequent and severe than those
of other phenothiazines—have, in the words of one report,
"limited enthusiasm for their use for outpatients," but the
enthusiasm is likely to recover. Since they were introduced a
decade ago, according to a conservative estimate, some 400,-

000 people have been treated with them, and the number continues to grow. The drugs are cheap to buy, cheap to administer, and cheap to control—they can, as the Prolixin ads say, "save time . . . save money, and . . . even save people." The trends in psychopharmacotherapy, said Ayd, suggest that

> in the future more and more psychiatric patients will be treated with long-acting oral and injectable preparations. This is understandable not only for scientific reasons but also because of the mounting pressure to provide mental health care outside of the hospital in the most expeditious, safe and economical way possible. An increase in this pressure is an inevitable and inextricable accompaniment of national health insurance, which will soon be a reality in the United States.
>
> National health insurance will automatically increase the workload of health care professionals [who] of necessity will resort to pharmacotherapeutic regimens that enable them to care for the largest number of patients in the most convenient, expeditious, and economic way feasible. There is every reason to predict that pharmacotherapy with long-acting oral and injectable drugs will escalate. . . [43]

Stripped of its jargon, the statement says that the less expensive the drugs, the more efficient their administration and the more people who can be brought into the system. In the Soviet Union, psychiatrist E. N. Vovina put it another way:

> By switching the patients over to prolonged-action preparations that frustrated their attempts to refuse treatment or circumvented irregularity in the taking of their maintenance dose, and that provided a means for continual "drug control" of the patients' condition, the patients' attitude toward work underwent an abrupt change, and they demonstrated a notable improvement in their activities in the workshops. . . . Those methods of treatment also demonstrated an influence on the patients' participation in the popular culture program and in family life.[44]

There may still be difficulty in making outpatients come in for their shots, but that can often be solved with pleas, coaxing, court order, or a team sent out with a needle. If people like Ayd are correct, the depot drugs will combine with national health insurance in the same fashion that the older tranquilizers combined with "mental health." They will make everything which preceded them look small and primitive.

# V

The great majority of the 35 million Americans who are regular users of psychoactive prescription drugs—an estimated 15 million others use over-the-counter medication—have probably never seen a psychiatrist or had any other formal contact with the mental-health system. Nearly half of those drugs are minor tranquilizers which are frequently prescribed by internists, gynecologists, pediatricians, and other nonpsychiatric practitioners, and, in some cases, by psychologists, social workers, and technicians who have been given blank prescription pads signed by a doctor. In 1975, some 61 million prescriptions were written for Valium, another 17 million for Librium, and an estimated 25 million more for other antianxiety preparations—enough, all told, to provide some 15 million pills a day—and their sales were growing at a rate of 5 or 6 million prescriptions a year. Those drugs did not exist a generation ago nor, with a few significant exceptions, have they replaced anything which was then on the market. Other than consuming alcohol or tobacco (whose per capita consumption has not declined), it is hard to recall what people did for "a case of nerves" before Frank M. Berger synthesized meprobamate in 1952 and Leo H. Sternbach accidentally produced chlordiazepoxide (Librium) in 1955.[45]

It was a considerable achievement. What they, their colleagues, the profession, and the industry accomplished was to medicalize and thus legitimize mood and behavior control for Everyman and, in the process, to teach him that he (or, more commonly, she) had not only a right but an obligation to be free of "anxiety," "tension," "nerves," and other forms of "psychic distress." Even if the complaint was patently nonmedical, the drugs appeared to make people feel better; they were safe—safer, certainly, than the barbiturates which they sometimes replaced as sleeping pills—and they were, in the words of one report, "virtually suicide-proof." "One would be loath," wrote Leo Hollister, "to withdraw a drug that a patient has found to be acceptable and beneficial, even though it might not be [the physician's] first choice." If they made the client feel good, there was no reason for the physician not to legitimize the transaction; and since there was evidence that with minor tranquilizers, as with a number of other drugs, the physician's attitude helped to determine whether the drug worked, "the moral is clear: if you are going to prescribe these drugs, at least try to work up some enthusiasm for them and try to communicate it to your patients."[46]

By now, at least a third of all adult Americans have had some personal experience with minor tranquilizers and they have, in that sense, become their own test subjects: they know whether or not Valium makes them drowsy or dizzy, whether or not it helps them sleep or calms "a case of nerves," and whether or not they wake up with a hangover in the morning. They may even know that it is not advisable for a woman to take minor tranquilizers in the first weeks of pregnancy: one study of some 19,000 live births found the rate of birth defects among children of tranquilizer-consuming mothers to be roughly five times as high as among children born to mothers who took no drugs during the first six weeks of pregnancy. What they may not know is that there are indications that extended use of large doses of minor tranquilizers may be addictive, that withdrawal in such cases may be as painful as withdrawal from heroin, that their side effects—anxiety or tension—are often similar to the conditions for which they were given in the first place, and that many physicians prescribe such drugs in amounts far above the recommended levels. At the Los Angeles County–University of Southern California Medical Center, a study of outpatient prescriptions filled in the hospital pharmacy found that one patient received 4,260 Librium pills in a 12-month period, that another got 3,142 Valium pills, and that more than 10 percent of the tranquilizers prescribed were in quantities higher than those recommended as a maximum by the hospital staff. No one knows whether those pills were consumed by the patients—in the one case that would amount to roughly ten times a moderate daily dose for a year —or whether they were given away or sold on the street. What is certain is that the minor tranquilizers now have a lively street market, and that in 1975 the National Council on Drug Abuse labeled Valium the most abused drug in America.[47]

Despite that abuse, they are not taken for kicks. Roughly two-thirds of the minor tranquilizers are consumed by women, among whom the heaviest users are unemployed housewives in the lowest strata of the economy. In the most comprehensive such survey ever conducted, 13 percent of the housewives in the bottom fourth of the economic scale acknowledged "regular daily use for at least two months" in the previous year.[48] (One study indicated that physicians prescribe psychoactive drugs to women partly because they believe that housewives can sleep and don't need to be mentally alert; in another study, researchers found that 87 percent of the physicians they interviewed considered daily use of Librium to be legitimate for housewives, but only 53 percent regarded such use as legitimate for college students.[49]) Yet, the housewife who uses drugs to cope, to get through the day, is hardly alone in what appears to be an organic system where physician, patient, and conditions collude and where the problem is an ailment like "stress," "fatigue," "pressure," or "psychic tension." In the past twenty years, prescription drugs, particularly tranquilizers and amphetamines, have become significant elements in coping with on-the-job stress and in the worker's attempt to fulfill the performance standards imposed by employers, especially in trucking, certain service jobs (waitresses, bus boys, stewardesses), and the clerical and sales fields. In a study conducted in 1971 for the New York State Narcotic Addiction Control Commission, Carl D. Chambers estimated that in New York alone, 51,000 workers were regular users of amphetamine-type pep pills, 117,000 regularly used amphetamine-based diet pills, 240,000 (3.2 percent of the work force) regularly used minor tranquilizers like Valium and Librium, one worker in ten used tranquilizers at least occasionally, and many of those drugs were being used on the job.[50] Subsequently, Chambers conducted similar surveys in other states and came up with similar data; the surveys are suspect because they sampled relatively small populations (7,500 people in the New York survey), but they are supported by other, narrower surveys and by extensive anecdotal reports from physicians, union leaders, and individual workers. Almost all the Bell System telephone operators confirm that many, if not a majority, of their fellow workers survive on Librium and Valium and that, in the words of a Communications Workers Union report, "the pressure applied to these employees has led to unnecessary absence because of nervous sickness or nervous breakdowns, widespread use of tranquilizers and a large turnover in the traffic operating force."[51] But perhaps the classic example is trucking, where, according to Senate testimony by one driver (1971), "possibly 90 percent of the drivers on long-line operations take pills [amphetamines]. They don't take them just to get hopped up. They take them so they can drive without running over people on the road."

It is either take a pill and go or quit. They tell you if you can't take it, you can quit. When you ask off, the first thing a [management] guy says is, "What's the matter, can't you take it?" This is not an exception. This is a condition of employment. . . .

The things that they put on the bulletin boards at these terminals, everything they say to you is apparently aimed at dominating you completely. This does away with a lot of a man's self-confidence. It puts him in a state of anxiety. When he climbs behind the wheel, he doesn't know whether he can do the job right or not. He is never told. . . . He is going from clock to clock, panic-stricken. If you can't make the run in the fog, the rain, ice conditions, they are always ready to tell you if you can't make it, we can hire a man that can.[52]

Most truckers feel that in the years since that testimony was given, conditions in the industry have improved; awareness among drivers and doctors of the dangers of amphetamines has increased; and the use of pills is down to the point where, depending on the estimate, only one in three or one in five or one in twenty uses them regularly.[53] The major trucking companies officially prohibit drug use on the job— they have, on occasion, been accused by drivers of following trucks in unmarked cars in an effort to catch truckers buying or selling drugs—but, in the words of a driver based in Memphis, "I wouldn't be too sure about the peckerwood outfits." Since 1972, when the Food and Drug Administration placed amphetamines on a tight government schedule of restricted drugs, which establishes production quotas and prohibits refills without new prescriptions, they have been somewhat harder to obtain. Yet they are still available—in the plant, on the street, on the road, or from certain doctors —and are still being used.

There are similar patterns in other areas: among electronics assembly workers, auto workers (particularly those on the night shift), paper workers, professional athletes—even in the lettuce fields of California's Salinas Valley, where some Chicano farm hands survive on speed during the peak harvest periods, working sixteen to eighteen hours a day, seven days a week, picking produce and filling and stacking boxes.

Sometimes, according to John Holmes, a psychologist in the psychiatric ward of the Natividad Medical Center, they are brought in at night suffering from amphetamine psychoses and hallucinations; they use the pills to stay "up" during the day, then take Seconal or other sedatives after work to bring themselves down. The pills are available for one dollar a tab, an exorbitant price, but considered worth it in a short season in which a chance of earning up to $75 a day is crucial. Until 1973, when he was found out and his California license suspended, the most prolific dealer in the area was said to be a circuit-riding doctor who once had a national reputation for his drug research. He is now practicing in another state.[54]

There is no evidence that American employers other than the military ever force or even encourage workers to take psychoactive drugs to speed them up or otherwise control them, but there appears to be at least some prescribing in industrial clinics and by private doctors to keep workers functioning. "One loom unattended," said a series of two-page advertisements which appeared in *Industrial Medicine* in the early seventies. "Valium to help break the cycle of skeletal muscle spasm. . . . When psychic tension adds to the burden of skeletal muscle spasm, the calming action of Valium can benefit total patient management. And when spasm and tension interfere with sleep, 1 tablet (in addition to regular daily dosage) usually permits a good night's rest."[55] Physicians who work in industrial settings all tell stories about workers in lead smelters whose private physicians prescribed Valium to deal with "irritability" that was probably caused by lead poisoning, workers who routinely take tranquilizers to cope with tension produced by factory noise or stress, and company physicians who prescribe tranquilizers and sedatives to "keep people with unique skills on board." "It's hard to tell self-medication from company medication," said Carl Chambers, who now runs an independent consulting firm in Washington, "and it's hard to tell who does the encouraging and who looks the other way. The airlines used to dispense amphetamines to pilots. They've quit, of course, but the stewardesses are still using them on their own." "If stimulants help get the job done," said a former assembly worker at Ford, "management will look the other way. If a guy knocks over his toolbox and five hundred reds fall out, everybody will be embarrassed, but unless it formally gets to the upper levels of management, they'll be pragmatic about it." In the end, moreover, it may not make all that much difference; the effects on the individual and the system are the same. The telephone operator who pulls the tranquilizers out of her purse, the boss-intimidated truck driver who takes speed to finish his run, the auto workers who pop Bennies and Black Beauties to get through the night shift, and the factory worker whose company doctor gives him Valium so that his "loom" won't be unattended—the volunteers, the seduced, the impressed—all make conditions tolerable and their impositions normative and legitimate by manipulating themselves.[56]

# VI

In the view of Dr. Ronald Fieve and a growing number of others, the "third revolution" in psychiatry has begun. The first was the acceptance of madness as an illness rather than a crime; the second was Freudian theory and analysis; the third is the use of lithium carbonate as a "prophylactic for recurrent manic-depressive illness." As professor of clinical psychiatry at Columbia University, medical director of the Foundation for Depression and Manic Depression, chief of psychiatric research at the New York State Psychiatric Institute, and director of its Lithium Clinic, Dr. Fieve, no ordinary psychiatric evangelist, is certain that "manic depression, this spectacular disease, now has an equally spectacular cure. Lithium is the first drug in the history of psychiatry to so radically and specifically control a major mind disorder. . . . It is truly spectacular to watch this simple, naturally occurring salt, lithium carbonate, return a person in one to three weeks from the terrible throes of moodswing to normalcy."[57] In his estimate, only 50,000 to 80,000 people are currently being treated with lithium, when some 3 to 6 million should be getting it. Quoting the enthusiastic endorsement of some of his patients, including theater director-producer Joshua Logan, Fieve explains that "the idea that there is a biochemical cause of their illness is reassuring. This is a new physical concept for patients who for years thought their highs and lows resulted from unconscious conflicts in their personalities."[58] Thus, they are freed from guilt—it is not their fault, it is not the result of conflicts with parents; it is simply chemistry.

There is no agreement on whether lithium has an effect on "unipolar" depression. Most of the published studies indicate that it has little, if any; even the American Psychiatric Association, while endorsing lithium for mania, recently declared that existing evidence is "not sufficiently conclusive to permit a clear definition of the value of lithium in acute depressions."[59] It is known that excessive lithium levels in the blood can lead to "lithium intoxication" and death, and that therefore blood levels of the salt must be carefully monitored; but there is little data on the long-term effects of lithium maintenance, nor is there any hard definition of what constitutes mania or manic-depressive illness. "I never saw a manic-depressive in medical school," said a California psychiatrist, "and I hardly ever heard of one until they started pushing lithium." Fieve himself recognizes that some of the most creative people in the world have been subject to "moodswing" and that their most productive periods were "manic." Is the artist who paints around the clock manic? The big spender? The high-energy executive? In Fieve's opinion Winston Churchill, Abraham Lincoln, and Theodore Roosevelt were all manic-depressives whose moodswings could have been controlled with lithium. What the country needs, in his opinion, is a proliferation of lithium clinics similar to his own where the traditional emphasis on the patient, the psychiatrist, and the fifty-minute hour two to five times a week has been changed to patient well-care, the rating team, and the brief ten-to-fifteen minute monthly visit. The net result of this new mental health system, if adopted on a larger scale, would be to expand the availability of psychiatric services without sacrificing effectiveness and to provide for early detection and treatment of recurrent manic and depressive moodswings.

The Lithium Clinic represents one of the first illustrations of a speciality clinic that could expand the services of community mental health centers if incorporated into their present structures. . . . In the next decade we shall probably see a completely new attitude toward mental illness in America. Traditional psychotherapy and analysis, as they have been practiced, will become, for the most part, obsolete.[60]

The irony of that position is that in making "traditional psychotherapy and analysis . . . obsolete, people like Fieve will make most of psychiatry obsolete. "It is now high time," said Dr. Nathan S. Kline, one of the pioneers in antidepressant medication and, like Fieve, no upstart in the ranks of the evangelists, "to turn a lot of psychiatric medicine back to the general practitioner. Therapeutically it is entirely feasible, and logistically it is the only way to solve the problem [of depression]."[61] Whether or not the world will be dotted with lithium clinics is unpredictable, but in forecasting the day when traditional psychotherapy becomes obsolete and in calling for a return of "psychiatric medicine" to the general practitioner, people like Fieve and Kline are not even prophetic. They are simply describing what, for the most part, is already going on: psychiatry or "mental health" may be the rationale, but the service is drugs. The only question is why the system needs physicians at all.

It is a complete system—the promotion, the pressure on the doctor to "do something" and his corresponding need to feel he is in control, the belief in medical miracles carried over from the antibiotics—but its fundamental historic importance is still consistently underestimated. Although psychotropic drugs have been used for thousands of years, the drug "revolution" that began with the tranquilizers democratized an idea which, through most of the twentieth century, had been regarded as the exclusive province of totalitarian societies and futuristic novels. In that context, it hardly matters whether the major tranquilizers are pharmacologically distinct from the minor tranquilizers, or whether the side effects of one particular class of drugs are more dangerous or debilitating than those of another. Indeed, the smoother the drug—the fewer the side effects—the more acceptable the idea of drugging becomes: virtually everyone is out of control, everyone is to some extent the unresponsible victim of his chemistry, and everyone's mind can be regarded as an object of manipulation, a mechanism distinct from the self (if, indeed, there is still a self). "The inviolability of the brain," said Jose Delgado, the neurophysiologist who experiments with brain implantations, "is only a social construct, like nudity."[62] Given such reasoning, the distinctions among classes of drugs and the distinction between drugs and electroshock or psychosurgery are only matters of technique to be determined by experts and not political or moral issues: all the techniques are part of the same continuum.

Clearly, the drugs are often useful—useful to the client; useful to the institution, the doctor, and the community. The disturbing questions arise from the uncertain relationships between the two classes of beneficiaries and out of the collective didactic effects of the behavior the drugs induce. When is the client the real, long-term beneficiary of his medication, and when is the doctor or the institution or the community? When does it liberate and when does it create indefinite dependence or teach the individual that he is just the victim of his own chemistry? Here the numbers themselves become significant: some 30 or 40 million Americans can't all be crazy or "sick." The very pervasiveness of the drugs has thus helped blur, if not eradicate, the already tenuous distinction between mental illness and mental health, between therapy and control, and between treatment and manipulation. In that respect, the new drugs are altogether different from alcohol or tobacco which, while they may be as pharmacologically specific as many prescription drugs, are consumed in innocence—free, that is, from the ideology of specificity—and without the blessings of medical mediation. In the West, the consumer of alcohol assumes personal responsibility for his drinking; the consumer of Valium yields it to a doctor who, in prescribing, legitimizes its use and validates the ideology of specific action. At the same time, however, the political and social ideas associated with the newer drugs—including the legitimacy of mood and behavior control itself—have gradually become attached to all sorts of other things, including alcohol, street drugs, behavior modification, and almost every narcissistic movement from encounter therapy to the Reverend Sun Myung Moon's Unification Church. It's not surprising, therefore, that many of those phenomena have been represented either as corollaries or alternatives to drugs, or that they are constantly involved in controversies as to whether they are really liberation or brainwashing. Each of them posits a belief in a dual personality: a hypothetically healthy, "together," genuine, adjusted self (past or future), and an existing sick, malfunctioning, chemically imbalanced self subject to treatment, manipulation, or control. (In such a demonology, "liberation" and "brainwashing" depend only on one's religious or political position.) This is the classic model of madness (just as it was once the classic model of heresy and demonic possession); but in blurring the line between the possessed and the saved, the mad and the sane, the drugs have helped extend the model and make it applicable to virtually everyone. Beyond the Valium is the breakdown, and beyond the breakdown the Thorazine, the hospital, and the shock treatments. The drugs connect everyone to the ideology of mental health, whether they are in the system or not; they make every physician into a parapsychiatrist; and they impose on all a reconfirmation of the normative standards which the dominant culture imposes. It is a closed loop: "mental health" legitimizes the drugs; the drugs legitimize mental health. In traditional psychiatry, mental health was largely talk and therefore subject to argument; with the drugs it becomes "specific" and scientifically legitimate, and it tolerates no debate.

# SIX

# Ultimate Weapons

## I

In the summer of 1966, Lloyd Cotter had what he would later describe as a deeply impressive experience. Dr. Cotter, a psychiatrist from Pomona, California, and teaching consultant in the Psychiatric Residency Program at Pomona's Pacific State Hospital, spent those summer months in Vietnam as a sort of medical missionary, "introducing," as he would later report in the *American Journal of Psychiatry,* "the latest in the treatment of psychiatric hospital patients" at Bien Hoa Hospital outside Saigon. The main problem at the hospital, he decided, was the chronic schizophrenics who were receiving nothing but custodial care and for whom, he believed, a mass treatment approach might be suitable. The hospital was crowded and individualized treatment was simply too slow, particularly since "the longer a schizophrenic is allowed to remain regressed, the less recovery one can expect." Accordingly, he and his Vietnamese colleagues told the patients that they wanted to discharge them; but because the patients would have to support themselves once they got home, they would first have to work around the hospital "to prove their capability." Those who refused to work—the great majority, as it turned out—would receive electroshock treatments at a rate of three per patient per week. The program was first initiated among a group of 130 men:

Gradually there began to be evident improvement in the behavior of the patients, the appearance of the ward, and the number of patients volunteering to work. This latter was a result of the ECT's alleviating schizophrenic or depressive thinking and affect for some. With others it was simply a result of their dislike or fear of ECT. In either case our objective of motivating them to work was achieved.[1]

Among the women, however, things turned out to be unexpectedly difficult. "Expecting the women to be more pliable," Cotter reported, "I hoped for quicker and better results. Instead, due perhaps to their greater passivity . . . at the end of twenty treatments there were only fifteen [of 130] women working. We stopped the ECT then and to the men and women still not working said, 'Look. We doctors, nurses and technicians have to work for our food, clothes, rent money, etc. Why should you have it better? . . . After this, if you don't work, you don't eat.' " There was some concern among the staff that "severely catatonic" patients might starve to death; but according to Cotter's report, none did. Instead, they all began to work, and the program was extended to several hundred more patients. In the succeeding weeks, Dr. Cotter and his colleagues were kept productively busy administering the program and giving "the several thousand shock treatments required as we started about one new ward a week on the program."

At this point, several problems arose. It had been decided to pay working patients one *piastre* (about one cent) a day; but as the number of workers grew, funds had to be found to meet the payroll. This difficulty was solved "by having some of the patients with woodworking ability manufacture Montagnard-type bows and arrows for sale to the American soldiers as souvenirs. Punji-stick manufacture and sale also increased revenues." A more serious difficulty—finding places to send discharged patients who had no relatives to take them—was solved when Cotter accidentally discovered that an American Green Beret colonel had been unsuccessful in obtaining Viet Cong prisoners to tend crops in the Third Corps Special Forces headquarters area.

When he learned that I could provide him with recovered patients, he said he would like 10-man agricultural teams to go to his A-camps, which are forts in Viet Cong territory manned by a 14-man American A-team and hundreds of volunteers from the local population who are willing to fight the Viet Cong. Growing crops at the A-camps would cut down on the cost of air transport of food and provide a better diet for the soldiers.[2]

The arrangement was made: a Green Beret trooper "was sent to the hospital to help select and train these teams," and Cotter toured the camps to explain to the military paramedics how to handle the ex-patients "in case any of them became irritable, withdrawn, etc." There was concern among the Americans that the ex-patients might "crack up under the stress of potential or actual VC attack or ambush," but Cotter assured them that during the blitz of World War II, there had been an "appreciable" drop in the number of Londoners developing mental breakdowns. Unfortunately, Cotter returned to the United States before the project was fully implemented; his report, therefore, provides no indication of how the ex-patients fared in their new camps, nor does he tell his reader whether the ex-patients who became "irritable, withdrawn, etc.," were to be sent back for more treatment. Nonetheless, Cotter could hardly have been more enthusiastic:

I was so impressed by the effectiveness of operant conditioning techniques for the motivation of difficult-to-activate patients that on leaving Vietnam I visited mental hospitals in Thailand, India, Lebanon, Egypt, Jordan, Turkey, Germany, Holland and England, sharing my experiences with the psychiatrists in these hospitals.

There is of course nothing new about work therapy per se in the treatment of mental illness. The novelty of operant conditioning techniques as applied in this area lies in the possibility or probability of its being utilized effectively with all patients not totally physically incapacitated. If the less effective, but more usually relied on, reinforcements of productive behavior do not work, then a more effective reinforcement, such as food for hungry patients, will produce the desired results. . . . The use of effective reinforcements should not be neglected due to a misguided idea of what constitutes kindness.[3]

Cotter's report can be used to prove a number of things—that mental patients are not sick, only irresponsible; that starvation is more therapeutic than electroshock or psychotropic drugs, which Cotter also used; that war is good for mental health; but perhaps its most important (and reliable) message is that it really does not matter whether psychiatric technology works by alleviating organic symptoms or simply by frightening subjects into compliance. Either way, as Cotter said, "our objective of motivating them to work was achieved." The purists in operant conditioning would probably deny that Cotter's treatments had much to do with what they would call behavior modification—there were no schedules of reinforcement, no proper procedures to extinguish undesirable behavior, no systematic recording of results—but that also is of little concern. The message, implicit in other reports on electroshock, is explicit here: the heavier the technology, the more difficult it is to distinguish treatment from torture. Bien Hoa was a real program of pacification.

It is a relatively simple procedure: the electrodes are attached to the subject's head, either at the temples (bilateral) or at the front and back of one side of the head (unilateral), and the current turned on for a half-second or a second, generally at a strength of 70 to 150 volts at 500 to 900 milliamperes—roughly the power required to light a 100-watt bulb. The consequence is a convulsive grand mal seizure, an artificially induced epileptic fit. Since most American patients are now given muscle-relaxant drugs and an anesthetic prior to the procedure, they are supposed to feel nothing, they have few physical convulsions—perhaps a twitch or two—and the chances for bone fractures or other orthopedic damage caused by the seizure are said to be minimal. (Cotter, who apparently did not use anesthetics, said he had no problems with his treatments: "Perhaps because of the smaller size and musculature of the Vietnamese people, no symptoms of compression fracture were reported at any time.") Nonetheless, many people who have been subject to ECT report excruciating pain during or after, and something approaching absolute terror—"the most horrifying experience of my life," as one of them said. "Although I was put to sleep during each treatment, when I awoke my head was throbbing with the most strange and inconceivable pain, something unimaginable to anyone unfamiliar with ECT. My mind felt like a blurred, pounding emptiness." Nearly all, moreover, suffer from loss of memory—whether temporary or permanent is a matter of dispute—and many complain that for days or weeks after treatment they walked around "like a zombie."[4]

In its varying forms, shock therapy is among the oldest psychiatric techniques in existence, dating back to Roman times when a man named Scribonius Largus tried to cure the emperor's headaches with an electric eel; in the sixteenth century, a Catholic missionary reported that the Abyssinians used similar methods to "expel Devils out of the human body"; and by the early 1930s, camphor, carbon dioxide gas, insulin, and the drug Metrazol had been used to induce comas or convulsions to treat schizophrenics and depressives. But it was not until 1938 that an Italian doctor named Ugo Cerletti developed what would today be regarded as ECT. Having experimented with dogs and having observed the "painless" slaughtering of hogs which had been rendered comatose with electric shock applied at the temples, Cerletti decided he was ready to experiment on man—in this case, "a catatonic schizophrenic . . . who spoke an incomprehensible gibberish."

The patient was brought in, the machine was set at 1/10 of a second and 70 volts and the shock was given. Naturally the low dosage resulted in a petit mal reaction. After the electric spasm, which lasted a fraction of a second, the patient burst into song. The Professor suggested that another treatment with a higher voltage be given. The staff objected. They stated that if another treatment were given the patient would probably die and wanted further treatment postponed until tomorrow. The Professor knew what that meant. He decided to go ahead right then and there, but before he could say so the patient suddenly sat up and pontifically proclaimed, no longer in jargon, but in clear Italian, "Non una seconda! Mortifere!" (not again, it will kill me). This made the Professor think and swallow, but his courage was not lost. He gave the order to proceed at a higher voltage and a longer time, and the first electro-convulsion in man ensued. Thus was born EST out of one man and over the objection of his assistants.[5]

Neither Cerletti (who died in 1963) nor his contemporaries ever learned how ECT worked, nor do any of their successors understand it today. Some early researchers believed that epilepsy and schizophrenia are rarely found together—that because of some "biological antagonism" between them, a person suffering from one is unlikely to have the other, and that, as a British physician observed at the beginning of the nineteenth century, "any considerable excitation, some new and violent action provoked in the course of the manic disease, often has the effect of considerably alleviating the mental disorder or of permanently improving it." Thus, people have been dunked in ice water, gased with carbon dioxide, and beaten with sticks. Benjamin Rush, the "father" of American psychiatry, founder of the American Psychiatric Association, and inventor of the "tranquilizer" chair in which the patient was strapped hand and foot, devised a "gyrator" on which patients suffering from "torpid madness" were rotated at high rates of speed.[6]

Yet none of the theories of "violent action" has ever been proven, nor does any of them explain the continuing enthusiasm for a form of treatment which is described by Elliot S. Valenstein of the University of Michigan Medical School, one of the most sober scholars in the field, as "nonspecific if not crude." The prime bases of validation for ECT are the notoriously vague standards of "clinical experience." (Perhaps the most widely reported of these clinical experiences is the case of an ECT machine in a British hospital which was used "successfully" on hundreds of patients over a two-year period in the early seventies before a nurse and a doctor accidentally discovered that it had never worked at all.) A decade ago, when she reviewed a generation of reports on the efficacy of shock treatment, Sylvia A. Riddell reported in the *Archives of General Psychiatry* that only two carefully controlled studies had been conducted on ECT, and that neither of them found a significant difference between people who were actually shocked and those who received a simulated shock. "It is apparent," she concluded, "that not only is there a distressing lack of acceptable research into ECT as a therapeutic agent, but that very few valid conclusions can be reached from the studies that have been carried out." The only two double-blind controlled studies conducted since that review was published have proved to be just as inconclusive.[7]

The paucity of evidence hasn't dampened the enthusiasm. Since the introduction of antipsychotics and antidepressants, the number of people subjected to ECT has undoubtedly declined; yet it is still regarded as the treatment of choice for "drug resistant" or other "intractable" patients, particularly those diagnosed as "suicidal" or depressive. No official statistics are kept on how many people get the treatment each year —here again, the government statisticians who count everything from appendectomies to tonsillectomies have no data —but estimates based on sample surveys range between 100,000 and 200,000 individuals annually, at least two-thirds of them women, of whom each gets an average of seven to ten treatments, though many get dozens and a few get hundreds—a total of at least a million treatments a year.[8] Most of these treatments are given for various forms of depression (which may be one reason why women outnumber men), but ECT has also been given to alcoholics, schizophrenics, "sociopaths," and, in at least one case, to a teenager who was hospitalized for smoking marijuana. John Friedberg, the author of a popular book attacking ECT, reports that he heard "from an ECT enthusiast who uses it for migraine, hay fever, asthma, eczema, allergic rhinitis, and conjunctivitis"; and Dr. Robert E. Peck, author of a defense of ECT called *The Miracle of Shock Treatment,* writes that "in my own experience I have seen such psychosomatic disorders as ulcers, spastic and ulcerative colitis, asthma, psoriasis [and] trigonitis all respond to shock treatment with remission."[9] According to the Network Against Psychiatric Assault (NAPA), an organization of ex-patients and anti-establishment psychiatrists that publishes the names of "shock doctors," at least 4,000 physicians give or prescribe ECT in America, among them one who claims to have given 50,000 such treatments in the past thirty years. What they offer, according to a statement by the American Psychiatric Association (1972) "has been a highly effective treatment for depressions since it was introduced in 1938. Not only is it a relatively safe treatment, but it has the great advantage of terminating an episode of depression very quickly—sometimes in a matter of days and virtually always within a month."[10]

There is no lack of material on the side effects, particularly on the confusion and amnesia which follow each treatment, which are reported to be nearly universal, and which are regarded by some practitioners as necessary (and therefore not really side effects at all). More important, however, is the possibility, as suggested in a number of studies and reported in scores of cases, that for some, the loss of memory may well be indefinite and irreversible. There is the case of Marilyn Rice, a Department of Commerce economist who, according to a law suit filed in 1974, suffered what her attorney charged was "permanent amnesia," which simply wiped out everything she knew about her work. There is the case of "David," a young man given twelve shock treatments after what may have been an accidental overdose of a drug prescribed by a Boston psychiatrist, who then diagnosed him as suicidal. "David," said his sister after the treatments, "was getting terrible headaches . . . such great pain. . . . During the treatments and after, David forgot everything. . . . He used to write these little fables—they were quite nice. Now he's forgotten his writing and his yoga and all his good things. They took all that away from him. [He's] without a personality, without a memory, without even knowing where the bathroom is." There is the case of Beatrice Rosenthal, who testified that after fifty treatments, "the greater part of my past life [was] either erased or rendered very vague. The mass of what I learned in college and high school, books that I had read and that I considered a part of my very being, were obliterated." There is the case of Ernest Hemingway, complaining, after a series of treatments just before his suicide, "What is the sense of ruining my head and erasing my memory, which is my capital, and putting me out of business? It was a brilliant cure but we lost the patient." In a survey conducted in Massachusetts in 1972, ten of sixty-six psychiatrists responding to a state commission asserted that "treatments leave irrecoverable gaps in memory and that a large number of treatments cause intellectual deterioration, seizures, or personality blunting akin to lobotomy," and virtually every study of ECT patients shows some deterioration immediately after treatment. Most practitioners insist that such damage is reversible, but there appear to be no studies which prove it, and at least two which indicate the damage is permanent.[11]

All of that, however—the pain, the loss of memory, the doubtful organic effects—may well be secondary to what, for many people, is sheer terror. By now the stories are banal: people who are threatened with ECT if they don't behave; people dragged in and strapped down; patients who "could look up the row of beds and see other patients going into epileptic seizures, one by one as the psychiatrists moved down the row. They knew their turn was coming"; people who are told that if they don't consent to the treatments, they will be incarcerated indefinitely or will remain ill forever; people in hospitals, in clinics, in doctors' offices, in prisons, in nursing homes. For many, if not most, the chances of successful "treatment" are incommensurate with the ailment —real or imagined—for which it is given. The Massachusetts commission, for example, found that more than a fourth of the patients given ECT in that state had been diagnosed as "neurotic," that private hospitals used shock on 28 percent of their patients, and that among them were several "shock shops" where as many as 70 percent were so treated. A nurse in California reported the case of a woman admitted for depression:

> Her husband had attempted suicide five years before and threatened daily to do so again. She worked at a job that she hated and had difficulty with her daughter. She had been seen as an outpatient [for six months]. She wasn't able to feel anger, although she said that pictures showed that her face was angry. Her expectations and her proposed treatment— electric shock. When I asked the doctor why he didn't treat the obvious with more reality testing, I was told that "women aren't ready to hear the truth."

In another case:

> A woman was admitted for hitting her husband. She had been physically abused by him and her father for years. Her treatment: shock.

In a series of other cases, reported by two former hospital staff members:

> 60-year-old female primary diagnosis alcoholism.
> 20-year-old female with marital problems.
> 70-year-old female upset over forced change of residence. She was forcibly restrained so treatment could be administered.
> 72-year-old male former athlete and physical education instructor upset because he was getting old.
> 26-year-old male diagnosed as mentally retarded, a management problem at home.

> 32-year-old female primary diagnosis multiple sclerosis.
> After treatments was unable to walk.[12]

"Terror," wrote Benjamin Rush 150 years ago, "acts powerfully upon the body . . . and should be employed in the cure of madness." The point of those horror stories, however banal they be, is that in practice diagnosis is often immaterial and that the distinction between treatment and terror remains almost as tenuous as ever. "Such fear," wrote a doctor who uses and advocates ECT, "is often described as intense even by people who have received EST during drug-induced sleep after having had medication to reduce their fear while awaiting treatment. I have heard a great many patients describe EST as one of the most fearsome experiences of their lives." Equally revealing is the fact that some people who have had ECT, probably a minority but nonetheless a significant number, believe they were cured by it. Typically, in a letter to *Psychology Today:* "I am one of the many people who, without electroshock therapy, would not be performing my responsibilities as a wife and mother of three, and holding down a full-time job. Many of us live under risks every day of our lives. . . . I doubt that there is any greater risk involved than there is in a gall-bladder operation or a hysterectomy, etc." Although such testimonials may simply validate Rush's ideas about the uses of terror, they also confirm the mystifying powers of the technology and those who possess it. The comparison with hysterectomy was unwittingly apt not only because that procedure has fallen under suspicion and is, by growing consensus, vastly overused, but also because it symbolizes the common faith in simple, "radical" procedures to deal with medical or pseudo-medical situations. Assuming, *arguendo,* that it is physically and psychologically possible to fully "perform" the responsibilities of wife and mother of three and still hold down a full-time job, such testimonials indicate how often people believe that they have so little self-control and, at the same time, so little control over the conditions of their lives, that they must be shocked into "performing my responsibilities."[13]

In the end, even the theory of ECT—however embossed with rationalization and justification—still squints toward fear and punishment. It is not simply that some brutal doctors or nurses or technicians have misapplied shock to the purposes of institutional management and client intimidation, but that the very essence of ECT—when it works—can more easily be explained in terms of learning theory (*i. e.,* punishment) than in any other way. A few years ago, Robert R. Dies, a clinical psychologist at the Institute for Living in Hartford, Connecticut, offered what still appears to be the most plausible explanation: "In social learning theory terms," he wrote,

> ECT can be characterized as having a decidedly negative reinforcement value. It is suggested that as treatment progresses . . . expectancy for the negative reinforcement [*i. e.,* punishment] increases as a function of repeated exposure to shock [and] expectancy for punishment becomes associated with those additional reinforcements resulting from shock, namely the profound but transient disorientation.

Dies suggests that the patient learns that "ECT has been recommended for him because of his pathological behavior . . . that his symptoms are generally unacceptable and must therefore be eliminated. . . . Conformity in this situation represents protective action to avert expected punishment."

Whether or not that theory is correct, it is at least plausible that since many practitioners, perhaps most, believe that suppression or erasure of memory, rather than being an unfortunate side effect, is the very essence of the treatment, that somehow it burns or blasts out the electrochemical brain data which caused the malfunction, and that it erases the memory bank of illness, its very nature is assaultive. From there it is only a small step to the theory of Dr. Richard D. Rubin of Trenton, New Jersey, who recently told the Canadian Psychiatric Association that the most effective use of ECT is to time the shock to coincide with the disturbing thought or behavior that the therapist is trying to eliminate.

One case [said Dr. Rubin] was that of a fireman whose particular hallucination was that he talked to Jesus Christ. I sat by his
bed for three hours, waiting for this to occur, while he remained wired up throughout this time, a syringe of succinyl-
choline inserted in a vein, and my finger resting near the
button. When his hallucination finally occurred, the succinyl-
choline was injected to prevent risk of fracture and, at the very
instant fasciculation was observed, the ECT was administered.[14]

The important thing, Dr. Rubin underlined, was what the
patient has in mind at the moment of treatment, a conclusion
he reached from earlier studies in animals of the effects of
ECT on conditioning and memory. "The results of such
studies showed that the retrograde amnesia produced by
ECT had its greatest effects on memories with which it was
contiguous." ECT generally works, he explained, for symptoms which are in a steady state (e. g., depression) but with
his method it will also work for "intermittent states," such
as hallucinations, delusions, and just possibly, for habitual
criminality and drug addiction. Although Dr. Rubin did not
explain how the method selects between desirable and undesirable "steady states"—between, for example, Ernest Hemingway's depression and the literary "capital" of his memory
—he has probably discovered the basic principle of ECT: any
behaviorist would recognize it as aversive conditioning. If
one zaps the rat often enough on its way to get a food pellet,
one can teach it to starve to death.[15]

# II

In his ice-cream jacket, white pants, white shoes, and dark glasses, M. Hunter Brown might be any Southern California doctor on his way to the golf course. There is nothing about him or the anonymous modesty of his little suite of offices in Santa Monica that gives any indication that, by his own undisputed claim, Dr. Brown is the most prolific psychosurgeon in America. In an average year, he performs between thirty and ninety such operations—he prefers to call them "target or multi-target stereotaxic surgery"—although in the first four months of 1976 he had already performed forty and was therefore slightly ahead of schedule. Those operations, in his judgment, bear little relationship to the primitive lobotomies which were performed by the thousands in the 1940s and 1950s, and which in his view continue to give psychosurgery an undeservedly bad reputation: "When I put a target in with a brain probe I know where the target is going with a high degree of accuracy," making the operation, in his opinion, "the safest of any neurosurgical procedure," with a mortality rate of one in a thousand and a "recovery or improvement rate" of nine in ten. Since there are no systematic controlled studies and no hard definitions of "improvement," the meaning of those figures is far from clear, but figures are not Hunter Brown's primary concern. What he deals with are those patients—people with "severe behavioral disorders, including aggression, severe neurotic disorders like obsessive compulsive neurosis and depressive neurosis, and major psychotic disorders"—and what he worries about are violence and crime—maintenance of the fragile social order—and the thousands of aggressive prisoners who he feels should be subject to his treatment.

The person convicted of a violent crime [he said in 1972] should have the chance for a corrective operation. A panel of doctors would give the pre-operation tests. After surgery, the patient would be kept in an institution for three months to see that the operation had worked. Then he would go before a parole board with powers to release him back to society. Each violent criminal incarcerated for 20 years to life costs taxpayers perhaps $100,000. For roughly $6,000, society can provide medical treatment which will transform him into a responsible well-adjusted citizen.[16]

Brown is one of perhaps ten or a dozen doctors who practice psychosurgery in the United States today—there are scores of others abroad, particularly in Japan, India, West Germany, Great Britain, and Canada—performing an estimated 600 to 1,000 operations a year, far fewer than there were a generation ago (before the introduction of phenothiazine tranquilizers) but carried out with an equally high sense of medical and social mission. Like Brown, many of the practitioners and their psychiatrist-associates from whom their patients are referred now believe that the technology represents what they regard as a great hope for curing society of crime and aggression. It is those prisoners they'd like to get, the murderers, the sex offenders, the psychopaths. On the wall behind the desk of H. Thomas Ballantine, Jr., a psychosurgeon who practices at Boston's Massachusetts General Hospital, and who specializes in severely depressed and obsessive-compulsive patients, there is a sign which could well be their slogan: "Stomp Out Violence."

The procedures vary, but the principles and objectives of psychosurgery are always the same: "The surgical removal," in the words of an NIMH report, "or the destruction of brain tissue or the cutting of brain tissue to disconnect one part of the brain from another with the *intent of altering behavior.*" (Thousands of neurosurgery operations, of course, are performed each year to remove tumors or deal with other organic problems; in addition, some—which fall into a marginal area between neurosurgery and psychosurgery—are performed to mitigate or eliminate the sometimes excruciating pain associated with the "phantom limbs" of amputees or with tic douloureux, a severe pain in a facial nerve.) Such procedures date back at least to the last decade of the nineteenth century, when Gottlieb Burckhardt, the director of an asylum in Switzerland, removed part of the brain of several patients in an attempt to calm them; but it was not until the Portuguese physician Egas Moniz performed the first frontal lobe operations in 1935—three years before Cerletti developed ECT—that psychosurgery began to spread. (Moniz himself was to win a Nobel Prize in medicine; he was also to be partially paralyzed by gunshot wounds inflicted by a lobotomized patient.) Optimistic reports of Moniz's procedures, combined with the support of the Veterans Administration, which encouraged psychosurgery for veterans of World War II with psychiatric problems, generated an enormous wave of lobotomy in the post-war decade, when it was used for everything from schizophrenia to voyeurism, delinquency to drug addiction: some 50,000 lobotomies were done in the United States alone—Walter Freeman of Washington, D. C., claims to have done 4,000 himself—many of them with the most unimaginably primitive methods. (In 1943, the VA asked its staff neurosurgeons to get special training in prefrontal lobe operations and directed that candidates for psychosurgery were to be those in whom "apprehension, anxiety, and depression are present, also cases with compulsions and obsessions, with marked emotional tension," for whom other forms of treatment, including ECT, had failed.) The target of those operations, the frontal lobes, were sometimes thought to be related to aggression or violence, but often the operations amounted to nothing more than crude attempts to destroy the brain. One physician recently recalled how, as medical students in 1946, he and his roommate would "hire out as emergency room 'docs' [hacks?] at a nondescript midtown hospital":

> After a hell of a Saturday night, replete with auto catastrophes, stabbings, poisonings, precipitous deliveries, rat bites, appendectomies, etc., I functioned as chief headholder

for a noted neurologist . . . who specialized in "ice pick" lobotomies. The patient would be wheeled into the operating room, where electrodes were strapped to his skull, and he would be zapped into temporary oblivion. During the post-ictal period, a carefully scored surgical "ice pick" would be inserted at the inner canthus of the conjunctiva [of the eye], tapped gently with a hammer, wiggled, tapped, wiggled. He would awaken deprived of a significant chunk of his intellectual capacity. We did three or four in an hour or so—it was a bloodless and thoroughly horrifying experience. I helped only once, but I am told it happened once a week for a few years.[17]

During the past decade, the practitioners have refined their methods beyond the ice-pick technology; they have tried chemicals, radioactive substances, ultrasound, and freezing to destroy brain tissue. Most now favor "stereo-taxic" techniques in which geometric coordinates and X-ray examinations are used to place a fine wire tipped with an electrode in the brain, thereby enabling the surgeon to reach not only the frontal lobes but the deeper brain structures which lie under them. Once the electrode is placed it can be used either to "stimulate" that part of the brain with a weak alternating current and thus, in theory, determine what mood or behavior is affected by that region, or to destroy it with a direct current. As a consequence, lobotomies have become relatively rare in the United States; the other structures are now the preferred targets—either one at a time or several at once—because such operations are believed to have more specific and limited effects.[18]

To say that psychosurgery is controversial is, quite obviously, an understatement. While evangelists like Hunter Brown believe it can be used to control aggression and violence in society, its more moderate advocates defend it as a treatment of last resort to be tried only on the most extreme cases, an act of desperation for people who would otherwise mutilate themselves or remain totally incapacitated for the rest of their lives. At the same time, however, the literature

—and the hospitals—are full of examples of individuals who were mutilated or whose intellectual capacities were destroyed by the lobotomies of the forties and fifties, and whose vegetabilized state gave the word "lobotomized" its most common meaning. Follow-up studies on lobotomized patients are, at best, inconclusive; in many cases, however, they indicate, in the words of one summary, that there is "no substantial scientific evidence that these psychosurgical procedures were useful." Yet the practice continues—usually with the patient's informed consent, sometimes without —and although the newer techniques are supposed to be more precise, more effective, and almost always safe, there are no systematic studies to verify that claim either and no theory against which it can be tested. No one knows with any precision which portions of the brain control which functions; moreover, since almost all the brain's structures are interconnected by many different anatomical circuits and since each portion appears to control several different functions, the possibilities of finding precise modes of intervention are minimal. Organically diseased tissue can be removed —tumors can be cut—because it looks different from other tissue, but the brain of a schizophrenic or of an "obsessive-compulsive neurotic" looks like any other human brain. There is, in the words of Elliot Valenstein, "no theoretical way at present of predicting the consequences of destruction of a particular structure. . . . Knowledge of the details of how the limbic system regulates the emotions is very general at best." Inevitably, therefore, success rates are founded on "clinical experience" based on the vaguest criteria—"improved" or "not improved," "good emotional balance," "symptom free"—which, in turn, depend largely on the self-serving judgment of the physician who performed the operation and those of the psychologists and psychiatrists who work with him. In his own evaluation of Brown's work, Valenstein marvels "that patients seem to be able to tolerate the extensive damage to their brain."[19]

The psychosurgeons frequently report cases as "successful" which, on a closer reading of medical records, and sometimes even by the surgeons' own descriptions, were tragic failures. Between 1968 and 1972, Vernon Mark, William Sweet, and Frank Ervin reported on a series of cases purporting to show the effectiveness of psychosurgical procedures. One of them was a woman who, after two such operations, became enraged and refused any further psychosurgery. The doctors dismissed the rage as "paranoid," but they removed the electrodes and, noting her good mood and "high spirits," released her from the hospital to go shopping. She went directly to a phone booth, called her mother to say good-bye, took poison, and killed herself. The doctors interpreted the suicide as an indication that she was functioning and therefore getting well, a "gratifying" result of the operations. In another case, Orlando J. Andy, a psychosurgeon at the University of Mississippi, reported on the success of a series of four operations performed on a nine-year-old boy who was diagnosed as "hyperactive, aggressive, combative, explosive, destructive, sadistic." The patient, he reported, "has again become adjusted to his environment and has displayed marked improvement in behavior and memory. Intellectually, however, the patient is deteriorating." (According to a psychologist who worked with Andy, the boy's memory was destroyed and his intelligence test scores went from 115 to 60.)[20]

In the halcyon days of ice-pick surgery, Walter Freeman and James Watts, the authors of the standard American psychosurgery text of the fifties, observed that "it is better for the patient to have a simplified intellect capable of elementary acts than an intellect where there reigns this disorder of subtle synthesis. Society can accommodate itself to the most humble laborer, but it justifiably distrusts the mad thinker." (The context of the statement gives no indication that any irony was suspected.) Since that time, drugs have tended to replace surgery, the annual number of operations has declined, and the ice pick has been abandoned. What the case reports suggest, however, is that while the techniques are professedly less crude, the criteria with which they are evaluated—to say nothing of the candor of the reports themselves —are often as casual and brutal as ever. Nonetheless, Mark, Sweet, and Ervin managed to persuade Congress in 1970–71 to appropriate $500,000 to their Neuro-Research Foundation for a study on "the control of rage seizure through implantation of electrodes in the brain and gradual destruction of tissue in the amygdala and other structures of the temporal lobe." At the same time, they received a grant of $108,000 from LEAA to develop medical screening methods for the potentially violent offender, among them the use of fingerprints which, they said, "exhibit specific variations in known genetic diseases including chromosomal abnormalities of the kind found in habitually aggressive offenders." They did not point out that extensive studies—many also financed by NIMH and other federal agencies—have been unable to establish any conclusive connection between "chromosomal abnormalities" and "aggressive offenders," but the grant indicated the direction in which they and the government hoped to go: if fingerprints could be used, almost everyone could be screened for violent tendencies.[21]

By 1972, when Mark, Sweet, and Ervin requested additional funds from the Justice Department and Congress—they wanted $1.3 million from LEAA alone and had already received congressional approval for an additional $1 million from the National Institute of Health—psychiatrist Peter Breggin and a handful of others had published enough data on the so-called new wave of psychosurgery to block further federal funding. Nonetheless, NIMH, which had negotiated a $500,000 contract with the Neuro-Research Foundation and which was later careful to point out that no psychosurgery was actually performed under it, has never abandoned its interest in the possibilities of screening and medical intervention for violent tendencies and in the genetic abnormalities which, in the words of David Rosenthal, chief of NIMH's psychology laboratory, "may . . . contribute toward a propensity to crime." The government has continued to

fund the search for a connection between chromosome anomalies—particularly males with an extra Y chromosome—
and violence, and it has never ended its flirtation with the
psychosurgeons.[22]

The same process that halted federal funding for Mark,
Sweet, and Ervin in 1972 was likely to resume it for others
in 1977 or 1978. In the spring and summer of 1976, the
National Commission for the Protection of Human Subjects
of Biomedical and Behavioral Research, which had been
established in response to protests about psychosurgery and
other experimentation, commissioned two "studies," one at
MIT, the other at Boston University, of psychosurgery subjects, most of them patients or former patients of Thomas
Ballantine or Hunter Brown. The results of those evaluations
were mixed and the conclusions qualified. The study teams
found that some patients had improved, sometimes dramatically; that some had not; but that even those who did not
benefit appeared not to have been further damaged by the
operations. That finding, however, was also qualified, since

> the operation added its effects not only to those of a persistent
> illness that preceded it, but to the cumulative impact of the
> massive earlier treatment efforts, which by themselves seemed
> to be interfering with certain higher functions, and often to
> an extent where it appeared futile to expect that the effect of
> [the surgery] as such might have been discernible within a
> welter of other handicaps that already weighed upon the
> patient as they entered upon his surgical course.

In simple language, many of the subjects studied were already in such bad shape from their condition and from earlier attempts to "treat" them that nothing the surgeons did
could have made them any worse.[23]

The major problem with the evaluations is that they were
not systematic studies at all. Of the sixty-one people examined by the two teams (most of them women), only eighteen
—less than a third—had been evaluated by the study groups
before the operation, and there was, therefore, no indepen-

dent judgment or diagnosis of the pre-operative condition of
most of the patients; judgment of their pre-operative conditions had to depend on the diagnosis and decisions of the
same people who put them on the operating table in the first
place. Equally important, there was no random selection of
patients, no way of knowing how many of those who were
unavailable for examination had improved or deteriorated,
how many were dead or from what causes, and how many
were vegetating in the back wards of hospitals. Those who
were evaluated were those who had been able and willing to
come to Boston for the tests. The two teams studied the
results of four different kinds of operations used by four
surgeons on a variety of patients—among them a number
who had the operations to mitigate chronic, intractable pain
(a procedure which falls only marginally within the definition of psychosurgery's scope of "altering behavior")—and
came up with similar conclusions for all four: the kind of
procedure used appeared to be immaterial to the results. As
a consequence, needless to say, there is still no theory; no way
of knowing why the operations work, when they work; and
no data on whether a pseudo-operation, a course of behavior
modification, some other form of intervention, real or simulated, or no treatment at all might have worked just as well.
Nonetheless, on the basis of these studies, the National Commission concluded that psychosurgery has "potential merit"
and recommended that the Department of Health, Education and Welfare "conduct and support research to evaluate
the safety and efficacy of specific psychosurgical procedures
in relieving specific psychiatric symptoms and disorders."

Given the commission's organization, mandate, and methods, the conclusion was predictable. One critic of its findings,
Ayub K. Ommaya, head of the Surgical Neurology Branch
of the National Institute of Neurological and Communicative Disorders and Stroke, told the commission that "I do not
find any worthwhile clinical trial or testable hypothesis [for
psychosurgery] either proposed or even perhaps possible." In
light of that failing and in light of the endemic vagueness of

diagnosis and criteria of evaluation, the commission's decision to evaluate the results of psychosurgical operations had, almost inevitably, to lead to the most banal of bureaucratic recommendations: further study. Even if it had the courage to make a conclusive decision in a highly controversial field, no group operating in the lush territory where "science" and government overlap is likely to respond with a flat no to the possibility of future government support. Just as predictably, the commission's report included recommendations to protect psychosurgery subjects with institutional review boards and elaborate informed consent procedures. The more fundamental questions about whether the government should be in the psychosurgery business at all—either as sponsor or evaluator—and, more important, about the ethics of even a "safe" and effective operation remained unanswered.

# III

It was the kind of experiment press agents dream about. When Jose Delgado, the Yale physiologist, stopped a charging brain-implanted bull by radio control, Delgado and the bull appeared in virtually every newspaper and magazine in America; and the idea of remote control of behavior—animal as well as human—moved out of the realm of science fiction into what appeared to be the domain of the imminently practical. A decade after Delgado published his results, for example, Boyce Rensberger reported in *The New York Times* that

> Dr. Delgado implanted a radio-controlled electrode deep within the brain of a brave bull, a variety bred to respond with a raging charge when it sees any human being. But when Dr. Delgado pressed a button on a transmitter, sending a signal to a battery-powered receiver attached to the bull's horns, an impulse went into the bull's brain and the animal ceased his charge.

After several stimulations, the bull's naturally aggressive behavior disappeared. It was as placid as Ferdinand. A similar device has been implanted in the brain of a man given to uncontrollable bursts of rage. When he feels an attack coming on, he presses a button on his battery pack and remains peaceable.

Such a demonstration indicated that

> though their methods are still crude and not always predictable, there can remain little doubt that the next few years will bring a frightening array of refined techniques for making human beings act according to the will of the psychotechnologists.[24]

Rensberger and others faithfully reported Delgado's claims for what he calls ESB—electrical stimulation of the brain— a technique he has tried not only on bulls, cats, and monkeys, but on humans. (What better way to show it off, however, than with a "brave" bull?) Nonetheless, the importance of those experiments does not lie in the technology itself—the hardware is similar to that in the implants used to monitor the brain activity of hospitalized epileptics (and similar to the implants of psychosurgery)—nor in Delgado's success in evoking certain kinds of motor responses: every high school freshman knows that it is possible to make a frog kick by applying an electric current in the proper place. It lies, rather, in Delgado's claim that ESB can control memory, mood, feelings, impulses, and will. In the case of the bull, Delgado, who started his work in Spain and moved to Yale in 1950, asserted that "the result seemed to be a combination of motor effect . . . plus behavioral inhibition of the aggressive drive." In other experiments, Delgado published photographs purporting to show that ESB had evoked "true rage" in cats and inhibited "ferocity" and "aggressive behavior" in monkeys. But the most intriguing claims concern the power of ESB to evoke hallucinations, illusions, memories, and feelings—including pain, fear, and pleasure—in humans. In his experiments, said Delgado, ESB has not only made people more friendly, open, and sociable; in one case, the subject started giggling and making funny comments, stating that she enjoyed the sensation "very much." Repetition of these stimulations made the patient more communicative and flirtatious, and she ended by openly expressing her desire to marry the therapist. . . . During control interviews before and after ESB, her behavior was quite proper, without familiarity or excessive friendliness.

Similar results have been reported by others: Mark and Ervin claim they can evoke relaxation and positive sensation in their patients; and Dr. Robert G. Heath, a psychosurgeon at Tulane University, reported that electrical stimulation can arouse patients sexually. Heath, who apparently holds the record for implantations—125 electrodes in one person at one time—says he uses his method to treat homosexuals and frigid women, and he hopes to use it to cure drug addicts who, in his view, suffer from a neurological deficit in their "pleasure centers."[25]

The scientific problem with such reports is that even when it is possible to distinguish motor effects and other physical effects from effects on feeling and mood, the results of the same treatment often vary from subject to subject, and, in many cases, even in the same subject at different times. Valenstein, examining films of Delgado's bull demonstration, observed "that the charging bull was stopped because as long as the stimulation was on, it was forced to turn around in the same direction continuously. . . . No evidence was presented to prove that aggressivity had been modified." Others have observed that while responses "of an emotional nature" have been reported—the most important is fear—"we have difficulty being certain whether fear actually was the result of stimulation or whether it was not simply the result of an unusual situation experienced under conditions that were alarming to the patient. In one instance fearfulness . . . practically disappeared as the patient became accustomed to the procedure of stimulation." More important, even when the researchers are confident that it was the stimulation and not the experimental environment which produced the effect, they have no way of predicting the effect, and no way of replicating it with any consistency.[26]

Despite its lack of reliability, however, the work of Delgado, Heath, Mark, Ervin, and others has generated no end of experimentation, speculation, and theorizing about the possibilities of direct behavior control through ESB and the creation of what Delgado calls a "psychocivilized society." Delgado claims that such techniques prove that "movements, sensations, emotions, desires, ideas, and a variety of other psychological phenomena may be induced, inhibited, or modified by electrical stimulations of specific areas of the brain." If the public would realize that "these facts have changed the classical philosophical concept that the mind was beyond human reach," it might make possible a "future psychocivilized human being, a less cruel, happier, and better man. The concept of individuals as self-sufficient and independent entities is based on false premises."[27] Some researchers like Mark and Ervin have produced tendentious reports —none of them validated—about the relationship of epilepsy and violence (one of the most primitive beliefs in Western demonology); but for the most part, the theorizing and experimentation have moved into a realm in which medicine and medical logic have become atavistic and where overt behavior control through brain stimulation is the wave of the future.[28]

The dream takes two forms: the further development of Heath's work in "self-stimulation"—a sort of neurological masturbation of the "pleasure centers" in the brain—and a combination of ESB, computer technology, and radiotelemetry to monitor and control epileptics, probationers, or anyone else that the doctor or the police or the state thinks should be watched. The core of the system is the so-called Schwitzgebel Machine, developed a few years ago by Ralph K. Schwitzgebel of the Laboratory of Community Psychiatry at the Harvard Medical School, and modified by his brother Robert at the Claremont Graduate School in California. The system consists of a "Behavior Transmitter-Rein-

forcer" (BT-R) worn on the belt which receives and trans-
mits signals to a central radio unit linked to a "modified
missile-tracking device which graphs the wearer's location
and displays it on a screen." In its various adaptations by the
Schwitzgebels and others, it can be used to communicate
with the subject (so far the effective distance is about a quarter of a mile), to record his pulse, monitor his heart, record
brain waves of epileptics, and monitor other physical or
neurological signs. Ralph Schwitzgebel saw the device as a
way of releasing high-risk prisoners into the community:

> A parolee thus released would probably be less likely than
> usual to commit offenses if a record of his location were kept
> at the base station. If a two-way tone communication were
> included in this system, a therapeutic relationship might be
> established in which the parolee could be rewarded, warned
> or otherwise signalled in accordance with the plan for ther-
> apy. . . . Security equipment has been designed, but not con-
> structed, that could insure the wearing of the transmitting
> equipment or indicate attempts to compromise or disable the
> system.[29]

Clearly, however, that is only the beginning of the possibilities. Combine that with devices for recording physiological
changes, with Delgado's implants, with computer technology, and the potential is almost unlimited. As promoted by
Barton L. Ingraham and Gerald W. Smith, criminologists at
the University of Maryland and the University of Utah,
respectively, certain physiological data "would be particularly revealing."

> A parolee with a past record of burglaries is tracked to a
> downtown shopping district (in fact, is exactly placed in a
> store known to be locked up for the night) and the physiologi-
> cal data reveals an increased respiration rate, a tension in the
> musculature and an increased flow of adrenalin. It would be
> a safe guess, certainly, that he was up to no good. The com-
> puter in this case, *weighing the probabilities,* would come to
> a decision and alert police or parole officers so that they could

hasten to the scene; or, if the subject were equipped with an implanted radiotelemeter, it could transmit an electrical signal which could block further action by the subject by causing him to forget or abandon his project. . . .[30]

Ingraham and Smith acknowledge that the technology is not yet sophisticated enough to do everything they dream about (possibly, however, the computer and the implant could keep the suspected burglar turning in circles, like Delgado's bull, until the police arrive), but they see no reason why such systems couldn't be developed and implemented. Not only would the offender gain his physical "freedom" from prison; society itself would be the beneficiary, saving the expense of his incarceration and exercising control "over behavior it defines deviant, thus insuring its own protection. . . . Because the control system works on conditioning principles, the offender is habituated into nondeviant behavior patterns." Just before its opponents managed to block the creation of the UCLA Violence Center in 1974, Jolly West and his colleagues were preparing to investigate those suggestions, and the government was preparing to fund them.

# IV

"A number of people would like to get their toes in this water," said Hunter Brown.

We see patients with massive gaping wounds—this is psychologically speaking—and the state gives us Band-aids. It is either this [psychosurgery] or a further escalation of violence and chaos in society that does not serve the best interests of the United States. I think it serves other interests. There is a political spectrum that is opposed to all forms of somatic therapy: that includes electroshock, drugs, target surgery—everything—for reasons, I think, to increase violence and chaos in society.

Did he mean that that political position advocates violence and chaos?

"That's right."

Did he then see opposition to psychosurgery and related methods as a conspiratorial movement?

"As one technique to produce disorder, and I have very good documentation, if you'd like to see it." He reaches into a box and produces old handouts from the Progressive Labor Party and a clipping from *Ebony* warning that psychosurgery could be used to practice genocide on blacks. "You certainly know that disorder within the continental United States does not serve the stability of our society. We both agree on that."

Did he see more surgery of this kind—did he expect more people would be treated this way in the coming years?

"There has to be more. No one suppresses scientific truth forever."[31]


The principle always seems to be the same: the more powerful the technology, the less it has to do with the treatment of specific illness and the more likely that the practitioners will see themselves as agents of control and shapers of the social order. "We have a grave responsibility," said A. E. Bennett, a Berkeley, California, psychiatrist, in a newspaper column, "to protect society, the so-called normal people, from the social disturbers, violent agitators, multiple murderers and drug addicts responsible for our increasing violence, crime rate and deterioration in respect for law and moral and social standards." "Violence," wrote Mark and Ervin, "is a public health problem" which the psychosurgeons can help mitigate. "Just as we have developed city planning," said Delgado, citing Skinner, "we should propose mental planning . . . to formulate theories and practical means for directing the evolution of man."[32]

Given those views and the fact that the heavy technologies —ECT, psychosurgery, and implants—assault the brain directly, it's hardly surprising that they have become the most emotional issue in psychiatry, that patients and former patients have organized against them, that a few states have passed laws restricting their use, and that, in response, the "shock doctors" have formed the American Society for Electrotherapy to "preserve the integrity of the practice of electrotherapy, the sacred privilege of treating our patients according to recognized standards, the preservation of the right to freedom of choice of physician, and maintenance of the confidentiality inherent in the doctor-patient relationship." The government, says the society, should not "regulate commonly accepted treatment modalities." If the government regulates ECT or psychosurgery, or if it restricts their use, it will deny people who really want such treatment a chance to have it. The practitioners insist that neither psychosurgery nor ECT should be considered experimental—that they have proven their worth in "clinical experience."

The issue of informed consent has plagued physicians and psychiatrists for generations, particularly since the Nazi experiments on human subjects and the promulgation, in the Nuremberg Code, of the principle that "the voluntary consent of the human subject is absolutely essential."[33] In the early seventies, that issue was sharpened with the disclosure of federally sanctioned sterilization of women on welfare, the revelation of the notorious Tuskegee experiments in which individuals with syphilis were studied but not treated (although they thought they were being treated), and the publication of a series of stories concerning drug and medical experimentation on "consenting" prisoners. In the realm of behavior control, however, the most celebrated case was that of an incarcerated "criminal sexual psychopath" in Michigan who was to become the first of some twenty-eight in the state's mental-health system—some "aggressive," some mentally retarded—who were slated for psychosurgery. The patient, who had been hospitalized for eighteen years after committing a rape-murder at the age of seventeen, had consented to the operation on the promise that he would be released from the institution. The operation was to be kept secret; someone, however, leaked the information to the press and to a Michigan Legal Services lawyer named Gabe Kaimowitz, who brought suit early in 1973 to stop the program. During the course of the hearings which followed, witnesses testified that in addition to the "experimental" group of psychosurgery subjects, there was to be a control group of sex offenders who would be treated with an experimental German drug; that one Detroit clinic had already sought information from the police on the number of local sex offenders to determine the market potential for the drug; and that therefore the whole program was an experiment and not a course of treatment. Although the promoters of the program said the patient was aggressive, one psychiatrist testified that the patient had shown no aggressive behavior since he had been incarcerated eighteen years before; furthermore, he had had no psychiatric treatment whatever during all those years although he was, in fact, treatable with routine psychotherapy. The prime issues, however, related to the patient's capacity to consent while he was locked up and to the question of whether psychosurgery was an accepted or only an experimental form of treatment. In July 1973, a three-judge court ruled that psychosurgery was in fact experimental and that

experimental psychosurgery, which is irreversible and intrusive, often leads to a blunting of emotions, the deadening of memory, the reduction of affect, and limits the ability to generate new ideas. Its potential for injury to the creativity of the individual is great and can impinge on the right of the individual to be free from interference with his mental processes.

The State's interest in performing psychosurgery and the legal ability of the involuntarily detained mental patient to give consent must bow to the First Amendment, which protects the generation and free flow of ideas from unwarranted interference with one's mental processes.[34]

The court, citing the Nuremberg doctrine, found that "the very nature of [the subject's] incarceration diminishes the capacity to consent to psychosurgery." Similar logic could probably be applied to ECT and ESB; but with the exception of statutory attempts in a few states, particularly Oregon and California, to make psychosurgery and electroshock for involuntary mental patients subject to review by outside physicians or to other restrictions, neither ECT nor psychosurgery nor implants are subject to such regulation by state or federal authorities. In Massachusetts, the state adopted regulations in 1973 requiring informed written consent from voluntary patients before ECT could be administered. As a consequence, according to Alan Stone of Harvard, "the responsible physician was stymied in the case of such voluntary non-consenting patients. Therefore, the regulations were altered to permit the hospital to move for commitment when such patients refuse shock treatment."[35]

Most states do not bother with even that much formality. In Alabama, where in 1972 U. S. District Judge Frank Johnson imposed stringent requirements on Bryce State Hospital in an effort to improve standards of treatment, doctors consistently violated a specific court standard that "patients have a right not to be subjected to . . . lobotomy, electroconvulsive treatment . . . or other unusual or hazardous treatment procedures without their express and informed consent after consultation with counsel or interested party of the patient's choice." In criminal proceedings conducted early in 1975, Judge Johnson found that "each instance in which ECT was administered to an involuntary patient without that patient's express consent constituted a clear and direct violation" of the previous court order. The court also found that there was no record that any of the patients, most of whom were black, were given an anesthetic in connection with ECT, that the hospital had adopted policies in clear violation of the order, and that all the doctors had clear and full knowledge of the court's standards. Nonetheless, Johnson, regarded as one of the most enlightened and courageous federal judges in the South, found that no evidence was presented to show that the doctors and administrators had acted with "contumacious intent or with a wrongful state of mind."[36] Although some physicians have faced civil suits from former patients who charge irreversible neurological damage from ECT, no doctor within memory has ever been successfully prosecuted for criminal assault against any of the thousands of people who, despite their refusal, were "treated" anyway.

Many, if not most, of the doctors themselves regard informed consent as something between a nuisance and a joke —"no more than an elaborate ritual," in the words of a report published in *The New England Journal of Medicine,* "a device that when the subject is uneducated and uncomprehending, confers no more than a semblance of propriety on human experimentation." In most areas of medical practice, the practitioners pay lip service to informed consent even when it is otherwise compromised or ignored. In psychiatry, however, which posits a hypothetical personality that would consent if it could only understand its real interests, even the formality is often regarded as unnecessary or unfeasible. "I always charm them into it," said Leo Alexander, a psychiatrist in suburban Boston and the author of a standard text on psychotherapy in the fifties.

> A surgeon never tells a patient, "I'm going to cut you with a knife." You de-emphasize the specific treatment; you say that there is an outside chance that there may be an operation that may help. It depends on a true doctor-patient relationship. A more or less institutional approach is always disastrous.

Dr. Alexander should know: he helped draft the Nuremberg Code, and it was his ideas upon which it was based.[37]

# V

There is, in fact, no brave new world of precise brain control —not yet, and not in the foreseeable future. The brain is simply too complex and the techniques too crude. Nor is it possible for anyone to start implanting electrodes in the brains of the citizenry without police-state coercion. Yet clearly, all the technologies that assault the brain directly— and many which, like drugs, assault it indirectly—have enormous impact on mood, behavior, memory, and intelligence; all have been used to pacify and tranquilize, to punish and terrorize. The fact that the heavy technologies other than ECT are rarely used these days in the United States does not diminish their political or social importance in reinforcing the dubious legitimacy of other techniques; the normative standards of behavior in whose service they are so promiscuously employed; or the assaultive ideology of people like Cerletti, Moniz, and Delgado which regards the brain as no more inviolate than the appendix. So far, the very crudeness of the techniques has been the most important barrier to wide implementation; but with rare exceptions, neither the government nor the profession has ever suggested that even if the techniques were genuinely precise and effective, they should not be used because they violate human rights and human dignity.

Although the practitioners complain about government controls and interference, they are themselves agents and beneficiaries of the state, both in terms of funds and other forms of support. It was the state, through NIMH and LEAA, which helped fund Mark, Ervin, and Sweet's Neuro-Research Foundation of Boston; it was the state, through the Public Health Service, the Office of Naval Research, and the U. S. Air Force Aeromedical Research Laboratory, which funded Delgado's work in the 1950s and 1960s; it was the state, through the California prison system, which sponsored psychosurgery experiments on three California prisoners in 1968; it was the state of Michigan which was preparing to perform psychosurgery on mental patients—the state legislature had appropriated $228,000 for operations on those twenty-eight people—and which defended its propriety before the court that ordered the program stopped; it was the state of California which sponsored the UCLA Violence Center until that project was halted by organized public opposition; it was a senior official of a Michigan mental-health clinic who said (echoing Mark, Sweet, and Ervin) that a certain percentage of the black Detroit rioters in 1967 had brain damage and that, to maintain social order, operations for aggression should be done on "dumb young men"; it is the states of Texas, Louisiana, Nevada, Arizona, and New Mexico, through public mental-health and prison officials and, in Hunter Brown's words, "an enlightened judge," which have sent Brown some of his patients; it is the state of Alabama which administers electroshock to mental patients without their consent—and without anesthetic—despite court orders to the contrary; and it is the state, through NIMH and other agencies, which funds aversive shock and other behavior-control experiments on prisoners, delinquents, and homosexuals.

The argument for each technique is the same: "What do you do," asked a psychiatrist in Los Angeles, "if a member of your family is a psychopath, a sociopath, an alcoholic, or a psychotic? What do you do with the recidivist who ruins his family? What do you do with the violent people? What do you do?" The question comes from doctors, from schoolteachers who want to drug unruly schoolchildren, from welfare administrators and social workers trying to cope with difficult clients, from lawyers representing mental patients, from judges, from cops, from the whole array of so-called dirty workers who have been charged with the task—or have arrogated to themselves the task—of "protecting society, so-called normal people" from the deviants, the misfits, the "violent agitators, social disturbers, multiple murderers," and from the ugly, the peculiar, the unclean, and the uncooperative. Even a dubiously valid procedure can be justified as a measure of desperation in the most desperate cases, yet inevitably the logic which makes it acceptable there begins to make it look attractive somewhere else. The society creates its superfluous people—the old, the young, the poor, the black, the middle-aged housewife, the unemployed adolescent—and then the state creates institutions and technologies to deal with them which, in turn, create still more categories of deficiency, still more people who need intervention and treatment.

What do you do? There are, as psychiatrist Lee Coleman said, "always real dilemmas; whatever we do we will have dilemmas." But "what do you do?" is a false question, a plea for sympathy from people who have no right to expect it, because the "you" (the "I" really) has already made false claims, either as an individual or as a member of the profession, about techniques and skills which he does not possess. Electric shock treatment, said Szasz,

> is paradigmatic of the interventions of institutional psychiatry: based on force and fraud, and justified by "medical necessity," the prime purpose of psychiatric treatments—whether utilizing drugs, electricity, surgery, or confinement, especially if imposed on unconsenting clients—is to authenticate the subject as "patient," the psychiatrist as a "doctor," and the intervention as a form of "treatment." The cost of this fictionalization runs high: it requires the sacrifice of the patient as a person; of the psychiatrist as a critical thinker and moral agent; and of the legal system as a protector of the citizen from the abuse of state power.[38]

In the end, the argument comes full circle to Lloyd Cotter's solution for chronic mental illness in Vietnam. That solution betrays the view that the "mental illness" of the patients was nothing more than their refusal to work for a

penny a day making souvenirs for American soldiers or
growing vegetables in the hospital garden and in the pacification compounds run by the Green Berets. Here Cotter comes
painfully close to begging questions that Szasz and R. D.
Laing have each answered in their own ways: that madness
(in Szasz's view) is either a form of irresponsible behavior or
a label of mystification and control, or that (in the context
of Laing's views) under Vietnamese conditions, it was the
most responsible behavior possible. More important, however, Cotter also comes close to stumbling on the highly
significant connection between "mental illness" and economic cycles, which has been almost totally ignored by his
fellow psychiatrists. In an extensive study of mental hospitalization in New York State between 1841 and 1967, M. Harvey Brenner of Johns Hopkins University found that hospitalization consistently showed an inverse relationship with
the economy: when the economy went up, hospitalization
went down; when the economy went down, hospitalization
went up. No matter how the categories are divided—by class,
age, sex, education, marital status—the pattern remains consistent. Brenner also found that in the generation since
World War II, the trend has become even more pronounced.[39] One of the "solutions" for unemployment or economic depression is madness.

All of that is probably obvious, but it illustrates the social
and economic functions of a system which, in the last generation, has become the ultimate of all social-service networks.
In their study of welfare practices and policies, Frances Fox
Piven and Richard A. Cloward found that welfare in America has been consistently used as a device to dampen or
destroy the possibilities of political protest and social unrest,
and "that when peace and order reign, the relief concession
is withdrawn." With the new technologies, and particularly
with drugs, the mental-health system performs a similar
function at less cost and with considerably more precision.
Whatever else it does, it takes superfluous people and pacifies
them. Here, conventional political attitudes are irrelevant: it

was Ronald Reagan who sponsored the Violence Center at UCLA; and it was the black liberal Kenneth B. Clark who, as president of the American Psychological Association, announced in 1971 that " we might be on the threshold of that type of scientific biochemical intervention which could stabilize and make dominant the moral and ethical propensities of man and subordinate, if not eliminate, his negative and primitive behavioral tendencies."[40] No one is exempt from the attraction of totalitarian belief.

Ideology obviates conspiracy. It swallows up whatever is left of professional restraint and limitations—the willingness to admit ignorance or to recognize the fact that "moral and ethical propensities" can have nothing to do with "biochemical intervention," and lose their meaning under its ministrations. "What do you do?"—taken at face value—is an absurd question if it seeks medical answers to social problems. But since it is absurd in those terms—because there are no validated medical solutions to most of those problems—it must necessarily be a rhetorical device serving social or political purposes. It no longer matters much how one responds to the assertion that mental illness is a myth: the semantic argument that follows simply cannot overcome the fact that diagnosis and technology are rarely specific enough to establish a therapeutic relationship between them. It is the person who is "treated," not the disease; it is behavior and mood which are controlled, not infection or some other medically precise organic problem. The question "What do you do?" always demands a social answer because it is a social (and political) question: get that dangerous person off the streets; get the wife and mother to "perform" her responsibilities; get the nuisance out of the housing office, or out of the home.

On the issue of outside intervention—on the question, for example, of whether the state should forbid psychosurgery— the doctors tend to have the best of the argument. If the choice is between a successful operation and a lifetime of misery or indefinite incarceration, the argument for the operation becomes at least defensible if not persuasive; if an individual is competent to refuse consent, he should also be regarded as competent to grant it. The suspicion arises out of the terms under which consent is given: To what extent is the patient in a coercive situation? How fully are the chances of success and the risks of damage explained? Considering the notorious shortage of validated data on psychosurgery, the lack of theory, and the insistence of some physicians that psychosurgery is almost always safe and effective, the grounds for suspicion are substantial. And considering the uncertain diagnoses which define the conditions for which psychosurgery or ECT is sometimes recommended, the suspicion is compounded. The doctor who treats the individual for a behavioral disorder also teaches the community how to behave. The more disproportionate ailment and intervention become, the narrower the tolerable norms of social behavior.

# SEVEN

# The Benevolent Eye

## I

The chain of events that led from the New Frontier to Vietnam and Watergate, and from the Great Society to "law and order" has made it clear that America enjoys no special immunity to Orwellian practices. The technologies and disciplines associated with apparently benevolent social objectives—and particularly the social and behavioral sciences—could, we discovered, be turned handily to the purposes of pacification, intimidation, obfuscation, propaganda, and war; could be used just as easily for control as for liberation; and could serve for mystification as readily as they could serve for enlightenment.

What was missed is the extent to which private organizations and the "benign" branches of government—universities, foundations, employers, credit bureaus, schools, the National Institute of Mental Health, the U. S. Office of Education, the Department of Health, Education and Welfare, and local and state welfare agencies—were, and are, in the business of surveillance and behavior control; the extent to which a police mentality, social welfare attitudes of "service," and medical-model "therapy" have fused; and the extent to which a substantial part—if not a majority—of the population has been taught to accept those impositions as routine: as the condition of a job, a welfare check, a loan, or a place in school. Those impositions, extensive enough in their own right, have begun to mesh with the new behavior technologies, with the rhetoric and ideology of mental health, and with the normative categories of acceptable behavior that those technologies sustain. The issue is no longer just conventional surveillance of an individual's acts—the cop with the camera or the bugging device attached to the telephone—but surveillance that extends to psychological states, to attempts—overtly or secretly—to extract confessions with lie detectors; to the collection and assessment of psychiatric data; and to the use of psychological techniques in welfare, schools, and other organizations with the intent of controlling behavior. The revelations of Watergate and the disclosures about the CIA and the FBI have made conventional surveillance practices familiar, but no one has yet begun to assess the extent to which both government and private agencies have, either by accident or by intent, grafted those practices to Skinnerian ideology and psychiatric theory. One can even suggest that the most important element in surveillance is not the information gained by the agency that conducts it, but the effect on the society or the group that thinks or knows it is being watched, and that every disclosure about surveillance, rather than impeding its effects, enhances them.

The surveillance is ubiquitous. "Everybody and his brother is making surveillance cameras," said a manufacturer in an advertisement in *Security World,* the trade journal of the industrial security field; and so, indeed, they are, but they are also making and selling ultrasonic detectors sensitive to noise or motion, electric eyes which activate cameras and silent alarms in stockrooms and other "high security areas," infrared detection systems, motion detectors, bugging devices, de-bugging devices, paper shredders, and virtually everything else the imagination can conceive. Parking lots, school corridors, classrooms, and production lines are watched with closed-circuit television systems; employee telephones are monitored; lunchboxes and lockers are

searched; and on occasion, workers have discovered micro-
phones in employee washrooms during union organizing
drives.[1]

Among the more arcane devices now in use is the Psychological Stress Evaluator (PSE) and other "voice analyzers"
which, according to their proponents, detect the tension in
the voice of someone who is lying (and which are sometimes
used to analyze surreptitiously made tapes). In one instance,
according to *Security World*, a company in Winston-Salem,
North Carolina, uses voice analysis in routine telephone
screening of job applicants. The firm hires a large number of
semi-skilled, high-turnover employees, which makes extensive pre-employment investigations expensive and impracti-
cal. Accordingly, the company asks an applicant to complete
a questionnaire, goes over the answers with him over the
telephone, and runs them through the voice analyzer to determine their truthfulness. "Some employers," according to
*Security World*, "also specify that they would like to know
the applicant's degree of stress when asked about drugs,
alcohol, and similar potentially disabling habits. . . ."[2]

It is a long list. In a survey of 1,200 corporate executives
conducted by the *Harvard Business Review* in 1974, 24 percent reported that their firms use "locker searches," 46 percent use "package checks," 39 percent use "electronic surveillance of high risk areas," 52 percent use "personality tests
—tests that measure characteristics, not abilities," 10 percent use lie detector tests, 49 percent use "drug abuse detection checks" (33 percent "occasionally," 16 percent "often"),
and 10 percent occasionally use handwriting analysis in
screening applicants.[3] In addition to the estimated 500,000
people subject to polygraph examinations every year—80
percent of them as a condition of their employment—hundreds of thousands of other job applicants are screened with
personality tests; surreptitious drug tests during routine
medical examinations; and the Reid Report, a pre-employment paper-and-pencil "lie detector" test which, like the
polygraph, is widely used in banks, discount stores, insur-

ance companies, drug stores, brokerage houses, trucking firms, and fast-food restaurants.[4]

Produced by Reid Associates, a Chicago polygraph firm, the Reid Report includes ninety-three factual questions on gambling, drinking, and drug habits, the amount and sources of the applicant's outstanding loans, the amount the applicant pays in alimony and child support, the current salary of the applicant's spouse, the "total value of merchandise or goods (that did not belong to me) that I have taken from jobs," and "the total amount of money (that did not belong to me) that I have taken from jobs."[5] In addition, the applicant is subjected to a 100-item inventory probing attitudes about theft and honesty. Reid scores the items, then reports to the employer that the applicant is either "recommended for employment," "qualifiedly recommended," "not recommended," or gives "no opinion." The report to the employer also includes a score indicating Reid's estimate of the chances that the applicant "would be involved in undesirable behavior." The inventory is retained by Reid, but the evaluation and the 93-item factual questionnaire with the data on alimony, debts, and drinking habits are returned to the employer for his personnel files and thus become part of the employee's record. Reid claims that in screening out dishonest job applicants, the report is almost as accurate as the polygraph.[6] Its major advantage is that it is cheaper than a polygraph test and that it is not covered by the statutes which, in a dozen states, restrict or prohibit the use of polygraphs in employment screening.[7]

There is considerable controversy about the accuracy of instruments like the polygraph and the Reid Report.[8] What is certain is that lie detector tests have been used to force workers to identify fellow workers whom they suspect of dishonesty, to dredge up irrelevant personal information, and to elicit personally embarrassing data that is sometimes given or sold to employers, credit companies, or anyone else in the market for dirt. But the power of the instrument to find cheats and liars, however accurate, is not nearly as important as the presumption of the practitioners that the innocent must prove their innocence, that 40 percent of all employees will steal given "need and opportunity," and that confession is one of the tests of truth. Philip Ash, a psychologist at the University of Illinois and director of research for Reid Associates, said recently that employers are often astonished that the Reid Report "works." Typically, Ash said, they fear that applicants will see through the test, but in practice many admit "to all kinds of delinquencies, defalcations, and crimes." Those admissions, he suggested, derive at least in part from "a strong tendency toward confession. . . . Confession reduces guilt; the act of confession itself seems to mitigate the offense confessed." Moreover, Ash said, "someone who steals will approve of punishment only for persons who steal more than he does . . . and sees as admissible more 'thoughts about stealing' than more rigidly honest respondents."[9]

The professional polygraphers—they like to call themselves "detectors of deception"—argue that such devices are not aimed at honest workers; that, in the words of a statement by the American Polygraph Association, "all intelligent people endorse the right of the innocent to prove their innocence, the right of the employer to protect his business —*and his honest employees*—from the occasional dishonest worker"; and that those honest workers "have a very personal stake in preserving the polygraph technique . . . so that their reputations, jobs and the public safety and welfare can be protected."[10] Yet it is all workers who are being watched and subject to search, all applicants who are screened, all who come under scrutiny, and all who are taught that in their relationship with the employer (and sometimes with their union), their records, personalities, behavior, credit rating, medical condition, mental health, drug habits, and in some cases, their living arrangements and sexual preferences are not private, and that if they lie about them they can be fired.

The principle is old, only the technologies are new; but

they themselves are so personally intrusive and, at the same time, so impersonal that they constitute a qualitative change in the relationship between the individual and his employer, the credit system, the schools, the welfare system, and any number of other institutions, public and private. In the small factory town—in Lowell and Lawrence and Haverhill—the employer, like everyone else, was often privy to local gossip about the private lives of his workers; could watch them at work and in the community; might even enforce curfews, church attendance, and appropriate moral behavior on the workers—and particularly the "girls"—who worked in his mills. Similarly, in company towns and mining camps, the company controlled not only the job but housing, credit, and virtually everything else. Yet all those forms of control, within the factory and out, whether in the name of employment or charity, presumed a "personal" relationship which, while it was often patronizing, exploitative, and brutal, made clear who was doing what to whom, made no pretense of scientific accuracy, and left no illusions about its lack of bias and general even-handedness.

The industry claims that tests like the polygraph are necessary in reducing industrial theft, particularly in situations where there is high employee turnover and satisfactory references are hard or expensive to get. (Industry estimates of employee theft range from $500 million to $16 billion a year.) What that means, among other things, is that the subjects include a disproportionate number of blacks, Chicanos, and other minorities who constitute the basic nonunion, high-turnover, minimum-wage work force in discount stores, fast-food stands, and similar establishments, many of them people already so conditioned to personal intrusions and so desperate for work that they can't afford the luxury of refusing to take the test, even if they thought of it. The choice, as one woman said, is "starvation or submission." Even in places where these tests are not routinely used for screening, they are sometimes used to intimidate. By their very nature, they favor the docile, the obedient, and the desperate, and they screen out the adventurous, the intractable, the union activists, the people who are simply not willing (or hungry enough) to submit to the indignity of proving their innocence, sacrificing their privacy, and relinquishing their principles. And that, in the final analysis, may be the test's real function. The test itself, and the individual's willingness to submit, are the most important criteria of acceptability. Confession and self-disclosure—the tests of truth—are the most important lessons.[11]

Despite the extensive surveillance and interrogation in industry, however, it has been government, and particularly the benevolent institutions of education, mental health, and social welfare, which have become the most promiscuous practitioners of behavior control. By the mid-seventies, social institutions were using all of the following: drugs; behavior modification, including aversive conditioning; systematic screening of children for psychological problems; electronic data processing to track welfare clients and "potential" child abusers; television and other surveillance devices to monitor school corridors and classrooms; mandatory reporting by teachers, doctors, and social workers of suspected child abuse and other family problems; mandatory treatment of "maladjusted" children and parents; mandatory reporting of the names of mental patients and drug-program clients to central registers; routine exchanges of personal information about clients among schools, welfare agencies, mental-health agencies, police, courts, probation, and other agencies; and mandatory medical and mental examinations of children on welfare. In industry the intrusions are theoretically limited to the needs of "security" or the proper placement of workers; in social service, where the client himself is supposed to be the beneficiary, there are no theoretical limits.

The common element is information itself. Information is the raw material of bureaucracy. Both the information and its collection and use legitimize and confirm the inequity between agency and client, and thus reinforce the power of the one over the other. The agency collects the data; the client must provide. Privacy is thus an issue in any transaction in which a bureaucratic institution or a "professional" (social worker, teacher, doctor) collects data about an individual, even if there is no possibility that the data will be overtly abused and even if every shred of it is necessary for the legitimate purposes of the collector. The fact that the information exists and that it is easily accessible generates a search for new ways to use it and, in turn, a "need" for still more information. In the two years after the FBI's National Crime Information Center (NCIC) was first established in 1971, the annual number of drunk-driving arrests in the United States increased from 640,000 to 940,000, not because there was a precipitous increase in drunk driving but because the arrests gave local police a chance to check suspects through the new computer. Similarly, and probably for the same reason, marijuana arrests increased from 225,000 to 420,000.[12] "As capacity for information handling has increased," said Arthur R. Miller, a Harvard law professor who has written extensively on privacy issues, "there has been a tendency to engage in more extensive manipulation of recorded data, which, in turn, has motivated the collection of data pertaining to a larger number of variables."[13]

# II

The plan, concocted somewhere in the bureaucratic morass between the New York State Department of Social Services and the U. S. Department of Health, Education and Welfare, was called Incentive for Independence. As outlined in September 1971, a few days (appropriately) before the publication of Skinner's *Beyond Freedom and Dignity,* it provided for the reduction of welfare payments to families in three districts in Rockland and Franklin counties and in parts of Harlem, and for the institution of a system of "incentive points" with which cooperating families could earn back some of the welfare money which had been withdrawn. During each two-week period, points could be earned as follows:

1. for each school-age child between five and fifteen who "cooperated" with his or her teacher (as determined by a Welfare Department caseworker): one point, worth $12.50.

2. for each child in school over fifteen years old who was cooperating with the teacher: ½ point, worth $6.25.

3. for each preschool child given all medically required vaccinations and boosters during the previous six months: one point, worth $12.50.

4. for each unemployable adult participating in one or more acceptable activities during the previous six months (among them assisting in establishing the paternity of children born out of wedlock; "participation in the location of a deserting parent"; "participation of children in citizen building activities, e.g., Boy Scouts, 4–H, community centers"; "utilization of community resources to overcome problems of child delinquency"; and "utilization of remedial medical services by the adult which is designed to enhance employability or self-functioning"): one point, worth $12.50.

5. for each youth over fifteen participating in a school work program: one point, worth $12.50, in addition to his or her earnings in the program.

6. for each employable member of the family who worked or took part in pre-employment training: one point, worth $12.50.[14]

Incentive for Independence was proposed under a section of the federal welfare laws which permits states to deviate from standard welfare formulas for "any experimental, pilot or demonstration project which, in the judgment of the Secretary [of HEW], is likely to assist in promoting" the objectives of the welfare program. Clearly, however, the New York State officials who proposed it regarded the three-district experiment only as a first step toward broader implementation. In response to protests from the National Welfare Rights Organization and other groups, the New York proposal was subsequently amended to exclude the Harlem district from the experiment, to replace it with a district in Brooklyn which was ethnically more diverse, and to modify the incentives to provide mandatory "counseling" for mothers of children with poor school attendance. If the counseling was rejected or the counselor's advice ignored, the family's welfare payments were to be "restricted"; if schoolchildren over the age of fifteen failed to perform at least six hours a month of community service, family grants were to be reduced by $12.50 a month.

The plan was never formally implemented, partly as a result of continuing protest, partly as a consequence of threatened legal action, and partly because it became clear that even in an organization with enormous tolerance for administrative confusion and uncertainty, the point system was just too cumbersome. Yet the elements are all there in the routine procedures of most welfare departments or in their informal relations with clients. In California every month, as in many other states, every welfare client receives her WR–7 from the Welfare Department, and every month it must be filled out and returned if she wants to continue to get her welfare benefits: IF THIS FORM IS NOT RETURNED TO THE WELFARE DEPARTMENT BY THE 5TH OF THE MONTH AFTER THE MONTH SHOWN ABOVE YOU MUST REPORT TO THE OFFICE ADDRESS BELOW FOR A PERSONAL MEETING BY THE 10TH OF THE MONTH AFTER THE MONTH SHOWN ABOVE. To receive that income, she must report every dollar of income and expenses, including hours and days worked, transportation costs, mode of transportation, child-care expenses, and other work expenses. She must report all changes in the household and family, including anyone who became pregnant, gave birth, or otherwise terminated pregnancy; anyone who started, lost, or quit a job or job training; anyone who became disabled, recovered from a disability, or died; and the name of any child over sixteen, indicating where he was attending school, how many hours or units per week he studied, and, if he was not attending school, explaining why. She must also list the name of the "youngest child having 6th birthday next month," an event which requires her to register for employment; and she must explain

> any change (bought, sold, received or transferred) in houses or land; campers, boats or trailers, jewelry, musical instruments, recreation equipment, other equipment or material, livestock or fowl (not for family use); motor vehicles; appliances, TV, radio, phonograph, tape recorder, any power equipment (garden, cleaning, tools), essential household items; future burial/funeral arrangements, life and burial insurance, or other personal property. If you bought an item, show how much you owe on it in the "Reason for Change/-Amount Owed" column.[15]

In addition, every year she must fill out an entirely new application complete with rent receipts; utility bills; wage stubs; copies of health, burial, and life insurance policies; bank statements; disability statements; and other documents. She must report if anyone in the household returns to school or drops out; when anyone moves in or out of the house; when anyone gets married or becomes pregnant; the names of the friends and relatives of any absent parent; the last known address of the absent parent; his or her social security number, driver's license number, physical description, occupation, employer; and the names of all the absent parent's children. If her sixteen-year-old son is not in school or job training, she can lose part of her benefits; if she does not register for work, she can lose part of her benefits; if she does not cooperate in helping to find the absent parent, she can lose all of her benefits. It is all reasonable—to provide proper service, to catch those cheats—but every month every client is reminded that she is being watched, that records are kept, investigations made, data verified. Every month she reports.

A few years ago, when a group of welfare mothers in Washington sued to stop what they regarded as "unreason-

able searches, harassing surveillance, eavesdropping, and interrogation concerning their sexual activities"—all the familiar practices of caseworkers looking for the man under the
bed—the court ruled that "any recipient has a perfect right
to slam the door in the face of the investigator. Of course,
he runs the risk then of being cut off the rolls."[16] Skinner,
putting it another way, saw no reason "why a husbandless
mother with some children given money [by welfare] should
not be made responsible for what she does. She has a job;
you're paying her for taking care of those kids."[17] But as the
capacity to collect and process data increases, taking care of
those kids is formalized into new categories—"cooperating
with the teacher," "participation in citizen building activities"—which impose new "services" on the client and which,
if they are not met, are likely to lead to still more intervention. The information technology not only enables the
agency to place, classify, label, and restrict but also to track
the client through other elements of the social-service network. What had been an individual client's relationship with
a clerk, a teacher, or a caseworker becomes an increasingly
impersonal, routinized, and "scientific" relationship with an
extended system.

Under those conditions it no longer matters whether the
agency's formal mandate is interpreted as "service," maintenance, or control. The collection and manipulation of data
enable the agency to pretend that it is fulfilling all the man-
dates simultaneously. It uses the information, on the one
hand, to provide "proper service" and, on the other, to keep
the client in line. It can, and does, use it to convince him to
accept services he doesn't really want—the school's psychological test, for example, to prove that his child is slow or
retarded or hyperactive and would therefore benefit from a
special class—and it can, and does, use the imposition of that
service to persuade the rest of the community that there is
a socially or pedagogically or psychologically justifiable way
of doing what the community (or the neighbors or the family) want done anyway: to keep the deviant and the difficult

under control—to render them invisible—usually by labeling and segregating them in special groups requiring special services: counseling, remedial education, social work, rehabilitation, resettlement, or pacification.

# III

The growing number of people who are made invisible to the community are highly visible to the institutions and organizations charged with their management. They have to be maintained or "served" without excessive force or brutality; at the same time, however, they can neither be allowed to disrupt the system in which they are enrolled nor, to whatever extent possible, to disturb the community. For this kind of bureaucratic dirty work, Skinnerian operant conditioning —common behavior modification—is an almost perfect instrument. It can be used on large populations; it is relatively cheap; it conforms nicely with administrative criteria (making beds, sitting still in class, obeying the rules); it creates the appearance of statistical and scientific precision; it obscures the contradictions between "service" or "treatment" and control; it obviates the civil-liberties and due-process issues raised by overt punishment; and it legitimizes institutional standards by making arbitrary demands appear normative and reasonable.

As a conscious "scientific" technique, its very essence is bureaucratic: the reduction of learning and human behavior to a series of discrete impersonal "behaviors" suitable for charts and checklists, and subject to counting and statistics. It hardly matters whether the behavior modifier imagines himself to be a "therapist," an "engineer," or a "teacher"; like the bureaucrat, who may indulge similar fantasies, he is not concerned with "inner states" or motives or organic disease, and certainly not interested in dealing with the complexities of personality: his concern is only with those chartable behaviors, with close and systematic surveillance of one or several distinct dimensions of the individual's performance, and with faithful adherence to the "schedule" and program which he or his superiors have established for the client. In the process, the surveillance itself becomes a major instrument of control. It creates not merely the much-discussed chilling effect—the subtle fear created by the knowledge or suspicion that one is being watched or overheard, and which itself tends to inhibit expression—but also reconfirms the power of the agency and the powerlessness of its subject. The more pervasive the surveillance, the more the environment is controlled.

As a clinical technique, behavior modification has been used—with varying degrees of success—in treating autistic children, bed wetters, smokers, "regressed psychotics," drug addicts, alcoholics, fat people, aggressive people, passive people, frigid women, male homosexuals, and a variety of "sexual deviants." Yet, since behavior modification depends on the ability of the shaper to control the subject's environment —depends, that is, on prior control—it works most effectively (as a management device, if not as a therapeutic technique) in schools, prisons, and other institutions. It is also more effective when there are substantial gaps in power between the shaper and the shaped: the teacher and the pupil; the jailer and the prisoner; the doctor and the patient; the agency and the client.[17] (In that sense, claims that the technique is "neutral," that it can be used by anyone on anyone else, are absurd: the jailers can use it on the prisoners; the reverse is almost inconceivable.)

In its most common institutional application—the token economy—points are earned on a systematic schedule for various good "behaviors" and can be exchanged for better conditions, additional privileges, or certain tangible rewards. In the federal START (Special Treatment and Rehabilitative Training) program, designed by the U. S. Bureau of Prisons for its facility in Springfield, Missouri, entering prisoners were stripped of all privileges and allowed to earn points for "shower on assigned day; shave on assigned day; haircut; personal appearance; room appearance (bed made, floor swept and mopped); accept industry assignment without controversy; clean industry area according to direction of industrial foreman; accept special assignment without becoming abusive"; and a score of other desired behaviors. The points could be exchanged, on a fixed scale, for fresh fruit, tobacco, matches, coffee or juice, pens, paper, newspapers, magazines, and other items. Each inmate carried a card on which points were recorded; when the points were exchanged, the appropriate number was punched out. A fixed number of points was also required for advancement from lower to higher levels of privilege which included, among other things, more exercise time in the yard, more opportunities to take showers, and more time in a prison industry which, in turn, made it possible to earn more industrial "pay."[18] In schools, acceptable behavior is measured and counted, sometimes with bells, automatic timers, and electronic decibel counters, and rewarded with points that can be exchanged for extra recess time, soft drinks, or dinner or a swim party at the principal's house. In institutions for the retarded, tokens issued for "clean toilets," "empty trash cans," "sweep and mop hall," "sort dirty linen," and scores of other institutional jobs can be exchanged for food, privileges, and better living conditions. (In one California institution modeled on a program in a neighboring institution, "we insisted that patients would have to earn tokens to pay for all aspects of their daily living accommodations, including food. We also proposed the control of parental visits."[19])

Usually such institutional programs begin with the "stripping" of the inmate, his reduction on entrance to a status where he lacks most of the basic amenities—cigarettes, coffee, free time, and in some instances, food—and from which he rises through tiers or levels on the basis of good behavior and institutional adjustment. In addition, some programs practice psychological stripping through verbal or physical abuse of inmates; forced confession of guilt, sin, inadequacy, or illness; and other forms of mortification and humiliation. The process has been common for centuries in convents, monasteries, and basic military training; it was fundamental to the success of the Chinese in brainwashing American prisoners during the Korean War (in 1962, M.I.T. psychologist Edgar M. Schein commended the Chinese techniques to American prison officials as "not so different and not so awful once we separate the awfulness of the Communist ideology and look simply at the methods and influence used"); and in various forms, it is common in prisons and mental hospitals.[20] What the Skinnerians have added to the traditional institutional methods are the systematic routines of the bureaucrat: points, charts, forms, numbers, schedules, and the accumulation of records. The essence of civil service is its system of points and tiers; it is the one thing that bureaucrats discuss incessantly and the thing they know best. The token economy is a form of civil service for inmates.

On the other side of the coin is aversive conditioning—systematic punishment. People like Skinner insist that such techniques are usually counterproductive—that by punishing one form of undesirable behavior, they will simply elicit another, that they repress rather than resolve. Nonetheless, in the past decade programs in aversive therapy and punishment have enjoyed an extensive revival not only in the laboratory but in clinics, prisons, and schools. "Punishment," wrote Barry F. Singer, a psychologist at the University of California at Long Beach, "can effectively suppress behavior, provided it is sufficiently severe. . . . The more severe the punishment, the more effective it is in suppressing behavior."[21] At the University of Tennessee, psychiatrist Gene G. Abel and his colleagues, supported by NIMH grants, have been "treating" homosexuals, exhibitionists, and other "deviants" with aversive electric shock; at a mental-health center in Wyoming, a group of therapists "treated" problem drinkers by trying to get them to associate "stimulating" pictures of bars, bottles, and drinks with the electric shocks they gave them; and in many places—clinics, doctors' offices, prisons—aversive shock is used on retarded children, voyeurs, alcoholics, drug addicts, self-abusive mental patients, homosexuals, and in at least one reported case, shoplifters.[22]

All that activity has generated a small industry of equipment manufacturers selling shockers, timers, "pants alerts" (a wired pair of underpants which causes a buzzer to sound "whenever urination is made 'in the pants' "), and other devices. The Farrall Instrument Company of Grand Island, Nebraska, one of the largest makers of behavior-control devices in America, claims that more than one hundred clinics, schools, and other institutions use its model AR–5 Receiver-Shocker and Transmitter for "remote wireless shocking of humans." The device is strapped to a patient's leg and is activated by a clinician standing on the other side of the room whenever the patient (usually an institutionalized retarded child) behaves in some way that the therapist considers inappropriate. The company also sells various desk model office shockers and sets of 35mm slides of homosexual acts, "young boys," nude males, "aggression," "gambling," "smoking," and other activities which can be used with aversive conditioning techniques to shape behavior.[23] The principle of these techniques is always the same: the therapist shows the patient a slide of the undesirable behavior and, at the same instant, delivers the shock. (Sometimes the shock is paired with a "secondarily aversive" sound which, after a time, replaces the shock in the treatments.) In the case of alcoholics, emetic drugs are sometimes used instead of shock: as the subject is about to vomit, the therapist hands him a drink.

In fact, there is almost no evidence that behavior modification of large groups in institutions has any therapeutic effect whatever. Abel and his colleagues reported that it is "clearly possible to measure changes of sexual object preference in the anticipated direction of treatment"—they measure the client's erections in response to various stimuli —but they concede that their techniques are inadequate "reliably and validly to reflect changes due to treatment, especially in the patient's behavior outside the laboratory." Clinicians working with alcoholics report only marginal success with aversive techniques, although some insist that those methods are at least as good as any other form of therapy (most of which are almost totally useless).[24] Yet whenever there is clinical "success"—notably in the classic cases of autistic or retarded children or "regressed psychotics" reported by psychologists like Teodoro Ayllon, Ogden R. Lindsley, and Nathan N. Azrin—it is founded on extensive, long-term work with individuals, not with large groups. The schoolchildren who complete those math assignments appear to learn no more mathematics than children not enrolled in behavior modification programs (though they may learn that math isn't worth doing unless extrinsic rewards are offered), and the delinquents and prisoners in the institutions where behavior programs have been initiated appear to behave no better once they are released than those who haven't been shaped by the behaviorists. There are hundreds of clinical studies on toilet-training children, teaching the retarded to function, helping adults overcome their fear of flying, and on "curing" child molesters with aversive shock and then training them with operant conditioning to favor more acceptable sexual practices; but there are virtually no long-term studies of large groups, no real theory, no definition of "learning," no agreement about techniques, and no evidence that institutional programs have any positive long-term effects. The behaviorists insist that teaching children is basically no different from training rats; the best that programming can claim is that it allows each student to proceed "at his own pace" along the one path that the programmer has set out. Yet, by definition, learning, which is an individual process with an infinite variety of styles, directions, and outcomes, is beyond anyone's imagination to program. The same applies to therapy, particularly where the problem is behavioral or psychological and therefore peculiar to each individual. An individual program may be therapy; a collective program, at best, is training.[25]

In many programs, behavior modification and overt punishment are so thoroughly confused—either by design or staff sabotage—that there isn't the remotest possibility of success. In one school for the retarded in Florida, for example, a token economy behavior modification program was combined with what an investigating committee called (in 1974) "programmed abuse," including

> forced public masturbation and forced public homosexual acts for engaging in proscribed sexual behavior; beating with a wooden panel for running away; and washing the mouth with soap for lying, for abusive or vulgar language, or sometimes for speaking at all. Further, food, sleep and visitation privileges were withheld as punishment; incontinence was punished by requiring residents to lie in soiled sheets and to hold soiled underwear to their noses . . . and one boy was required to walk around publicly clothed only in female underpants.[26]

What the investigators found most remarkable in the Florida school, however, was that all these punishments were regarded as part of the program, and that they were "recorded . . . in great detail in well-kept records, with the encouragement, or at least the acquiescence, of the chief psychologist." Yet even where the program is relatively pure, it is so intimately associated with the deprivations and humiliations of the institutional environment that the possibilities of long-range "therapy" are almost nil. On the outside, as Goffman says,

> the inmate could probably unthinkingly decide how he wanted his coffee, whether to light a cigarette, or when to talk; on the inside such rights may become problematic. . . . He can spend the day, like a fanatic, in devoted thoughts about the possibility of acquiring these gratifications or in the contemplation of the approaching hour at which they are scheduled to be granted.[27]

Outside the institution, the residual effects of behavior modification are minimal and, where they occur, are likely to be very different from those intended. Almost inevitably the institutional situation creates its own "counter-mores"— its counterculture—which teach the inmate to cheat (in schools or universities); to sneak food or drugs past the guards (or candy past the mother superior); or, as Goffman said, "to combine all strategies and play it cool." Once released, the former inmate quickly learns to take for granted the rewards and privileges around which institutional life was organized. The proof for behavior modification comes from individual successes with individual people—autistic children, for example, who begin to function again, or retarded children, who are taught to perform household tasks —and which may themselves derive not from the program but rather from the extensive attention paid to the individual patient—a Hawthorne-type effect. But there is no proof that behavior modification works for large groups.

Since the fundamental objective of institutional behavior modification—however "scientific" or Skinnerian—is not therapy but control, and since behavior mod is a technique of management, of order, which is generally useless once the subjects leave the environment established to control them, it always requires dependence and submission. The practitioners and defenders of behavior modification often have an exasperating tendency to exaggerate their powers in one context and to minimize them in another: what the Chinese did to "re-educate" American prisoners during the Korean War proves how powerful it is; what the schoolteacher can't do to reshape her pupils indicates, as one behaviorist said, that "it is questionable that an individual will do anything contrary to his values to obtain a reinforcer."[28] The behaviorist, like the bureaucrat who is held accountable for the behavior of his clients, will therefore attempt to enlarge his power to shape the client's environment; to enlist (as some schools have done) the cooperation of parents in the child's behavior modification program and thereby extend the schedule of reinforcement from the school to the home; to involve other agencies in collaborative projects "in the best interests of the client"; to send caseworkers to the home; to require periodic visits to a probation officer; and to establish data banks and reporting systems to monitor and track individuals through the community.[29]

Most of the behavior-control programs of the seventies—many of them funded by the federal government—are not rationalized as "in the national interest" but as therapeutic or diagnostic medical-model efforts in treatment and "early intervention." In Orange County, California, (1970–75) there was VISA (Volunteers to Influence Student Achievement), an LEAA-funded project in which teachers of first- and second-grade children were instructed to identify "potential delinquents" among their six- and seven-year-old children for assignment to "big brother counselors" in the community (and where the criteria for potential delinquency included "father away from home" and, in one case, breaking pencils); in Montgomery County, Pennsylvania, until it was ordered stopped by a federal court in 1973, there was CPI (Critical Period of Intervention) to "identify children who may be susceptible to drug abuse" through "diagnostic testing" in schools which included questions about intimate relationships between pupils and their parents and which encouraged young children to identify classmates who made "odd or unusual remarks"; and all over the country behaviorally oriented youth bureaus and "diversion" programs are created and maintained for adults and juveniles who have been accused (but usually not convicted) of minor crimes, drug abuse, or status offenses—truancy, running away from home, "incorrigibility"—which would not have been crimes at all if the perpetrators were older.[30] What most of these people are told—explicitly or implicitly—is that if they don't enroll in those "voluntary" programs, they'll go before the judge; and that if they don't complete the program and are arrested or detained again, the cops will throw the book at them. In 1975, Michael Goldman, a student working for the

American Civil Liberties Union in New York, observed the
screening and selection of candidates for diversion:

> All the people inside the cell are black. Nearly all those
> outside are white—lawyers, cops, program staff. The prison-
> ers are all males, from about eighteen to twenty-five years old.
>
> They are held for many hours, sometimes for a full day, six
> or seven people to a small cell. They seem to be "street kids,"
> and they get along famously with one another. They are also
> obviously tired as hell and quite understandably edgy and
> irritable.
>
> The screener calls a defendant over to the barred door of
> the cell. She has checked his arrest sheet and found that he
> may be eligible for the program. She asks him question after
> question, and writes down all the answers. Did you commit
> the crime you are accused of? Were you ever arrested before?
> (She already knows the answer from his arrest sheet.) What
> for? Were you guilty then? Tell me about your family, school,
> job. . . . All these questions are informally, almost casually put
> —and, usually, quite casually answered.
>
> This particular defendant claims he is innocent. That does
> not mean the screener tells him not to enter the program, even
> though the program is supposedly only for offenders who are
> to be rehabilitated. (It later turns out that the police indeed
> picked up the wrong fellow, and that this accused person *was*
> innocent.) The screener still tells him that he has a better
> chance to be "free" if he enters the program.[31]

Goldman pointed out that many innocent defendants are
afraid to choose trial because they fear that they'll be convicted anyway, and they therefore agree to the program even
though they can still be prosecuted if they fail to conform to
its rules.

Consistently, the pressure is to enroll people in the system
at earlier and earlier stages of their hypothetical deterioration into deviance and therefore to find them at younger and
younger ages: the delinquent before he becomes the criminal,
the pre-delinquent before he becomes the delinquent, the
hyperactive child before he becomes pre-delinquent, the

child with perinatal problems before he becomes hyperactive, the infant *in utero* before he becomes anything at all. In 1976, NIMH announced that it planned to study infants as "psychosocial organisms" and to establish a Therapeutic Infant Development Project to "develop ways to work with community-based systems in identifying, before birth, infants who will be vulnerable to mental-health problems."[32]

# IV

The most common hostages are children. Because they are already enrolled in the social-service system—and because they are children—they, and through them their parents, are easily accessible for observation, screening, and intervention. Whereas welfare or public housing or Medicaid is restricted largely to the poor or to other minorities, public schools touch at least half the population at any given time. Through psychological tests, questionnaires of family history, medical reports, anecdotal reports from teachers and counselors, and state and federally mandated medical and developmental screening instruments, it is the school which sits at the center of the service network and represents the most pervasive and broadly intrusive institution in America.

Much of it is a familiar process: schools which look for the "ego disturbed" or the "Oedipally conflicted"; schools which test for "minimal brain dysfunction" and "developmental disabilities"; schools which segregate "hyperactive children" and coerce parents into having them drugged to keep them still; schools which record parents' political activities and sexual habits in pupil files; schools which, in the name of "affective education," psychologically molest children and require them to talk not only about their own fears, dreams, nightmares, and passions, but also about family fights, parental relationships, and the most intimate details of their parents' lives; schools which regard themselves as "diagnostic centers" assessing the mental health and social adjustment of their pupils and their parents, and which routinely refer deviants to psychologists, physicians, and social agencies; schools which have become central to the exchange of information and referrals between police, welfare, and other social agencies, and which have already fulfilled a prediction made in the official magazine of the National Education Association that "schools are becoming 'clinics' whose purpose is to provide . . . psychosocial treatment for the students."[33]

In the past four or five years, however, one "social disease" —child abuse—has generated such an extensive network of intervention and, along with it, such an intensive barrage of "public service" promotion—much of it sponsored and financed by the federal government—that it requires special attention. Much of it is well intentioned; but what began in concern about some 125,000 serious cases of child abuse each year (some preventable, some not) has grown into an enormous system committed to finding not only real abuse but "neglect," "potential abusers," and virtually any parent whose lifestyle, child-rearing practices, or social circumstances fail to accord with the expectations of the social agents who operate the system. There is obviously child abuse, but if it is defined as anything but the small number of genuinely severe cases—cases so damaging that the child's life or health is in immediate danger—then no intervention of social service is demonstrably better than the conditions of the parental home. According to the American Civil Liberties Union, "of the hundreds of thousands of children that family courts annually judge maltreated, an estimated 4 percent are the victims of serious physical abuse." Nonetheless, that small number of severe cases, some of them fatal, has given rise to systems of intervention so broad that virtually no parent and no form of ordinary child rearing is fully exempt.

The process is pervasive. In Montgomery County, Maryland (suburban Washington), all school employees are required to report all suspected cases of physical abuse, sexual abuse, and "neglect" to a social agency and a central register. The neglected child is defined as one who is ill-clad and dirty, unattended, emotionally disturbed due to friction in the home, emotionally neglected through denial of "the normal experiences that produce feelings of being loved," or exposed to "unwholesome or demoralizing circumstances." In New York State, it is a misdemeanor for a teacher or physician not to report any child who he or she has "reasonable cause to suspect" is "maltreated" by a parent in such a way that his "emotional health" has been impaired or that he suffers "diminished psychological or intellectual functioning in relation to but not limited to such factors as failure to thrive, of control of aggressive or self-destructive impulses, of ability to think or reason, or acting out, or misbehavior, including incorrigibility, ungovernability, or habitual truancy. . . ." In New Jersey, the criteria of suspected child abuse are "disruptive or aggressive" classroom behavior, "withdrawn or quiet" behavior, "poor attendance or chronic lateness," and dirty or torn clothing. In Adams County, Colorado, the parameters are extended to include children who are reticent in class, who are aggressive, or who have "poor peer relationships, poor hygienic habits [or] a fear of adults." And almost everywhere, teachers and school officials are instructed to look for symptoms of child abuse in parents as well as in other teachers. *Guidelines for Schools,* a widely used booklet published by the American Humane Association, a national child-abuse organization, defines such parents as "apathetic or unresponsive" or who "fail to participate in school activities or to permit the child to participate."[34]

Reporting procedures vary; almost always, however, the reports are transmitted from teachers or physicians or, in those states where everyone is required to report suspected abuse, from private citizens, to social workers and police, and then to a central register of abusers and "potential" abusers. In California, where, in 1974, nearly 121,000 children were reported as abused or neglected, the typical schoolteacher who suspects abuse will call in the school nurse or some other designated staff member to talk to the child and, if warranted, to report the matter directly to the police. Thereupon an officer comes to the school to interrogate the child, remove clothing, examine the body and, if he deems it necessary, to take the child directly into protective custody. In some districts, parents are notified before the child is taken away; in others, they are not called until the child has been interrogated, photographed, and entered into the rolls and case records of the agency to which he has been taken: in some instances, a welfare agency; in others, a juvenile institution associated with a court. In Hayward, California, according to Diane Divoky, who investigated the child-abuse network for *Learning* magazine:

> social agencies are [then] checked by phone to see if the family has a history of problems, because at some point the children's division of the county probation department must decide whether the child will be returned home immediately or put at least temporarily into a children's shelter or foster home. Again, guidelines are fuzzy, a "judgment thing," but the attitude of the parents when they get to the station or shelter—how contrite they seem—is a major factor. . . .
>
> Within 36 hours of phoning the police, the school employee must make a written report, including information about the nature of the injuries and the student's statement. Copies of this report go to the police, the probation department, the school district office, the school principal's "confidential" file and, when appropriate, the welfare department. One copy gets sent on to a state register of suspected child abusers maintained by the Department of Justice.
>
> Even when they are found to be unsubstantiated, these written reports are never removed or expunged from the various agency files. The Hayward school district personnel do not know which of the reports in their own files represent actual abuse and which are false alarms. What services the family receives as a result of reporting and what impact there is on the child aren't known by the school staff either.[35]

There are no firm guidelines as to what signs justify the transfer of a child from the school to the police station or other agencies; nor is there much evidence that, in the great majority of cases, the intervention which follows—foster placement of children, counseling, or "therapy" for parents —is better than no intervention at all. But once a case has been reported, intervention is sure to follow. A few lavishly funded model programs claim some success in counseling abusive parents and reducing the "reabuse" rate (at a cost of some $2,000 per case). But most programs have no such resources; the institutionalization of children or parents is notoriously brutal and ineffective; foster-home placement creates its own psychological difficulties (and is often perceived by the child as a form of punishment); and the chances of successful "treatment" of neglectful parents—however defined—are almost nil. Moreover, it is almost impossible to establish any relationship between child-rearing practices and the psychological health of the child—no way, in short, to determine what kind of abuse or neglect is sufficiently severe to justify the trauma (to parents and children) of removing the child from his natural parents. "There is substantial evidence," wrote Michael Wald, a professor of law at Stanford who studied the child-abuse network,

> that, except in cases involving seriously harmed children, we are unable to improve a child's situation through coercive state intervention. In fact, under current practice, coercive intervention frequently results in placing a child in a more detrimental situation than he would be in without intervention. This is true whether intervention results in removal of the child from his home or "only" in mandating that his parents accept services as a condition of continued custody.[36]

Despite all those uncertainties, the practices Divoky describes in Hayward are not exceptional. Some forty-four states already have formal child-abuse reporting procedures, which, in some states, make it a misdemeanor not to report suspected abuse. Children have been removed from their parents' custody on grounds that include sloppy housekeeping, failure to cooperate with welfare workers, and "emotional neglect." Should the reports prove to be false or unfounded, they nonetheless become part of the central register, all with name, address, and other pertinent data. Under a proposed Child Protective Services Act drawn up within the Department of Health, Education and Welfare as a model state law, every state would be forced to require all teachers, social workers, physicians, religious healers, daycare workers, and a variety of other public employees to report to a toll-free number "their reasonable suspicions" of parents or others who abuse or mistreat children. Among those to be reported would be parents who create or permit "to be created a substantial risk of physical or mental injury to the child, including excessive corporal punishment" or who "fail to supply the child with adequate food, clothing, shelter, education [as defined by state compulsory school attendance laws] or medical care." The "mental injury" to be reported includes "failure to thrive; ability to think or reason; control of aggressive or self-destructive behavior; [and] acting-out or misbehavior, including incorrigibility, ungovernability, or habitual truancy." As in California and in New York State (upon whose child-abuse laws the model act is itself modeled), the police or a social worker would be able to place a reported child in protective custody and have him examined without notifying parents; if the parents subsequently refused to cooperate in the required investigation of the case, if they failed to allow the investigators into the child's home, or if they refused to participate in carrying out an agency-designed "service plan," legal action could be taken against them. The investigation would also be linked to a statewide data bank through which prior reports of "abuse" or "neglect" could be checked; all such reports, even if proven false, would become part of the permanent data file, and all, no matter how absurd, would have to be investigated. In addition, the act would authorize local agencies "to suggest a service plan for the family even when the children are not believed to be suffering from abuse or maltreatment, if such services appear to be useful or beneficial."[37]

Early in 1976, HEW's Office of Child Development (OCD) came within a hair of having state adoption of the model law made a condition of continued receipt of certain federal child-development funds; its promulgation as official government doctrine was blocked only by Stanley J. Murphy, a lawyer in HEW's Office of Civil Rights who, alerted by protests from a variety of organizations, managed to keep the act from getting final approval by HEW Secretary David Mathews. The act, however, still exists as a possible model; and under a new and more activist administration, OCD is likely to try again. In the meantime, nearly all states already have laws and practices which, like those in New York and California, come painfully close to the model. Each year the names of a million children and their parents go into the registers.[38]

The issue of child abuse may be one of the most revealing (and least reported) examples of the way in which private organizations and the "benign" agencies of the federal government manipulate data to turn what is undeniably a genuine problem into national hysteria and then, in turn, convert the hysteria into intervention. Late in 1975, for example, the *CBS Evening News* reported on this "social problem of epidemic proportions." Roger Mudd, filling in as anchorman for Walter Cronkite, introduced it:

> Not until this week has anyone known the extent of child abuse in this country. Now the first national study has been made of child abuse, and the Health, Education and Welfare Department says it is a social problem of epidemic proportions. More than a million children are victimized each year by abuse or neglect. . . .[39]

CBS correspondent Steve Young went on to report the story with a mixture of pathos, sympathy, quotes from "experts," and what appeared to be hard statistical data: "Authorities say as many as three thousand children were killed by their own parents last year in America, that fifteen thousand were brain damaged for life. . . ." What the viewers were not told was that there was no hard statistical information to support these assertions, that no "national study" had been completed, and that the figures were pulled out of a hat by HEW bureaucrat Douglas Besharov, who heads the National Center for Child Abuse and Neglect (itself a part of OCD) and who was then trying to promote the model act. The CBS story came on the heels of a UPI report which ran on the wires the preceding weekend. The story, carried by hundreds of newspapers, reported that

> more than a million American children suffer physical abuse or neglect each year and at least one of five of the young victims die from their mistreatment, the Government announced today. Disclosing tentative results of the first nationwide child abuse study, an official of HEW said the figures represented a "social problem" of "epidemic" proportions.

*The New York Times,* which ran the story on November 30, 1975, the day before the CBS item, headlined it "Child Abuse Rate Called Epidemic—U.S. Says Fifth of the Annual Million Victims Die." The story went on to elaborate details of the "study," citing a dozen different kinds of figures and quoting Besharov as saying that "200,000 children a year die from circumstances associated with abuse or neglect." Neither the *Times,* UPI, nor CBS saw "the nationwide study," which the UPI story said had been conducted for HEW by the American Humane Association—nor could they have seen it, since it didn't exist. None of them challenged the figures or the definitions, and none questioned HEW's reasons for releasing them. Some reporters, puzzled by the 200,000 alleged fatalities (in fact, fewer than 108,000 children in the United States die each year from all causes), called Besharov at home for an explanation. The figure, he explained, was a "typographical error," and, he said, UPI had been given a correction reducing the figure to the "three thousand" that CBS reported, but no correction ever appeared in the *Times.*[40]

What was more important, however, was that the "more than a million," which Besharov continued to insist was accurate, was unfounded. The American Humane Association, which was conducting a study for HEW (which in turn was a long way from being finished), flatly advised callers "not to pay any attention to the news stories." AMA statisticians estimated that there was a "top limit" of one million reports of abuse or neglect in 1974, of which 650,000 were investigated, of which 16 to 18 percent—roughly 100,000 to 125,000—"were diagnosed as abuse." A total of 620 abuse-related deaths were verified.[41] There was, in fact, no evidence of an epidemic, nor was there any way to define what constituted abuse or neglect, and, in most cases, no way to treat it even if it could be defined. There was, however, a proliferating network of programs, agencies, and reporting systems; there was a growing pot of federal money (Besharov's National Center on Child Abuse and Neglect alone spent some $19 million in 1975); there were those "more than a million" cases reported to social agencies and listed in state data banks; and there were those local "child protective service teams" hauling the kids off, taking Polaroid pictures of their bodies, and telling the parents they better cooperate, answer the questions, fill out the forms, and comply with the "service plan" if they didn't want to lose custody of their children altogether. In a few years, the matter of protecting a small number of badly beaten children from genuinely dangerous parents—the most vulnerable, of course, are those who are younger than school-age and therefore not subject to observation in schools—had turned into a vast reporting system that regards millions of parents as "potential abusers" and so lists them in its files, and that increasingly manages to ignore or conceal the fact that in the vast majority of cases, the real source of abuse is poverty, improper nutrition, bad housing, inadequate day care, poor (and often abusive) schools, and social violence and neglect—not psychopathological parents. "Getting beaten," said James Kent, a pediatric psychologist who runs a demonstration child-abuse project in Los Angeles, "is the least of these kids' problems.

The bones will mend and the bruises will heal. It's everything else that goes on in their families that's overwhelming."[42] The child-abuse issue—a "red herring," Kent called it—is another way of blaming the victim.

Almost every program is promoted with the best of intentions: a less stigmatizing, more humane form of intervention that replaces the harsh sanctions of prison, school suspension, eviction from public housing, family court, or hospitalization. In practice, however, each consistently enlarges the possibilities of intervention; each brings thousands of people under the umbrella of social service who would never have been there otherwise; and each creates—in the name of treatment, of prevention, of diversion, of service—a wholly new level of intervention. The principle is always the same: the less restrictive or punitive the intervention, the easier it is to bring people into the system and the more difficult it becomes for the client to exercise his constitutional rights. However well intentioned, therefore, "treatment" becomes an attractive façade for what in fact is punishment or social control, and almost inevitably the two become confused. As new methods and institutions are created, and as new reasons for intervention are found, they complement what existed before. They rarely replace it.

# V

On February 10, 1976, Andrea Martin, who was then 26 years old, gave birth to a seven-pound, two-ounce girl in a public hospital a few miles from downtown San Francisco. Before she left the hospital, she verified and signed a standard California birth-certificate form, which included her name and address, the father's name and address, the baby's name and birth weight, and the other standard items for the child's birth record. All of that, she knew, would be filed and entered in the Recorder's Office for Alameda County, where it was available for inspection as a public record. What she did not know—and what she probably still does not know—is that the certificate also included a bottom portion which she was never shown and which she wasn't asked to verify. That portion includes, among other things, space for such items as: number of other children now living; number of other children born alive but now dead; number of fetuses born dead after twenty weeks gestation; date of the last fetal death; date the last normal menses began; month that prenatal care began; complications involved in this pregnancy; birth injuries to the child; and congenital malformations of the child. In Martin's case, a casual visitor to the Recorder's Office could learn that her last menstrual period had begun on May 2, 1975; that she had had two abortions; and that during pregnancy, she had had "many drugs via psychiatrist." For mothers of other children born in the same hospital during the same week, the casual visitor could have learned that one was suffering from "heroin addiction," another had "recurrent monilia," a third had "mid-trimester bleeding" and "post-partum hemorrhaging," a fourth had "premature rupture of the membranes," delivery in the case of a fifth involved "fetal distress," a sixth was on Valium through most of her pregnancy, and a seventh once had a mid-trimester abortion. Probably none of these women knows that any of that information is part of a public record which is filed not only at the county courthouse but also at the local health department and in the files of the State Health Department in Sacramento; nor are most of them ever likely to find out. If they or their children request a copy of the birth certificate, they will receive only the top portion. If a mother is affluent enough to go to a private hospital or if the physician is sensitive to privacy, the bottom portion is likely to be blank; if neither is the case and the children are born in public hospitals, anyone can find out about the mother's drug habits, abortions, and psychiatric health.[43]

*          *          *

On the north side of San Francisco Bay, in suburban Marin County, a 44-year-old garage mechanic is hit and killed by a truck as he is walking along a dark highway on a winter evening. To the officials in the county coroner's office it looks like an "apparent suicide," and a "psychological autopsy" of the victim is ordered. A team of consulting psychologists is commissioned to interview the "significant others" in the mechanic's life—his wife, children, employer, and several of his friends. Was he depressed? Had there been previous suicide attempts? What was his state of mind before he died? Had there been any recent changes in lifestyle? In the case of the garage mechanic, the psychologists concluded that the victim had been a prisoner of war in Korea; that the experience "apparently took a lot out of him"; and that as a consequence, he suffered from "periods of disorientation, . . . disturbed sleep patterns, and insomnia." The psychologists also decided that since he suffered from bad eyesight and inadequate visual perception, he had probably become confused by the truck's headlights, had jumped the wrong way, and that his death should therefore be ruled accidental. Nonetheless, he now has a file an inch thick somewhere in the county coroner's office—all of it collected posthumously —about his life, his mental health, and his relatives. According to Edwin S. Shneidman, a psychologist at UCLA and the country's leading "suicidologist," a fourth of all deaths in Marin County involve some "participation" by the deceased, and Shneidman would like to see psychological autopsies performed on every American who dies under ambiguous circumstances.[44]

They begin on this side of the cradle and end beyond the grave: birth records, school records, police records, tax records, social security records, voter records, military discharge and veterans records, employment records, medical records, and death certificates, among others—many of them available with a little legwork or through a request and a small fee to the appropriate agency. With a name or just a car's license-plate number, almost anyone can obtain the vital information that appears in any motor-vehicle record—age; height, weight; eye color; certain physical infirmities; and in many states, whether the individual has ever been treated in a mental institution or served time in prison, whether his license has ever been suspended or revoked, and his present, and in many cases past, addresses. If the individual has ever applied for a loan from a bank or finance company, some of the details will be on file in the county clerk's office; if he has ever been treated by a mental-health agency, the Department of Mental Hygiene or the Department of Health may, according to an internal memo from a consumer-credit company, "furnish some details without a medical release"; if he has ever defaulted on a debt or been involved in a law suit, a disputed unemployment or workmen's compensation case, or an automobile accident, or if he has ever received a business or professional license, the details of these transactions will be available somewhere in a public record; and if he was discharged from military service between the early 1950s and 1974, a code on his discharge papers will indicate whether he was discharged for "character or behavior disorders," "bed-wetting," "homosexual tendencies," "apathy, defective attitudes, and an inability to expend effort constructively," "inadequate personality," or simply for "inaptitude." (In 1973 alone, some 35,000 men were so labeled.) Although all those individuals have honorable or general discharges "under honorable conditions," most of them were never told about those codes—the so-called SPN numbers—but many employers know them. In 1974, the SPN numbers were eliminated, yet most veterans still have not been informed that they can request new papers without the numbers; and many of those who have received new certificates are still required by prospective employers to sign waivers allowing access to their SPN numbers.[45]

The bureaucratic appetite for personal information has always been enormous. In the past generation, however, it has been further stimulated by the possibilities of electronic data-processing technology, the interventionist theories of social science, medical-model ideas of early diagnosis and treatment, and the growing search for predictive instruments and information that will identify deviants before any deviant act has been committed. People who had once been clerks begin to see themselves as diagnosticians, and those who once did little more than issue licenses begin to operate like social engineers. In Washington, D.C., the Department of Transportation and the District of Columbia are sponsoring a $2-million experimental project to "identify potential problem drinkers" when they renew their driver's licenses through a 121-item psychological "profile" which asks, among other things: "About how many years has it been since your last out-of-town vacation?" "How many large debts do you have?" "Would you describe yourself as being lonely a good deal of the time?" "With whom do you live?", and (true or false), "Sometimes I feel very guilty," "I usually sweat at night," and "I wish people would stop telling me how to live my life." The theory, according to James Nichols, a psychologist with the National Highway Transportation Safety Administration, is that "there is a correlation between income and problem drinking. Lower socioeconomic people appear to have more problems with alcohol than higher socioeconomic people." Moreover, said Nichols, "alcoholics have unstable family situations and are very often divorced." The hope is to identify them early, then give them some form of "medical evaluation" and "alcohol education" as a condition for obtaining a license.[46]

Similarly, legitimate congressional concern about the health of poor children has prompted a comprehensive mandatory medical, developmental, and psychological screening program in state or county facilities which collects information on everything from dental decay to mental retardation and mental illness for all of the nation's 13 million Medicaid-eligible children. Under amendments to the Social Security Act passed in 1972, every state must participate in EPSDT (Early and Periodic Screening, Diagnosis and Treatment).

Children (as in the Minnesota program) are evaluated in such areas as "bad temper . . . wanting too much attention, comfort, support . . . disobedient . . ." and parents are screened for "troubled marital relationships . . . excessive demands from spouse . . . low self-esteem . . ."; or (as in North Dakota) questions are raised as to whether the child is "too active . . . too shy . . . cries too much . . . daydreams . . ." and whether "his behavioral problems may bring the individual in conflict with community laws"; or (as in Oregon) questions are raised whether the child seems "restless," has "difficulty learning," or gets "upset when he/she has to do something different"; or (as in West Virginia) information is obtained on the "marital status of parents, living arrangements [and] housing conditions" of the child; or (as in South Dakota) on "evidence of emotional, intellectual or psychiatric problems"; or (as in Florida) on signs of "emotional stress, among them tongue chewing, hair pulling [and] ear twisting." (In addition, there are hundreds of other local and state programs to screen children for learning disabilities, "mental defects," and psychological problems. Among these is a California requirement that "each child, upon enrollment in the first grade, present satisfactory evidence . . . that he has received specified health screening and evaluation services within the prior two years." The California program includes affluent as well as poor children.)

Although many of the conditions for which children are screened are not susceptible to treatment—many, of course, are not medically definable conditions at all—and although many which could be treated are, in fact, not treated (usually because of the expense), and although many could easily be spotted without screening, all of the EPSDT information is collected in county-wide and statewide computerized Medicaid files to which almost any agency which provides medical or social services has access. In Illinois, for example, each of the state's 560,000 EPSDT children has an individual record maintained by the Illinois Department of Public Health to which any "provider" of social or medical services authorized to do EPSDT screening—clinics, schools, day-care centers—can gain access. Increasingly, moreover, individual states are hooking their own data files to the Department of Health, Education and Welfare's national Medicaid Management Information Service (MMIS) computer, thereby making it possible to follow each child—and his family—from state to state. "You just punch a button," said a state EPSDT coordinator, "and there it is, the whole history of the family."[47]

# VI

More important than any single set of records or kind of records is the combination of all of them and the conditioning which that combination generates: the total is greater than the sum of the parts. It has become difficult even to estimate the full scope of those records, their contents, the way they are used, or the extent to which information flows from one data system to another. (The federal government alone maintains some 4 billion individualized records in 6,700 data banks.) The average child's school record may be a couple of inches thick and contain details on virtually every aspect not only of his own life in and out of school, but also on those of his parents and his siblings. The dossier on the average welfare client includes between 50 and 300 sheets of paper on everything from her mental health to the condition of her refrigerator. (An application for food stamps alone requires six pages of material, including a complete inventory of all income, expenses, and assets; disclosure of affiliation in any "drug-addict or alcohol rehabilitation" program; and a blanket release authorizing the local food-stamp office to collect all information necessary to verify the application.)

The data flow from the doctor or the hospital to the insurance company and the employer; from the juvenile probation department to the school; from the credit bureau to the insurance company; from the school to the police; from the police to the FBI, the credit bureau, and the employer; from the employer to the union; from the school to the welfare department and the division of mental health.[48] Many of these exchanges are informal or even surreptitious—friendly transactions between fellow dirty workers trying to help each other out: the secretary of a community tutoring project in New York City who calls an elementary school to check on a student's grade placement and listens as the principal gratuitously reads from the record that the child is a bed wetter and that his mother is an alcoholic who sleeps with a different man every night; the moonlighting cop in Southern California who works for a local department store as a security officer and who goes through the department's files of adult and juvenile arrests to check the records of people who have applied for jobs with the store; the credit investigator who walks into the records room of the local police station in Wheaton, Illinois, asks about a person who has just applied for a loan, and is quickly informed that the subject has an arrest record.

Locally, many individual agencies that are reluctant to cooperate are under constant pressure from police, licensing boards, employers, and various state and federal agencies to disclose the identities of program participants. In New Hampshire in 1974–75, Governor Meldrim Thomson directed the superintendent of New Hampshire (mental) Hospital to turn over detailed patient records to his office for a drug-abuse investigation; and in New York City in 1975, Robert G. Newman, then the city's assistant commissioner for Addiction Programs, reported that in the preceding two years he had received "hundreds of demands" for confidential information on patients in drug-abuse programs from the FBI, federal and state narcotics agents, the New York State Department of Social Services, parole and probation officers, family court, the city fire marshal, local welfare centers, the police, the district attorneys of all five boroughs, private employers, and insurance companies.[49] Newman resisted those demands—he himself was sentenced to jail for refusing to comply with a court order to give the police photographs of heroin addicts in a methadone program—but in most jurisdictions, social agencies have few such compunctions; and in many, the records systems are organized in such a way that even if the physician, the social worker, or the school principal is scrupulous about protecting confidentiality, he has little control over the information.

Increasingly, the system takes the information out of his hands: the exchanges become formalized through shared data banks or through mandatory reporting to central registers. In New York, state-operated mental-health facilities must file a detailed report on each psychiatric outpatient with the State Department of Mental Hygiene (an M–5 report) containing the patient's name, social security number, "problem appraisal," "problem severity rating," and other personal data. The "problem appraisal" includes "sleep problems," "eating problems," "enuresis, soiling," "social relations disturbance," "suicidal thoughts," "obsessions, compulsions," "social withdrawal, isolation," "grandiosity," "suspicion, persecution," "delusions," "hallucinations," "anger, belligerence, negativism," "anti-social attitudes, acts," and many others—all of them, according to the Department of Mental Hygiene, necessary for accounting and record purposes. New York also requires pharmacists and physicians to furnish copies of all prescriptions for certain restricted drugs—codeine, Ritalin, Percodan, and morphine —complete with the name, age, and address of the patient and the name of the doctor to a central state data bank. (The system was created to apprehend drug abusers who, using their own names, go from doctor to doctor to get prescriptions for abused drugs; but after nearly two years of operation in which 100,000 prescriptions a month went into the computer, the system turned up two suspected cases of abuse.) In other states, physicians are required to report the names of women receiving abortions to a central "fetal death" register; and in others, doctors and local clinics are required to submit the identity and status of every drug addict under treatment to a central drug-abuse register.[50]

The systems track, they exchange, they follow; and in the process of that tracking and exchanging, the information they collect is no more secure than the most accessible terminal in the agency with the least concern for confidentiality.[51] The managers of such systems usually insist that the central records are secure from unauthorized access, but no one makes any claim for the individual agencies which can legitimately tap into it. It has become almost commonplace for juveniles to find that their delinquency records have been passed on to military recruiters or employers, and for adults to discover that details of their medical and psychiatric records have been passed by their medical insurance company to their employers, to their auto-insurance carriers, and to various elements of the credit system: a surgeon, after being hospitalized for a heart attack, is informed that his auto insurance has been canceled because, as he later learns from his broker, his hospital insurance report had been passed to his auto-insurance carrier; an executive learns that he was passed over for promotion after his employer, through his insurance company, had learned that he was seeing a psychiatrist. According to a report by the American Psychiatric Association, "There are many patients, covered by insurance, who will not use their benefits because it will get back to their employers. We receive reports that there are many more who need care but cannot afford it unless paid for by the insurance they have, but forego treatment rather than take a chance." In one survey of some 900 psychiatrists, half said they were certain that insurance companies do not preserve confidentiality of psychiatric information provided by doctors about their patients; less than a fourth were confident that the information was protected.[52]

Given such exchanges of data, it becomes almost impossible to distinguish between legitimate and illegitimate uses. If the information exists and if there are easy means of passing it along, someone will find its use legitimate: for research, for accounting, for statistics, for police investigations, for drug-abuse control, for "quality control." Privacy laws passed in the wake of Watergate—the Buckley Act on school records, the Fair Credit Reporting Act, the Federal Privacy Act, and a variety of state laws—have given the individual some access to his own records, a modicum of control over who sees them, and a chance to collect damages from credit bureaus circulating false information collected in violation of federal standards. In addition, a number of the central registers and the mandatory reporting requirements have been challenged in the courts on constitutional grounds by individual physicians, patients, and civil-liberties organizations; but in light of the changing temper of the Supreme Court under the Nixon and Ford appointees, and in light of the cancerous growth of new information systems, the prospects for constitutional challenges of public-agency data banks have become increasingly dim. In New York, for example, the Mental Health Law Project and the New York Civil Liberties Union sued to stop the state from collecting those identified mental-patient records and pharmacy prescriptions, charging (in the case of the M–5) that

> there is some indication that any doctor or employee of any state facility can obtain the information on any patient in the state simply by dialing a specific telephone number and requesting the information. By law the information is available to any court of record, and . . . with the sole consent of the Commissioner to any agencies which make payments on behalf of the patients such as Medicare or Medicaid, missing persons agencies, criminal agencies, and the Firearms Control Board of the City of New York.[53]

In the first round of litigation, the challengers obtained a federal court order stopping the state from requiring submission of the pharmacy prescriptions to a central register on the ground that this "regulatory scheme . . . has a needlessly broad sweep," but they lost in the U. S. Supreme Court. They also lost in a state court on the required reporting of mental-health data; and there were indications that the Supreme Court would be no more sympathetic on the M–5 than it was on the prescriptions. In Supreme Court arguments on the prescription law in the fall of 1976, Justice William H. Rehnquist sardonically asked attorneys for the New York Civil Liberties Union if they were suggesting that "if it's made easier through new technology, then it's unconstitutional. . . . You want the state to show a compelling reason for any information system it begins." In two previous cases, Rehnquist, writing the majority opinion of the court, had placed increasingly narrow boundaries on constitutionally protected privacy. Those protections, he argued, should be limited only to "certain basic matters of procreation, marriage and family life."[54] For the poor, who had never been able to afford privacy, almost every intrusion has always been regarded as legitimate; now, increasingly, privacy and confidentiality become luxuries even for the affluent.

Frequently, the professionals who claim to be most interested in protecting confidentiality are also the most adamant about keeping information from a client, who, according to the common logic, is not capable of understanding the information because he is too ignorant, too ill, too disturbed psychologically, too old, too young, or too limited to cope with it. "Apart from his obligation to maintain a 'safe atmosphere' for all patients," said Maurice Grossman, chairman of the American Psychiatric Association's Task Force on Confidentiality, the doctor "has an obligation to protect the individual patient *even from the patient himself.*"[55] There are things that the doctor (school principal, social worker, counselor) simply cannot tell the client for the client's own good. Sitting across the desk from the client, he may read selected portions, offer to "interpret" the record for the client, or "summarize" it for him; but he will rarely allow the client to read it for himself. The medical industry has been particularly successful in imposing that logic on public policy: medical data is specifically exempt from the provisions of the Fair

Credit Reporting Act, but the logic extends to many other areas.

Most clients, in any case, are simply too busy, too poor, too dependent, or too conditioned to accept what the doctor, the teacher, or the social worker tells them even to ask for the record. The law may require (as does the Buckley Act) that the agency inform the client of his rights or that it obtain informed consent before providing information to third parties; but in practice, most agencies find it easy to conceal such provisions in fine print, to obtain blanket releases, or simply to disregard the law altogether. And as information flows from one data bank to another, from file to file and agency to agency, it accumulates too quickly, moves too fast, and goes too far for any individual to control it. In the end, the data in the file may be so extensive and so full of unsubstantiated gossip, trivia, and innuendos that it is no longer possible to tell where it originated, leaving the client little if any means to correct it. Some states now make it possible to expunge police arrest records in cases which do not lead to conviction, or juvenile records when the subject reaches maturity; but there is almost no way to expunge such data from the other dossiers to which such information has spread and virtually no provisions for deleting or correcting information in mental-health, welfare, child-abuse, or school records. Once the label is affixed or the information recorded, it is likely to be permanent.

# VII

There has been no end of debate about the effects of computerization on individual records. Privacy experts like Alan F. Westin have argued that computers, despite all dire prophecies, have not produced "revolutionary new powers of surveillance," that most computer systems lend themselves only to internal use, that they are more limited in capacity and at least as accurate as the paper files they replace, and that it is usually easier to walk off with a set of paper files than to get information out of a computer.[56] But such arguments tend to ignore the virtually unlimited capacity of computers to sort people by categories and to exchange information with other data systems and agencies. The person who can walk off with an individual's dossier can also walk off with a print-out of all of an agency's clients, together with the codes indicating the nature of their problems. The paper record is perishable and unwieldy; the electronic record is permanent, and with proper programming, instantly accessible. Particularly where they deal with "soft" material—psychiatric diagnoses, teachers' judgments of schoolchildren, or anecdotal reports of deviance in credit reports—paper records have a self-betraying modesty deriving from the literary limitations—the inky scrawls, the faulty grammar, the misspellings—of the clerks, nurses, teachers, cops, and social workers who create them. The computer converts such material into codes and crisp uppercase letters, creates the aura of impersonal objectivity, and infuses the process with the trappings of scientific and technical precision. The further those subjective impressions move from the source, the more objective and precise they appear; qualifications vanish; certainty replaces doubt; and impression becomes fact. In the spring of 1974, for example, Barbara Shaffer-Kelley of Montgomery County, Maryland, was visited by two policemen who had been summoned by a neighbor who suspected child abuse. Normally the woman's baby cried in the afternoon, but on this particular afternoon the child was quiet. The cops inspected the house and examined the baby, found nothing wrong—the child had not been harmed—and left. A few days later, however, Shaffer-Kelley was informed that a worker from the Bureau of Social Services would conduct a further investigation which also proved to be negative. Even though no abuse had been found, information about the case was fed into a child-abuse register, where it became part of the state's permanent records and to which almost every social agency has access. What had been the suspicion of a nosy neighbor thus hardened into a "suspected," "potential," or "unfounded" case of abuse.[57] If, in the future, a teacher, policeman, or social worker should discover a bruise on the child or suspect an emotional problem due to "friction at home," a query to the data bank will turn up the record.

It is the data systems which, as much as anything, make possible the "institutionalization" of individuals who are not inmates of institutions, people who can be tracked from place to place, case to case, agency to agency, and who, in one form or another, never vanish from the ubiquitous surveillance of the network of agencies which have access to the system. The state of Michigan now operates an Automated Client Information System (CIS), which "contains information on all residents who are currently receiving any form of state social-services or who have received such benefits in the past two years," and which links all of the clinics, welfare offices, and other agencies throughout the state's eighty-three counties through video keyboard terminals to a statewide data center in Lansing.[58]

Those systems do not represent the realization of the single data bank containing everything about everybody which had once been so confidently (or ominously) predicted; but they do constitute major "sub-systems"—criminal justice (police, prosecutors, courts, probation, and corrections); financial (municipal licenses, taxes, real estate); social service (welfare, health, mental health, rehabilitation, education)—which represent the beginning of a network of total intervention from which no aspect of the client's life is secure and through which each agency is in a position to know what every other agency knows. First the agency confirms its power over the client by requiring him to provide the personal information —necessary or unnecessary—for "proper service"; then it creates a chilling effect by subtly reminding him that it knows a lot of things from sources that he didn't offer and which, in many instances, he doesn't even know himself.

Thus, the information never exists in a vacuum: it is always used, even if that use is manifest only in confirming the power relationship implicit in its collection and dissemination—directly, through the exercise of the bureaucrat's power to make the client provide it; and indirectly, through surreptitious surveillance and the heady feeling generated by the agent's access to confidential material. In bureaucratic thermodynamics, the chilling effect on the client is almost always accompanied by the warming effect on the agent engaged in the surveillance. To the extent that the surveillance diminishes the subject, it gives the person who engages in the surveillance a concomitant sense of power. Either way, the more anonymous or distant the source of information, or the more "scientific" its base (in a test, for example, or a screen or a diagnosis), the more difficult it will be for the client to challenge it and the more suitable it will be for the climate of inexorability in which bureaucracies thrive. It's relatively easy to talk to the teacher, the caseworker, or the billing clerk; it's difficult to talk back to an "objective" test or a computer, and it's harder still to challenge an unknown source. The problem is familiar to subjects of police investigations in totalitarian states; but as computers institutionalize the exchange of data among agencies, they create similar situations in open societies as well: "We would like to help you, I am personally sympathetic, but according to your record . . ." The information takes on a life of its own, an independent existence that transcends the transaction between a client and one particular agency, and which permits (and sometimes requires) the agency to operate like an outpost of an enormous and anonymous system of clerks, accountants, diagnosticians, and other functionaries in which it is just as helpless as the client.

Since the very limitations of the computer—its demand for a common language with seemingly precise terms—help to reify ambiguous abstractions into concrete labels, to conceal shades of meaning and disagreements of interpretation, and, as data are shared and exchanged, to encourage the use of such labels by all participating agencies, the data systems themselves tend to institutionalize and legitimize the criteria of acceptable and deviant behavior by which individual social-service agencies operate. Thus, the issue is not merely an abstract form of surveillance, but surveillance in the concretized terms that the data system imposes: child abuser, schizophrenic, hyperkinetic, maladjusted, or, even more succinctly, a 601 ("pre-delinquent" in California) or a 316.1 ("social maladjustment" in the classifications of the American Psychiatric Association, the mental-health institutions, and the insurance companies). In that process, the impact of mystification may be almost as powerful on the agency as on the client: on the schoolteacher or the social worker, for example, who, in learning to use the label also learns to distrust her own observations and judgments and to ignore the qualifying and contradictory evidence which suggests the label is wrong. If the test says the kid is retarded, he must be retarded; if the diagnostic report says that Rosenhan's pseudopatient is "schizophrenic," he must be schizophrenic. As the data are exchanged, it becomes increasingly difficult for the individual to escape the label and increasingly likely, as nearly all labeling studies have shown, that he will behave accordingly. And as the data systems proliferate, it becomes increasingly difficult for him to find areas of life in which he doesn't have a record.

Clearly, both the law and economics limit the possibilities of direct intervention outside closed institutions. But just as clearly, they have a major impact in teaching their subjects that there is nothing unusual in being watched, tested, questioned, and labeled; in training them to accept as normative the criteria that the bureaucracies impose; in conditioning them to the idea of a permanent, universal, lifelong record; and if they are in the system long enough, in getting them to speak a kind of institutional language. Enrollment in the system thus becomes its own form of institutional conditioning. In the end, even the horror stories—now so banal—become part of that conditioning: we are all being taught what can happen if we have a bad record. As it becomes harder for the client to escape the network and as more clients are created, more and more people are institutionalized through the records which follow them through the community and through their lives and through the partial re-creation of the conditions—the stripping, the surveillance, the little ceremonies of humiliation—which make behavior control possible in closed institutions. For a growing number of people, and to some extent for all Americans, everyday life on the outside becomes a little more like life on the inside.

# EIGHT

# The Lessons of Intervention

## I

Each element reinforces the others; they work together. The drugs support the belief that the behavior for which they are prescribed is really disease. Mental hospitals confirm the need for mental health. Hospitalization is a measure of illness. The data bank scientizes the diagnosis and legitimizes the label; both look better in codes and uppercase letters coming out of a machine. Therapy in the clinic encourages treatment at the Department of Social Services and screening at the Board of Education. Surveillance technology in industry habituates the adult to surveillance by the police; surveillance technology and testing in school conditions the child to surveillance and testing everywhere. If treatment fails, it proves only that it was too late, not that it was ineffective, unwise, or unnecessary; earlier intervention was necessary. The medical ideology justifies the practices, and the practices the ideology.

Collectively, those elements constitute an enormous and continuing shift in the way government and other institutions control individuals and in the way individuals are taught to control themselves: from the overt to the covert, from the punitive to the therapeutic, from the hortatory to the manipulative, from the moralistic to the mechanistic. In some instances, that change simply represents the replacement of one mode with another. In some it is incremental and therefore not a change at all but an addition; the two operate together in such a way that the old is an inducement to the new—is it going to be prison or therapy?—and in many the two are so thoroughly confused that therapy, punishment, and control become indistinguishable. "In certain refractory cases," said Richard D. Parlour, director of day treatment at the Riverside (California) Mental Health Services, "deliberate painful applications are an absolutely necessary part of the treatment. . . . The concept of punishment is largely a semantic, philosophical problem which may be avoided in practice by substituting new phrases such as 'aversive conditioning' or 'negative consequences.' "[1]

It is not a complete system—there is too much bureaucratic slippage, too much confusion, too many rivalries, too many inconsistencies. But the assumptions, lessons, and attitudes are all the same. "What," asked Judge Bazelon, "can psychiatry offer a beleaguered mother with no income, bad housing, and children who lack rudimentary care? . . . Should she be treated with antidepressants for her depression, tranquilizers for her hallucinations, and therapy for her alcoholism? One does not need to be a psychiatrist to see that treatment is doomed to failure unless the conditions fostering such disabilities are ameliorated."[2] But the conditions are not to be ameliorated—not now, anyway, and maybe never—and something must be done. In the most favorable terms, her pain and misery require treatment. "Of course I know that part of the problem is jobs and housing," said the director of a mental-health center, "but I'm a doctor; that's my job." Does a military physician campaign for peace or treat the wounded on the battlefront? In less favorable terms, it is all pacification, sedation, and repression. If she does not receive treatment, she may burn down the neighborhood or blow the welfare money or organize a movement; she has to be taught that while the problem is not her fault, it lies in her. As Bazelon said, "The same patient labelled 'schizophrenic' for purposes of the mental health center might be stamped 'neurotic' in the forensic division, 'sociopathic' in the prison system and 'heroin addict' in the drug treatment system."[3] But the messages are the same: bring in your sick relative, bring in your alcoholic, bring in your difficult client, bring in your unruly child. Let us work on you; let us teach you to work on yourself. It can be the beginning of a career.

Everywhere there is government, its institutions, and its benevolent agents. As moral authority declines, its therapeutic authority grows. As people become economically superfluous and therefore immune to the discipline of the economic system, they must be disciplined by the social-service system. As recipients of social service, welfare, or mental health, the clients are responsible to the state, "employees" of government. And what of those who are not taking care of kids but who are being supported or "serviced" anyway? Is the state paying them to take care of themselves, to behave themselves, to stay out of trouble? More often it pays someone else or it gives them drugs, but the objective is the same. Every year there are more of them: more clients, more therapists, more techniques of control.

At some point in the past ten years, it reached a critical mass—the point at which the psychological screen, the tranquilizer, and the behaviorist's jargon had, at the very least, achieved parity with the club of the cop, the stick of the schoolmaster, and the moral strictures of the judge. It was not simply, as Parlour suggested, that punishment could be dismissed as a "semantic, philosophical problem" and Newspoken into "aversive conditioning," or that it became increasingly difficult to distinguish among therapy, punishment, and control, but that the great American faith in social betterment and perpetual improvement had itself been transformed into a technical problem for the growing army of psychiatrists, psychologists, social workers, and others in the "helping professions" charged with the management and control of officially certified "social problems." While the last great outburst of the American faith in transportation— the New Frontier and the Great Society—had been repudiated as chimerical and consigned to benign neglect, it left a broad and, it appeared, indefinite mandate for service and intervention. The residual mandate, however, was not so much to reform conditions or institutions—to build better housing or devise more effective programs of education or guarantee incomes—as it was to work on individuals. "The tendencies," said John R. Seeley, one of the founders of the mental-health movement in Canada and a sociologist at Charles R. Drew Medical School in Los Angeles,

> were the existence and rapid proliferation of what claimed to be social and psychological sciences with hegemonic claims as the exclusive royal roads to the understanding of humanity *qua* human, the cure or mitigation of its major ills; the nearly universal acceptance of the view that underlying all human stress or distress is merely a "problem" or set of problems capable in principle of solution, and, in practice [given enough means and money], proximately so. . . .

and, finally, the existence of a sort of religious quest for "the ulterior secret that would transfigure human life."[4]

Some of that, of course, was older than America itself; but in less than three generations, the faith once placed in Providence and in the inexorable, mysterious dynamics of the new nation itself—the belief in the American as the new Adam and in the country's ability to "transfigure human life"— became, first, a growing mandate to reform institutions and thereby "solve" problems and, more recently, a therapeutic vision which replaces moral stricture, retributive punishment, and a romantic faith in human perfectibility with an ideology of treatment, service, and preventive intervention directed toward individuals. The teacher as moralist thus becomes the teacher as "behavior modifier," therapist, and psychologist; the "moral treatment" of mental illness becomes chemotherapy; and character is reduced to conditioning, neurons, synapses, and enzymes beyond freedom and dignity. Along the way, the clinic tends to become a model for many other social institutions and, in some mea-

sure, for society itself. While the factory transmutes the own-
ership-based authority of the boss and his managers into a
system in which human control is structured into the technology of production, the school, which for nearly a century
had been operated as a training ground for industrial labor,
is transformed into a sort of pre-clinic that conditions its
clients to accept screening, diagnosis, service, and "treatment," and that teaches them that to be good patients (or,
at the very least, passive clients of services) is to be good
citizens.[5] In both cases, authority is increasingly disguised as
part of the nature of things as revealed by the practitioners
of medicine, psychology, and behavioral science; one form of
"natural law" replaces another; and mystery supplants mystery.

But there is a difference between mysteries and forms of
mystification. The original American mystery was, at least in
theory, and at least for white men, a celebration of the ability
of Everyman to cope for himself and of the society to create
conditions—mainly by leaving him alone—in which he
could successfully do so. It was not until the last decades of
the nineteenth century that industrialization, urbanization,
and, in America, the great waves of "new immigrants" from
Southern and Eastern Europe shaped the evolution of a science of behavior occupied with the analysis, measurement,
and control of human differences. Throughout the West, the
erosion of older structures of class and authority, and the
claims and challenges of new classes and ethnic groups,
stimulated the work of the phrenologists, the testers of intelligence, the eugenicists, and the analysts of deviance—Lombroso, Binet, Madison Grant, and, in the first half of the
twentieth century, Cyril Burt, Edward L. Thorndike, H. M.
Goddard, Lewis M. Terman, and Sheldon and Eleanor
Glueck; but it was in America—necessarily in America, that
most democratic, "classless," and ethnically pluralistic society—where they became most influential.

Given the historic American faith in transformation, and
given the facts of urban industrial life (and, indeed, the facts

of life generally), the shape of that behavioral science may have been inevitable. Although many of the practitioners managed to shake their more blatant assumptions about class and ethnic differences—the fear, for example, "that if the present differential birth rate continues, 1,000 Harvard graduates will at the end of 200 years have but 50 descendants, while in the same period 1,000 South Italians will have multiplied to 100,000"—neither they nor their intellectual descendants ever relinquished their belief in the power of science to test for deviance, to measure intelligence, or to predict madness, crime, and what used to be called "pauperism."[6] The purists of the twenties and thirties became firm believers in restrictive immigration, eugenics, and sterilization programs for "defectives"—all those people who, because of their genetic inferiority, were impervious to the transforming power of America. For them, intervention was limited to the control and restriction of defective populations.[7] Their progressive, liberal colleagues, however, reinvoked the historic American faith and linked it to their professions of medical and social science in programs of individual treatment and transformation: stress, mental illness, low intelligence, misery, depression, delinquency, and crime were "social problems" that were aberrations from the normative human condition subject to measurement and analysis, and given the proper resources and techniques, to prediction, prevention, and therapy. "Social problems" could be treated or behavior modified away.

# II

There are no simple solutions or quick prescriptions for eliminating or reducing the growing impositions masquerading as "therapy" or "service." If one accepts deviance, mental illness, or "maladjustment" as problems to be resolved rather than as dilemmas to be lived with, then the currently fashionable remedies will often appear more attractive or efficient than the cruder methods they replaced. The difficulty is that individual remedies grow into collective problems; that what is advertised as therapy is, or becomes, dependence and maintenance; and that treatment in hard-core cases becomes an appealing method of intervention in marginal cases. Nearly every remedy generates a tendency to redefine comparatively benign situations into terms that will make them applicable to that remedy. When a chemical antidepressant is introduced, more people will be diagnosed as depressed; when a child-abuse reporting system is established, more and more individuals will be identified as potential abusers; when a community mental-health clinic is offered as an alternative to closed mental hospitals, it soon becomes an invitation to other agencies to redefine their difficult cases as mentally ill.

Each remedy and each system has a tendency to deliver less and less to more and more. A clinic established to handle a thousand cases finds itself dealing with two thousand on the same budget and with the same staff; a social-service network founded on the premise that poverty, poor housing, and social pathology were temporary problems to be resolved finds itself serving a permanent, growing underclass with little if any hope of extricating itself from its situation. In each instance (and regardless of the good intentions of those who work in the system), there will be a search for more efficient means to "treat" and serve and, wherever possible, for ways to define problems that will render them suitable for such intervention. As a consequence, every system expands to the point at which something breaks down—the point where a scandal in a prison or a hospital, or where some new evidence about the damaging side effects of drugs, generates just enough pressure to reform practices without essentially changing them, to re-achieve the uneasy balance among budget, "service" (particularly the absence of blatant brutality), and social control. Because the new technologies are often cheaper and more humane than simple restraint or incarceration, they are obviously attractive in maintaining that delicate equilibrium.

Most of the alternatives are obvious: full employment and a shift of resources from therapy and "medical" intervention to the improvement of the social conditions which often cause the problems in the first place; a conservative insistence that intervention be limited to serious cases; a willingness to tolerate diversity as difference and not as deviance; and absolute prohibitions on "service" or treatment for unwilling clients. Community mental health has become a substitute for community itself. As one former hospital inmate insisted, what many, if not most, mental patients want is not a doctor or a drug but simply a place to live—a "fraternity" or a "sorority" house which provides reasonably comfortable accommodations and something of a retreat from stress. Less obvious, but more important, is the complete separation of psychiatry and "mental health" from the power and resources of the state—the disestablishment of mental health —through the elimination of involuntary commitment laws, the abolition of government mandated mental-health screening, a shift of public funds from the control of doctors and institutions to the control of clients who can then choose whether to use them for formal therapy or housing or simply a month at the beach (which is likely to be at least as therapeutic as a month in the state asylum), and above all, a redefinition of "mental health" itself from something that suggests certain normative standards of behavior to something that celebrates community and diversity. The first obligation of any genuine professional is to understand and clarify the limits of what his profession can do; to insist on the scrupulous observation of limits; to be able to say, "Sorry, but I can't help"; and to distinguish between matters of morals, politics, or culture and matters of science, technology, or medicine. It is patently absurd to establish enormous developmental screening networks for young children or to organize mandatory child-abuse reporting systems when there exist no remedies even for the problems which have already been identified; it is manifestly dangerous to drug millions of people with medications which, while they might be marginally justified as alternatives to manacles or self-mutilation, are totally unjustified as instruments of social sanitation and community aesthetics; it is fraud to advertise an intervention as "treatment" when its only demonstrable effect, if not its intent, is nothing more than indefinite mainte-nance and control. The most important side effect of any form of intervention—drugs, surgery, incarceration, screen-ing—is social and political. No matter how smooth the method, no matter how little medical damage it inflicts on the individual, it will shape not only his behavior and atti-tudes but also those of the society at large.

The ultimate base of resistance is simply the information and the right and power to say no. It lies in the ability to ask basic questions about effects, to demand reasons, to look for alternatives, and to retain responsibility. Hypothetically that right is generally granted, but practically it is almost always constrained by the social pressure to conform, by economic pressure, by the reassurances of the practitioner that the remedy is medically legitimate, by the incessant propaganda of the drug industry and the mental-health establishment, and by the illusions of science.

There is precious little behavioral science, nor are there cures for the individual behavioral "syndromes" or for the "social problems" into which they are collectively defined. Tests are conducted, diagnoses pronounced, labels attached, hypotheses suggested; but the science and understanding of "mental illness," intelligence, and criminality have hardly grown at all in the past seventy-five years.

Yet, if there is little science and little in the way of cures, there is the scientific mystique—the Latinized labels; the epidemiological theories of social contagion; the rhetoric of diagnosis, prevention, and treatment—and along with it, the ideology of intervention and the mushrooming technologies of maintenance, surveillance, and control. In their application to "hard" cases—those individuals who, for whatever reason, had previously been locked up or tied down—those technologies are in many ways "smoother," less obviously punitive and restrictive than what they replaced. But for the same reason, they are also more easily applied to people whose form of deviance, if any, is too marginal to justify the harsher, more direct, and more expensive forms of intervention and who had never been formally labeled deviant before the technologies were available.

Ideology and technology combine to create cases and clients out of individuals who had once been left alone; they blur the distinction between (mental, physical, social) "illness" and "health," and they reinforce the authority of the therapist and the agency. Since the ideology runs consistently through most areas of intervention, and since those areas are often linked through exchanges of personal client information, each reinforces the power and legitimacy of the others. Education shades into social welfare, criminal justice, and mental health: the same "objective" which justifies testing the child in school also justifies the visit of the child-abuse team to the home; the same theory which justifies an examination for dental cavities also justifies it for "anxieties" or "neuroses" or delinquent tendencies; the same medical ideology that justifies Elavil for the mother's inability to cope with her mops and brooms also prescribes amphetamines for her son's inability to sit still in class. The historic American faith in transformation and problem solving, already converted into the interventionist's "cure," is converted again into maintenance and applied to the dirty work of social sanitation. The come-on is cure, but the merchandise is management; and what had been a mystique of human perfectibility becomes a rationale for keeping the imperfect from causing trouble. The vision is of a society whose greatest virtue is a kind of sanitary efficiency partly modeled on the rationalized factory where, as historian Georg Lukacs said, "the human qualities and idiosyncracies of the worker appear as mere sources of error."[8] By definition, such a society cannot neglect its deviants, nor can it punish them; it can only treat them or render them invisible.

Skinnerian behaviorists often protest that the press and public apply the term behavior modification to techniques which they don't practice and in which they don't believe (and that, as a consequence, they sometimes wish that their methods had been given another name); yet every one of those techniques operates with similar aims and grows out of the same assumptions. Although the professed objective may be strictly limited—the chemical treatment of a particular depressed person, the management of one obstreperous client, the investigation of one suspected case of child abuse —the practices collectively create a climate whose inevitable effect is to teach its subjects and those around them (who, but for the grace of God, might be clients also) that their freedom and will are limited, that they are prisoners of their own chemistry or their own conditioning, and that the requirements of the culture are scientifically normative. "When behavior modification is elevated to ethics, to a philosophy of culture," said psychoanalyst Rollo May, "it becomes destructive." The behaviorists often appear to be embarrassed by Skinner's grandiose claims about his technology—they don't want to talk about shaping the culture—yet even without his ideological professions, they operate in a climate where the very proliferation of behavior technologies has elevated behavior modification into something just short of an ethical principle.

# III

For nearly a generation, the course of legal due process and the history of the search for new techniques of behavior control have run in opposite but related directions. In the past decade particularly, judicial decisions and legislative enactments have made it more difficult to lock people up arbitrarily; to expel children from school without a hearing; and to justify incarceration in juvenile detention homes and mental institutions on the ground that the individual needs "treatment," without, at the same time, providing treatment. Minors in the juvenile justice system now have certain due-process rights—the right to counsel and to cross-examine witnesses (but not the right to a trial by jury)—and mental patients can no longer be institutionalized solely on the ground of "mental illness." Moreover, the lower courts have begun to rule that institutions which offer "treatment" have an affirmative duty, sometimes defined in extensive court-mandated standards, to provide such treatment. (In theory, all mental-commitment cases and all juvenile cases are civil proceedings not subject to all the protections of criminal procedure and therefore, as one court recently ruled, "the government must afford a *quid pro quo* to warrant the confinement of citizens in which the conventional limitations of the criminal process are inapplicable."[9]) Yet most major developments that extend new legal protection to minorities —the poor, the black, the mentally ill, the old, the young— appear to be accompanied (perhaps as cause, perhaps as effect, perhaps fortuitously) by a search for extra-legal means to maintain to whatever extent possible the previous order.

The principle is self-evident, and in various forms it has been a familiar part of recent American history. In the past twenty-five years, however, the ideology of medical-model intervention and the increasingly "smooth" technologies of control have transformed the various forms of behavior modification into highly attractive methods to maintain the status quo. Harvard law professor Alan Dershowitz argues that the courts have not led in this area but have responded to the introduction of chemotherapy and legislative pressure to cut institutional budgets. Either way, old categories of disqualification are translated into new, apparently noninvidious labels of medical or social disability, punishment into treatment, discrimination into retardation, service into surveillance. Thus, psychiatrist Leopold Bellak can dream about his "central registries" where "the social, emotional and medical histories of every citizen who had come to attention in any way because of emotional difficulties would be tabulated by a computer."[10] As the law makes it more difficult to lock up deviants arbitrarily, "science" makes it easier to define them as sick and to divert them into programs of treatment—"outpatients" of the mental-health system, the education system, the social-service system, or the criminal-justice system. And as it becomes more difficult to discriminate on the basis of race, class, age, or sex, "research" finds new labels to replace the old—the parapsychiatric, the predelinquent, the potentially abusive—and technology new ways to control and watch these "deviants."

This is not to say that all of those services are discriminatory or that most forms of social therapy are really attempts to punish (although some are) or that there is a general conspiracy to keep people in line. There is no Big Brother. Most of these services are well intentioned—genuine attempts to serve or "treat" those who appear to need treatment; and even when they are not, they are more likely to be the consequence of a little professional aggrandizement, a search for another grant, some government money, a contract, or an excuse for previous failure than some political plot. But ideology and technology make it ever more difficult to distinguish among punishment, treatment, and control and, in some respects, increasingly unnecessary. "Behavior modification" obviates the distinction. This is what makes behavior mod comparatively smooth and attractive and what, as the various techniques become smoother, makes it easier to impose on the unwilling and easier to administer to volunteers. The ultimate technology is the one in which the individual is unaware that his behavior is controlled by an outside agency—in which he no longer knows (or cares) whether he is a recruit or a volunteer—the behaviorist Utopia in which free will and determinism vanish as practical or philosophical considerations.

In a series of sardonic speeches and interviews, John R. Seeley argues that since the social-problems industry is organized and financed on assumptions of permanence and long-term growth, every "problem" with which it is supposed to deal has to be more or less intractable and is therefore defined in such a way as to build insolubility into its very structure. Ideally, therefore, the terms should be vague; the ideology sufficiently obscure to make it possible to fend off challenges as "playing politics"; the definition broad enough to sustain expansion and promise refinement, "particularly the development of a great new technology"; and the problem endowed with "a large capacity to divert attention from problems of a more fundamental order." Also, it "should involve an available helpless population or one that can be made available." In mental illness, mental retardation, crime, and delinquency,

> the essence of each term lies in its lack of any anchoring point that does not (or would not) shift with any solution of the "present problem." The problem is the problem of the [sufficiently] below-average performer on any scale. . . . What we mean at best by any of these terms is the problem presented by the approximately 5 percent (or whatever the facilities for dealing with or even sympathizing with the problem will permit) at the lower tail of whatever distribution we are talking about. If we were to attempt a radical solution by simply shooting those now held to be mentally retarded, it is unthinkable that anything would happen to the problem except that psychologists would need to re-score present intelligence tests so that they again found mean, mode and median at 100.[11]

Sociologist Kai Erikson of Yale has argued that concepts like crime and delinquency are themselves necessary to define the boundaries of acceptable social or cultural behavior and therefore structurally inherent in every society. (In the same way, one would imagine, "madness" may be necessary to the definition of reasonable behavior.) Yet the theories of Seeley and Erikson only partially explain the fact that those most affected by the new technologies of intervention

—in numbers, and perhaps in degree—are not the hard-core cases who have often been subject to punishment or outside control but those on the margins of deviance and on the fringes of undesirability who, in earlier times, would either have been subject to overt discrimination (as blacks or as schoolchildren or as women) or simply left alone. The propaganda and ideology of preventive social or mental medicine trade on the new technologies to move the locus of intervention toward the mainstream and to convert the bell-shaped curve of the psychologists and statisticians into an epidemiological concept of universal affliction. In that sense, no "radical solution" of the problems of those at the "lower tail" of the population is required. As the new technologies become cheaper and smoother, and as the economy renders more people superfluous, the everyday problems of people further up the line are medicalized into new ailments, and the whole idea of the normal distribution of human traits turned on its conceptual head. The curve begins to represent not the normal spread of human characteristics in which some minority at the lower end is arbitrarily defined as pathological but rather a scale of pathology on which no one is completely normal and on which everyone can use some help. From schizophrenia grow "latent," "pseudoneurotic," "pseudopsychopathic," "borderline," and "creeping" schizophrenia. From organic brain damage grow "minimal brain damage" and "minimal brain dysfunction." From crime comes delinquency, from delinquency "pre-delinquency." At the same time, the discovery of a mode of "treatment" for a specified ailment invariably increases the number of cases so diagnosed. The vagueness or intractability of the core problem—crime or "schizophrenia" or the failure of some children to learn—makes the creation of anticipatory marginal, "latent," or "borderline" problems that much more inviting: it provides a rationale for failure even while it legitimizes the arbitrary definition of the original ailment and enlarges the empire of intervention. As usual, failure justifies escalation.

There is no logical end to the process. The only limitations lie in the shortage of resources and the relative crudeness of the techniques themselves: in the failure of therapy and behavior modification to reduce crime and juvenile delinquency; in the negative side effects of drugs; in the administrative difficulties of a welfare scheme like Incentive for Independence. There is probably far more public awareness of the dangers of medication than ever before, more stories in the press, more law suits, more pressure for government regulation. At the same time, there has been a swing back to more overtly punitive methods in criminal justice: a trend away from the dominant pattern of rehabilitation-oriented indeterminate sentencing of convicted felons (the therapeutic model) toward legislatively mandated fixed sentences (the "justice" model), pressure to try 16- and 17-year-old adolescents charged with serious crimes in adult courts, and general public disenchantment with the possibility of converting or reforming serious offenders.[12] Yet that pressure has not been accompanied by any reduction in programs of early intervention or in any significant legislative effort to keep marginal and status offenders out of the criminal-justice and social-service systems. If anything, the general "war on crime" and official recognition of the futility of rehabilitative programs for hard-core criminals is likely to further institutionalize prevention and early identification of "pre-delinquency," child abuse, minimal brain dysfunction, mental illness, and the panoply of other ailments which, according to one theory or another, are the first steps to crime.

Almost invariably, the attacks on drugs and other behavior technologies are directed at their medical side effects or at their lack of efficacy, not at the ideology of intervention or the medicalized "problems" for which they are prescribed; they therefore constitute a demand for more elegant, medically efficient methods of accomplishing what the profession claims it can do already. And because many of the challenges are based on the concept of a "right to treatment," they not only tempt the courts to impose what is, in effect, a duty to treatment but, more significantly, reaffirm the theory that there is such a thing as scientifically valid intervention with scientifically valid results. In fact, nearly all discussion of the effects of behavior technology involves confusion between cure and maintenance, and therefore between "liberation" and dependence. (Once there is a physician in the transaction, concern about drug addiction and dependence is mystified away; almost no one speaks about phenothiazine junkies or diazepam addicts.) On both counts, therefore, the medical mystery and the authority of the "helping professions" go virtually unchallenged, and their narrowing definition of what constitutes normative behavior stands unquestioned. As due process, equal protection, and civil-liberties measures mitigate what de Tocqueville called the tyranny of the majority, "science" converts cultural and social standards into natural law and deviance into disease. One can rebel against the cops, the teachers, the doctors, and perhaps even the community, but there is no rebellion against nature.

# IV

It is a subtle, erosive process. Almost every agency of education, social welfare, and mental health talks the seductive language of prevention, diagnosis, and treatment; and almost every client is a hostage to an exchange which trades momentary comfort and institutional peace for an indefinite future of maintenance and control. Although cases are sometimes dramatic—the severely beaten child, the murderous mental patient, the violent feral adolescent—and therefore apt headline material for the mythology of intervention, they do not necessarily illustrate general principles, much less prove that a broad scheme of intervention is or might be successful. But out of the limelight, the cases accumulate undramatically in a therapeutic environment which invites (or coerces) more and more people in for care or management and which teaches even those who remain outside that if they misbehave, they will get the treatment too. Each instance of intervention narrows the bounds of acceptable behavior for the rest of the population; each person formally declared deviant brings the next person closer to the margin. Even the best-intentioned practitioners participate in the exchange. Perhaps it is the fault of the system, the economy, the whole society; perhaps it would be better if we left this person alone; but the system can't be changed, and this person needs help now. Dependency, conformity, responsibility, are abstractions; but the pain is immediate, the disturbance is real, the institution can't function with this man acting up, his family is not safe. Thorazine for peace, Prolixin for safety, behavior mod for institutional order. By the time the system changes, if indeed it ever does, he'll have failed in school, lost his job, murdered his children. Every pill makes it less likely that the system ever will change.

There is no way to estimate the extent to which this process creates superfluous people and the extent to which it only pins scientific labels of disability on those who have already been rendered economically, technologically, or psychologically superfluous by something else. Clearly, it helps maintain the balance and preserve order not only by keeping people in their place but also by creating an extraneous, diversionary rationale for those who are in it. The reason you don't have a job is because you are untrained, mentally ill, retarded; the reason you can't feed your family on welfare is because you have not learned the proper domestic skills; the reason you can't learn is because you are learning disabled; the reason you can't clean house is because you are depressed; the reason you are thinking of suicide is because you are sick.[13]

Each year more people are kept busy in the increasingly complex occupations of therapy consumption and system coping; and more and more are taught that their minds, psyches, and behavior are organic objects to be worked on. Like anything else made by man, the ideology, however pervasive, is probably resistible and reversible. The technologies are still relatively crude, their validity more myth than science. There is, moreover, the beginning of a counter-movement—still weak and rudimentary, but growing—of "radical" therapists, former mental patients, civil libertarians, welfare clients, and others who are trying to attack not merely the formal impositions of mental health, mandatory screening, and child-abuse reporting but the subtler, "voluntary" invitations to treatment and management. If enough people recognize that social sanitation cannot cleanse the community of crime or deviance or ugliness, let alone pain and misery, and that, in any case, the political price of the effort is increasing control, there is a chance to confront the ideology in legal and political terms. Yet every day the various means of intervention and surveillance and the standards they impose appear more normative; and every day, therefore, they become harder to resist.

With the passage, now probable, of some form of compulsory national health insurance covering psychiatric problems, it will become more difficult still. Such insurance can never pay for extended counseling or talking therapy, but it may well provide just enough coverage—as Medicaid does now—to pay for long-term medication and cheap institutionalization. (There is already extensive pressure from organized clinical psychologists, through the American Psychological Association, to have their services covered by national health insurance, as some private group plans already do, and to give them parity with psychiatrists as primary health providers in virtually every respect, including the legal power to write prescriptions for psychotropic medication.[14]) More important, the ideology and the concomitant conditioning of people to accept services are themselves reinforced by what appears, at least for the moment, to be the growing need to store, manage, and control the enormous number of people no longer subject to more traditional controls or who, because of changing standards of community acceptability and social hygiene (which are themselves promoted by the new industries of intervention) have been declared presently or potentially deviant. For them, medical and social science obviate the protections of due process and make unnecessary the overtly invidious (and therefore more easily resistible) distinctions of class, race, age, or sex. Slowly, subtly, humanely, "science" repeals the Constitution. In the long run, its subjects will no longer know, or care, whether they are being served or controlled, treated or punished, or whether they are volunteers or conscripts. The distinctions will have vanished.

# Notes

## Introduction

1. Erving Goffman, *Asylums* (Garden City, N.Y.: Doubleday and Co., 1961), p. 38.

## Chapter One

1. West's letter was leaked to alternative newspapers in California a few months after it was written, along with the state's rejection of the request as too "delicate." It has since been published by the Subcommittee on Constitutional Rights of the Senate Judiciary in *Individual Rights and the Federal Role in Behavior Modification* (Washington, D. C.: U. S. Government Printing Office, 1974), p. 357.

2. The proposals for the Violence Center went through at least four versions, three of which have never been published. The quotes in this section come from a version I obtained from staff members of the California State Senate and from a "Project Description" dated September 1, 1972, and published in *Individual Rights,* pp. 324–48.

3. For a fuller description of the Schwitzgebel device, see Chapter Six. There is also a discussion of the device in Barton L. Ingraham and Burton L. Smith, "The Use of Electronics in the Observation and Control of Human Behavior and Its Possible Use in Rehabilitation and Parole," *Issues in Criminology* 7, no. 2 (1972): 35–53; Ralph Schwitzgebel et al., "A Program of Research in Behavioral Electronics," *Behavioral Science* 9 (1964): 233; Ralph Schwitzgebel, "Electronic Innovation in the Behavioral Sciences: A Call to Responsibility," *American Psychologist* 22, no. 5 (1967): 364; and *Anthropotelemetry: Dr. Schwitzgebel's Machine,* 80 HARV. L. REV. 403 (1966).

**4.** Vernon H. Mark, William H. Sweet, and Frank R. Ervin, "Role of Brain Disease in Riots and Urban Violence," *Journal of the American Medical Association* 201, no. 11 (September 11, 1967): 201; Vernon H. Mark and Frank R. Ervin, *Violence and the Brain*, (New York: Harper and Row, 1970), pp. 156, 158.

**5.** There is a more complete discussion of psychosurgery and electroshock treatment in Chapter Six.

**6.** Jose M. R. Delgado, *Physical Control of the Mind: Toward a Psychocivilized Society* (New York: Harper and Row, 1969), p. 259.

**7.** Mark and Ervin, *Violence and the Brain*, p. 161. For a more complete discussion of the Hutschnecker proposal, see Peter Schrag and Diane Divoky, *The Myth of the Hyperactive Child* (New York: Pantheon, 1975), pp. 3–5. All such attempts to predict future crime or violence through tests, screens, or brain-wave examinations have always been, and continue to be, subject to serious doubt.

**8.** Mark and Ervin, *Violence and the Brain,* p. 147. They did not explain how "behavior" that included careful planning, the purchase of a mail-order rifle, and patient waiting for Kennedy to come into range could be called "uncontrolled." Their prime illustration of such behavior was Oswald's propensity to beat his wife, an attribute that could hardly be regarded as a proper predictor of future presidential assassins.

**9.** Mark, Sweet, and Ervin, *Role of Brain Disease,* p. 201.

**10.** Some of the federally funded behavior modification programs are described in *Individual Rights;* the chromosome studies, including research at Johns Hopkins, the University of Wisconsin, the Educational Testing Service, and Boston Hospital for Women, are listed by the NIMH Center for Studies of Crime and Delinquency under its "Active Research Grants" (July 1, 1973); the HEW program of Early Periodic Screening, Diagnosis and Treatment (EPSDT) is described by Sharland Trotter in "Massive Screening Set for Nation's Poorest Children," *APA [American Psychological Association] Monitor* 6, no. 9 (September/October 1975): 1, 5, 23.

**11.** *Individual Rights,* pp. 49–54. The Senate Subcommittee on

Labor and Health, Education and Welfare Appropriations had been persuaded—no one is quite certain how—to earmark $1 million in its 1973 appropriation bill for "studies of violent behavior related to brain disease." When Senator Warren G. Magnuson, the subcommittee's chairman, received "several disturbing published reports" indicating that an earlier appropriation was being used for studies in psychosurgery, he asked NIMH to delay further funding. The "disturbing published reports" were largely the work of Dr. Peter R. Breggin, who then headed the Washington-based Project to Examine Psychiatric Technology. There is considerable material on the psychosurgery issue in U.S. Senate, *Quality of Health Care— Human Experimentation: Hearings of the Subcommittee on Labor and Public Welfare* (Washington D.C.: U.S. Government Printing Office, 1973), pp. 357–63, 435–80; and there is a summary in Jean Dietz, "Senate Urged to Kill Brain Study," *Boston Globe,* 24 September 1972. For more on psychosurgery, see Chapter Six.

12. Arthur L. Mattocks and Charles Jew, "Assessment of an Aversive Treatment Program with Extreme Acting-Out Patients in a Psychiatric Facility for Criminal Offenders" (Unpublished paper to the California Department of Corrections), quoted in Shapiro, *Legislating the Control of Behavior Control: Autonomy and the Coercive Use of Organic Therapies,* S. CAL. L. REV. 237, 245–46 (1974). The original paper is on file, and available, at the University of Southern California Law Library, University Park, Los Angeles, CA 90007.

At least five inmates were treated "against their will." The Connecticut prison program with aversive shock is reported in *The New York Times,* 21 May 1974, p. 43; for details on the Iowa program, which was ordered stopped by a federal court, see Knecht v. Gillman, 488 F.2d 1136 (1973); for a report on the Michigan psychosurgery case, see Kaimowitz v. Department of Mental Health for the State of Michigan, Civ. No. 73–19434 (Circuit Court, Wayne County, Mich., July 10, 1973); for an account of California's psychosurgery on prisoners, see Leroy F. Arons, "Brain Surgery Is Tested on 3 California Convicts," *The Washington Post,* 25 February 1972.

13. Quoted from *LEAA News Release,* 14 February 1974, p. 1; on

the same day, LEAA issued a "guideline" which stated that "because the field is still experimental and because LEAA personnel generally do not possess the technical and professional skills . . . to evaluate and monitor" behavior modification, there would be no further funding in the field.

14. As late as April 1974, the Violence Center proposal, by then renamed the Center for the Reduction of Life-Threatening Behavior, was still very much alive. It was extensively debated at the annual meeting of the American Orthopsychiatric Association and defended in *The UCLA Project on Life-Threatening Behavior: Some Facts* (Westwood, Calif., April 4, 1974), a UCLA statement that charged that the opponents had set up a "barrage of misinformation" and "issued a steady flow of distortions." A revised proposal was then being drafted for submission to NIMH, but by then it was too late.

15. Interview with Skinner at Harvard, May 14, 1976.

16. Perry London, *Behavior Control* (New York: Harper and Row, 1969), p. 4.

17. B. F. Skinner, *Beyond Freedom and Dignity* (New York: Alfred A. Knopf, 1971), p. 149. Almost all the ideas, as well as the "scientific" conclusions, were elaborated in Skinner's *Science and Human Behavior* (New York: The Macmillan Co., 1953). In the acknowledgments for *Beyond Freedom and Dignity,* Skinner credits NIMH for support in preparation of the book; he had, in fact, received more than $280,000 from the federal government.

18. Interview, May 16, 1976.

19. Goffman, *Asylums,* p. 51.

20. Frederick Winslow Taylor, *The Principles of Scientific Management* (New York: W. W. Norton and Co., 1967), p. 117–18. The book was originally published by Harper and Brothers in 1911.

21. Ibid., p. 40. The full story, and the various descriptions of Schmidt, appear on pp. 41–47.

22. Ibid., p. 53.

23. Ibid., p. 63.

24. Ibid., p. 120. Taylor used the school model in making his argument: "No efficient teacher would think of giving his class

of students an indefinite lesson to learn. Each day a definite, clear-cut task is set by the teacher before each scholar, stating that he must learn just so much of the subject; and it is only by this means that proper, systematic progress can be made by the students." Broken down to even smaller steps, this is the essence of "programmed instruction" as promoted in the 1960s and incorporated in Skinnerian "teaching machines."

**25.** Ibid., p. 119.

**26.** "Testimony Before the Special House Committee to Investigate the Taylor and Other Systems of Shop Management," in F. W. Taylor, *Scientific Management* (New York: Harper and Brothers, 1947), pp. 211, 189. The hearings at which Taylor testified were held in 1912.

**27.** Peter F. Drucker, *The Practice of Management* (New York: Harper and Row, 1954), p. 280. There have been arguments that scientific management is all but passé, but only in the sense that it has become so fundamental that it is no longer noticed in industry. "Scientific management," said Drucker, who is probably still the leading management intellectual in America, "is all but a systematic philosophy of worker and work. Altogether it may well be the most powerful as well as the most lasting contribution America has made to Western thought since the Federalist Papers."

**28.** Ellwood P. Cubberley, *Public School Administration* (Boston: Houghton Mifflin Co., 1916), p. 338.

**29.** *National Association of Corporation Schools* [*NACS*] *Bulletin* 6 (March 1919): 103. Skinner's writing is not only similar to scientific management literature in content and ideas, but in prose style. "It is possible," said the *NACS Bulletin*, "through recently developed tests, to determine in a measure at least whether or not the individual possesses mechanical skill, salesmanship, or other special talents. This branch of the science is just being developed. The business world will be amazed when the final story of the development and usefulness of the personnel division of the war department is known."

"A science of behavior," said Skinner, "is not yet ready to solve all our problems, but it is a science in progress, and its ultimate adequacy cannot now be judged. When critics assert that it cannot count for this or that aspect of human behavior, they usually imply that it will never be able to do so, but the analysis continues to develop and is in fact much further advanced than its critics usually realize." Skinner, *Beyond Freedom and Dignity,* p. 160.

30. The statement was made by Karl U. Smith of the University of Wisconsin in testimony before the Senate Subcommittee on Constitutional Rights, June 8, 1965, and quoted in *The American Psychologist* 20, no. 11 (November 1965): 911.

The list of standard commercially published "instruments" is vast: "social maturity" scales, "personality inventories," "dimensions of temperament" inventories, "psychological screening inventories," "infant intelligence scales," "employee attitude scales," tests of "behavioral rigidity," "social insight" tests, "adjustment inventories," "security-insecurity inventories," measures of "ego development," vocational preference scales, measures of dexterity, and hundreds of others.

31. Ibid.

32. The chronology and relationships are revealing:

1908: The American Breeders Association, organized five years earlier in response to Mendel's discoveries in genetics, establishes a Section on Eugenics and a Committee on Immigration. Henry H. Goddard translates the Binet intelligence test from the French and uses it to identify and study the "feeble-minded" in a training school in New Jersey. Clifford W. Beers publishes *A Mind That Found Itself,* the story of his three years in mental institutions and, later that year, founds the Connecticut Society for Mental Hygiene, thereby launching the mental-health movement in America.

1909: Freud comes to America to deliver lectures at Clark University, and the first American edition of Freud's work is published. In New York, Beers and others organize the National Committee for Mental Hygiene (now the National Association for Mental Health).

1911: Taylor's *Principles of Scientific Management* is published. A group of distinguished American lawyers and professors publishes an American edition of Lombroso's *Crime: Its Causes and Remedies,* which draws "analogies" between the "born criminal," the "moral imbecile," and the "epileptic";

describes the criminal as "a savage and at the same time a sick man"; lists the physical characteristics of the born criminal; and prescribes various forms of "penal treatment" for the different categories of criminals.

1912: The National Committee for Mental Hygiene urges Congress to "provide for adequate mental examination of immigrants." The committee names Dr. Thomas W. Salmon as its medical director. Dr. Salmon, who began his psychiatric career conducting mental examinations of immigrants at Ellis Island, had been among the first to study the relationship of insanity to the country from which the individual came.

1914: The First National Conference on Race Betterment, including some of the most important figures in American medicine, social science, and education, is held in Michigan. The purpose is to "assemble evidence as to the extent to which degenerative tendencies are actively at work in America, and to promote agencies for race betterment." Among the basic principles, according to Dr. Stephen Smith, conference president and vice-president of the New York State Board of Charities, are "the education of idiots," "the reform of criminals," and the "curative treatment of the insane."

*Proceedings of the First National Conference on Race Betterment* (Battle Creek, Mich.: The Race Betterment Foundation, 1914), pp. 5–22. On the origins of the mental-health movement, see Earl D. Bond, *Thomas W. Salmon, Psychiatrist* (New York: W. W. Norton and Co., 1950); Thomas W. Salmon, "Immigration and the Prevention of Insanity," *Boston Medical and Surgical Journal* 169, no. 9 (August 28, 1913): 297–301; Thomas W. Salmon, "Insanity and the Immigration Law," *State Hospital Bulletin* 4 (1911): 379–98; Jeanne L. Brand, "The National Mental Health Act of 1946: A Retrospect," *Bulletin of the History of Medicine* 39, no. 3 (May/June 1965): 231–47; Nina Ridenour, *Mental Health in the United States* (Cambridge, Mass.: Harvard University Press, 1961); and J. K. Hall, ed., *One Hundred Years of American Psychiatry* (New York: Columbia University Press, 1944).

On eugenics and genetics, see Henry H. Goddard, "Heredity of Feeble-Mindedness," *American Breeders Magazine* 1, no. 3 (1910): 62–73. On testing and eugenics, generally see Clarence J. Karier, "Testing for Order and Control in the Corporate Liberal State," *Educational Theory* 22 (Spring 1972): 155–80.

33. Karier, "Testing for Order"; *Official Proceedings of the Second National Conference on Race Betterment* (Battle Creek, Mich.: The Race Betterment Foundation, 1915); Lewis M. Terman, *The Measurement of Intelligence* (Boston: Houghton Mifflin Co., 1916), p. 11.

34. Edward L. Thorndike, "How May We Improve the Selection, Training and Life-Work of Leaders?" *Addresses Delivered Before the Fifth Conference on Educational Policies* (New York: Columbia University Press, 1939), p. 32.

35. The Garrett quote is from Henry E. Garrett, *Breeding Down* (Richmond, Va.: Patrick Henry Press, n. d.), p. 10. The pamphlet was circulated in 1966.

   The Goddard quote is from "The Levels of Intelligence," in Lionel D. Edie, ed., *Practical Psychology for Business Executives* (New York: H. W. Wilson Co., 1922), p. 48.

   The statement about the feeble-minded was made by H. H. Laughlin of the Committee on Sterilization of the Eugenics Record Office and is quoted in Mark H. Haller, *Eugenics* (New Brunswick, N. J.: Rutgers University Press, 1963), p. 133.

   The testers of the twenties and thirties were all certain that, as Thorndike said, "there is a substantial positive correlation between intelligence and morality. . . . No group of men can be expected to act one hundred per cent in the interest of mankind but [those superior in ability] will come nearest to the ideal." Thorndike, "How May We Improve the Selection," p. 32.)

36. Stephen Smith, "The Basic Principles of Race Betterment," *Proceedings of the First National Conference on Race Betterment,* pp. 10–11.

37. Henry Alden Bunker, "Psychiatry as a Specialty," in Hall, *One Hundred Years,* p. 494.

38. George S. Stevenson and Geddes Smith, *Child Guidance Clinics: A Quarter Century of Development* (New York: The Commonwealth Fund, 1934), p. 155.

**39.** Robert H. Felix, *Mental Illness* (New York: Columbia University Press, 1967), pp. 28–29. On World War I intelligence testing, see N. J. Block and Gerald Dworkin, *The IQ Controversy* (New York: Pantheon, 1976), pp. 4–44.

**40.** Leopold Bellak, "Toward Control of Today's 'Epidemic' of Mental Disease," *Medical World News,* 6 February 1970, p. 41. There have been scores of similar statements from "responsible" physicians, psychiatrists, and public officials. They will be discussed more extensively in Chapter Two.

**41.** On chromosome abnormalities, see, e. g., W. H. Price et al., "Criminal Behavior and the XYY Male," *Nature* 213 (1967): 815; P. A. Jacobs et al., "Aggressive Behavior, Mental Subnormality and the XYY Male," *Nature* 208 (1965): 1351; and M. D. Casey et al., "YY Chromosomes and Antisocial Behavior," *Lancet* 2 (1966): 859.

On brain-wave patterns, see Mark and Ervin, *Violence and the Brain;* and E. Rodin, "Psychomotor Epilepsy and Aggressive Behavior," *Archives of General Psychiatry* 28 (February 1973): 210–13.

On hyperactivity and crime, see Allen Berman, "Learning Disabilities and Juvenile Delinquency: A Neuropsychological Approach" (Paper presented at the Regional Conference of the Association for Children with Learning Disabilities, Los Angeles, February 2, 1973); and William Mulligan, "Dyslexia, Specific Learning Disability and Delinquency," *Juvenile Justice,* November 1972. On child abuse, see Chapter Seven.

**42.** Jacques Ellul, *The Technological Society* (New York: Vintage Books, 1964), p. 398.

> The psychotechnicians have recognized that adaptation is not possible for everyone. In a completely technicized world, there will be whole categories of men who will have no place at all, because universal adaptation will be required. Those who are adaptable will be so rigorously adapted that no play in the complex will be possible. The complete joining of man and machine will have the advantage, however, of making the adaptation painless.

**43.** Noam Chomsky, "Psychology and Ideology," in *For Reasons of State* (New York: Pantheon, 1973), p. 337.

**44.** Chomsky, "Psychology and Ideology," p. 363. There is nothing mysterious about the process of relabeling socially or culturally deviant behavior in medical terms; once the labels are there, whole pseudoscientific systems replete with statistical machinery are set up. But the statistics can have no meaning, since the terms they serve are themselves meaningless and elude scientific validation.

**45.** Interview with Skinner. See note 15.

## Chapter Two

**1.** *Staffing of Mental Health Facilities* (Washington, D. C.: National Institute of Mental Health, 1974), p. 16. NIMH lists a total of 454,000 mental-health workers for 1974, with a full-time equivalent of 403,000. These numbers do not include psychiatrists, psychologists, and social workers in private office practice. According to the 1970 census, there were 340,000 police officers.

**2.** Frank J. Ayd, Jr., "The Impact of Biological Psychiatry," in Frank J. Ayd, Jr., and Barry Blackwell, eds., *Discoveries in Biological Psychiatry* (Philadelphia: J. B. Lippincott Co., 1970), p. 232.

**3.** National figures for prescription drugs are derived from Hugh J. Parry et al., "National Patterns of Psychiatric Drug Use," *Archives of General Psychiatry* 28 (June 1973): 769–83; Glen D. Mellinger et al., "Psychic Distress, Life Crisis and Drug Use: National Drug Survey Data" (Paper of the Institute for Research in Social Behavior, Berkeley, Cal., 1974); Mellinger et al., "An Overview of Psychotherapeutic Drug Use in the United States," in Eric Josephson and Eleanor E. Carroll, eds., *Drug Use: Epidemiological and Sociological Approaches* (New York: Hemisphere Publishing Corp., 1974); Herbert I. Abelson and Ronald B. Atkinson, *Public Experience with Psychoactive Substances* (Princeton, N.J.: Response Analysis Corp., 1975); "Tranquilizer Usage" in *NDTI Review*, June 1973, pp. 1–2; and the *National Prescription Audit* for 1975 (Ambler, Pa.: IMS America, Ltd., 1976), a confidential survey of the drug market based on pharmacy prescriptions. IMS also publishes a *National Hospital Audit* of drugs used in hospitals (not included in the figures cited in the text) and the *National*

*Disease and Therapeutic Index,* based on drug "mentions" in periodic surveys of physicians. The IMS figures, not available to the general public or in libraries, are regarded as the most reliable in existence, although even they have been challenged as being based on inadequate samples. The federal government collects no prescription-drug data of its own (other than gross Commerce Department figures for shipments in broad categories). The Food and Drug Administration uses IMS data. For a general discussion of prescribing patterns, see also Milton Silverman and Philip R. Lee, *Pills, Profits and Politics* (Berkeley: University of California Press, 1974); Henry Lennard, *Mystification and Drug Misuse* (New York: Harper and Row, 1972); and the reports of the Task Force on Prescription Drugs of the Department of Health, Education and Welfare, and the U. S. Senate Subcommittee on Monopoly.

4. Darrel A. Regier and Irving D. Goldberg, "National Health Insurance and the Mental Health Services Equilibrium" (Paper presented at the American Psychiatric Association annual meeting, Miami, Fla., May 13, 1976. It has long been established that nonpsychiatrists prescribe more psychoactive medication than psychiatrists. In their survey, Regier and Goldberg also found that 67.3 percent of office visits to nonpsychiatrists who make a "principal diagnosis of mental disorder" involve a drug prescription as part of the treatment, while "drug therapy" is involved in less than half of all office visits to psychiatrists.

5. Parry et al., "National Patterns of Psychiatric Drug Use."

6. The figures are from the American Psychiatric Association. Whenever Congress talks about reducing money for training grants, the APA and its members issue warnings that serious shortages will develop in professional manpower which will have to be filled by foreign-trained doctors.

7. The data on "episodes" are from the NIMH *Statistical Notes* and other information supplied in interviews or published by the Survey and Reports Section of the NIMH Biometry Branch. The data on the percentage of psychiatrists who work for public agencies is from Robert F. Lockman, "Nationwide Study Yields Profile of Psychiatrists," *Psychiatric News* 1, no. 2 (January 1968): 1.

8. Steven S. Sharfstein, Carl A. Taube, and Irving D. Goldberg,

"Private Psychiatry and Accountability: A Response to the APA Task Force on Private Practice," *American Journal of Psychiatry* 132, no. 1 (January 1975): 43–47.

9. Brand, "The National Mental Health Act of 1946: A Retrospect," p. 237.

10. Felix, *Mental Illness,* p. 29.

11. By 1975, the total NIMH budget was $420 million, but that did not include $220 million for the National Institute of Drug Abuse, $134 million for the National Institute on Alcohol Abuse and Alcoholism, and $50 million for the operation of St. Elizabeth's Hospital, the government's mental hospital in Washington. The Vannevar Bush estimate is in his *Endless Frontier: A Report to the President* (Washington, D. C.: U. S. Government Printing Office, 1945), p. 1.

12. John F. Kennedy, *Message from the President Relative to Mental Illness and Mental Retardation,* 88th Cong., 1st sess., 1963, H. Rep. Doc. No. 58, p. 2.

13. Gerald Caplan, *Principles of Preventive Psychiatry* (New York: Basic Books, 1964), pp. 94–95.

14. Leopold Bellak, *Handbook of Community Psychiatry and Community Mental Health* (New York: Grune and Stratton, 1964), p. 459. Bellak, among other things, advocates "legislated psychotherapy." His book is dedicated to John F. Kennedy, who gave America "a Magna Carta of Community Mental Health. . . . The campaigns of his lifetime as well as his tragic death bear testimony that we can ill afford political lunacy of any kind."

Harold Visotsky, "Social Psychiatry Rationale: Administrative and Planning Approaches," *American Journal of Psychiatry* 121 (November 1964): 434; Stanley Yolles, "Community Mental Health: Issues and Policies," *American Journal of Psychiatry* 122 (March 1966): 980.

The Bertram Brown statement is quoted from Franklin D. Chu and Sharland Trotter, *The Madness Establishment* (New York: Grossman, 1974), p. 13.

15. Quoted in David F. Musto, "Whatever Happened to 'Community Mental Health'?" *The Public Interest,* no. 35 (Spring 1974): 55.

16. For the Yolles statement, see *Hearings on Community Mental*

*Health Centers Act Before the Subcommittee on Public Health and Welfare of the Committee on Interstate and Foreign Commerce, November 18–20, 1969* (Washington, D. C.: U. S. Government Printing Office, 1970), p. 38.

For the Brown statement, see *Hearings Before a Subcommittee of the Committee on Appropriations, House of Representatives, Departments of Labor and Health, Education and Welfare Appropriations for 1973, March 8, 1972, Part III* (Washington, D. C.: U. S. Government Printing Office, 1972), p. 97.

The statement about "breaking the back of the asylum system" was made by NIMH official Frank Ochberg in a telephone interview in June 1976.

17. The average pharmacy prescription for Thorazine provides for an 18-day supply; figures for other drugs are comparable. Thus, a total of some 60 million prescriptions for antipsychotics, antidepressants, and combinations of the two (which, according to the best available figures, were written in 1975) would be enough to supply 3 million people full-time.

18. The data were obtained in interviews with officials of the organizations involved. The Los Angeles clinics budgeted more than $1 million for medication in 1975 for some 194,000 patient "contacts," or units, each of which could be a visit or telephone call, or enough money to buy the equivalent of one prescription every time a person walked into a clinic. In San Francisco, officials estimated that 52 percent of all outpatients received medication.

19. Paul Lowinger et al., "Does the Race, Religion or Social Class of the Psychiatric Patient Affect His Treatment?" in J. Masserman, ed., *Science and Psychoanalysis* (New York: Grune and Stratton, 1966), pp. 129–47. See also Paul Lowinger and Shirley Dobie, "The Attitudes of the Psychiatrist About His Patient," *Comprehensive Psychiatry* 9, no. 6 (November 1968): 627–32; and Herbert S. Gross et al., "The Effect of Race and Sex on the Variation of Diagnosis and Disposition in a Psychiatric Emergency Room," *The Journal of Nervous and Mental Disease* 148, no. 6 (1969): 638–42, which concludes that "as the sociocultural distance between the clinician and his patient increases, diagnoses become less accurate and dispositions more nonspecific."

**20.** Joan H. Cole, "Institutional Racism in a Community Mental Health Center" (Ph.D. diss., The Wright Institute, 1975), pp. 229–30.

**21.** The information is from Health Applications Systems, Inc., (HAS) of Burlingame, California, which has contracts to process portions of the Medicaid programs in Arkansas, Florida, North Carolina, parts of California, parts of Colorado, and several other states.

**22.** The California Medi-Cal data are on file in the library of the State Health Department, Sacramento; they are broken down by drug, number of prescriptions, cost, and number of "dosage units." Significantly, while the total volume of all drugs prescribed under Medi-Cal and Medicaid is proportionately somewhat higher than that for the rest of the population, it is only certain psychotropics, and particularly the phenothiazines, which are prescribed at rates three or four times that of the general population. Part of that disproportion may be accounted for by the fact that in California, the Medi-Cal figures include medication in nursing homes, which, according to one U. S. Senate survey, includes an average of $60 worth of tranquilizers (roughly ten prescriptions) per year per inmate. For a summary of the California data, see "Medi-Cal Prescriptions by Therapy Class," in *Data Matters* (Sacramento: California Center for Health Statistics, February 5, 1976).

**23.** Cole, "Institutional Racism in a Community Mental Health Center," pp. 229–30.

**24.** U. S. Bureau of the Census, *Census of the Population, 1950* 4, Special Reports, Part 2, "Institutional Population" (Washington, D. C.: U. S. Government Printing Office, 1953), tables 4 –10; and *Census of the Population, 1970,* Subject Reports, "Persons in Institutions and Other Group Quarters" (Washington, D. C.: U. S. Government Printing Office, 1973), tables 4 –10.

**25.** Andrea Sallychild, *"Mental Health in California, An Orientation with Policy Implications"* (Internal report of the California State Health Department, February 9, 1976), p. 8.

**26.** For a discussion of the "latent functions" of drug prescribing, see Lennard, *Mystification and Drug Misuse,* pp. 26–30.

**27.** U.S. Senate Special Subcommittee on Aging, *Drugs in Nursing*

*Homes: Misuse, High Costs and Kickbacks* (Washington, D. C.: U. S. Government Printing Office, 1975).

**28.** Thomas R. Fulda, *Prescription Drug Data Summary* (Washington, D. C.: U. S. Department of Health, Education and Welfare, 1976), pp. 15, 20. Public funds—including state and local sources—accounted for $2.9 billion of the total $6.2 billion spent for prescription drugs in the United States in 1974.

## Chapter Three

**1.** *DSM–II: Diagnostic and Statistical Manual of Mental Disorders* (Washington, D. C.: The American Psychiatric Association, 1968), p. 51.

**2.** Karl Menninger, "Sheer Verbal Mickey Mouse," *International Journal of Psychiatry* 7, no. 6 (1969): 415. This issue of the journal was devoted to a discussion of the new edition of *DSM* and includes analyses and criticism of its categories and definitions.

**3.** The hearing was conducted May 1975 in the Family Division of the Superior Court of the District of Columbia. The client was an inmate confined to St. Elizabeth's Hospital, the NIMH-operated mental institution in Washington, who was moving for his release.

**4.** Thomas S. Szasz, *The Manufacture of Madness* (New York: Dell, 1970), p. 208. See also Thomas S. Szasz, *The Myth of Mental Illness* (New York: Harper and Row, 1974). For similar analyses, see E. Fuller Torrey, *The Death of Psychiatry* (New York: Penguin, 1975); Phil Brown, ed., *Radical Psychology* (New York: Harper Colophon, 1973); and R. D. Laing, *The Politics of Experience* (New York: Pantheon, 1966).

   Among the best critiques of the "myth" position is Michael S. Moore, "Some Myths About 'Mental Illness,' " *Archives of General Psychiatry* 32 (December 1975): 1483–97.

**5.** Szasz, *The Myth of Mental Illness,* p. 12.

**6.** Ivan Illich, *Medical Nemesis* (New York: Pantheon, 1976), p. 169.

**7.** Szasz, *The Manufacture of Madness,* pp. 38–39; Karl Menninger, *The Vital Balance* (New York: Viking Press, 1963); pp. 27–28.

8. See, e. g., William C. Menninger, *Psychiatry in a Troubled World: Yesterday's War and Today's Challenge* (New York: The Macmillan Co., 1948). The quotation is from Joseph Ziskin's review in the *Journal of Nervous and Mental Disease* 112 (September 1950): 270–71. In the generation since Menninger's book was published, there has developed a general consensus, even among the evangelists, that Menninger's criteria and definitions were off base and that they misidentified thousands of cases. The British Army, with a much lower rate of psychiatric rejections for military service, suffered no higher rate of psychiatric problems among its troops.

9. *Schizophrenia: A Multinational Study* (Geneva: World Health Organization, 1975), p. 28. See also Morton Kramer, "Cross-National Study of Diagnosis of the Mental Disorders: Origin of the Problem," *American Journal of Psychiatry* 125, Supp. (April 1969): 1–12; and other papers in the same issue.

10. Loren R. Mosher et al., "Special Report: Schizophrenia, 1972," *Schizophrenia Bulletin,* no. 7 (Winter 1973): 34, 21. The basic study, conducted in Denmark by American researchers with NIMH funds, indicates a genetic (and therefore biochemical) source of schizophrenia. The study is reported in Seymour S. Kety et al., "Mental Illness in the Biological and Adoptive Families of Adopted Schizophrenics," *American Journal of Psychiatry* 128, no. 3 (1971): 302–06; and David Rosenthal, *Genetic Theory and Abnormal Behavior* (New York: McGraw-Hill, 1970). The genetic connection, however, has been argued for only 10 percent of the cases, leading some researchers to conclude that there may be a "genetic predisposition" to schizophrenia, which, in most cases, never manifests itself.

   The most comprehensive recent text on schizophrenia is Silvano Arieti, *Interpretation of Schizophrenia* (New York: Basic Books, 1975). The most concise attack on the mythic function of "schizophrenia"—the way the label is used as the ultimate justification for psychiatric intervention and the imposition of unwanted treatment on involuntary patients—is Thomas Szasz's *Schizophrenia: The Sacred Symbol of Psychiatry* (New York: Basic Books, 1976).

11. William T. Carpenter, Jr., "Current Diagnostic Concepts in

Schizophrenia," *American Journal of Psychiatry* 133, no. 2 (February 1976): 175.

12. On psychiatric labeling of Goldwater's politics, see pp. 62–63. On Soviet psychiatry, see Vladimir Bukovsky and Semyon Gluzman, *Manual of Psychiatry for Political Dissidents* (New York: Amnesty International, 1976); on residual labeling, see Thomas J. Scheff, "Schizophrenia as Ideology," *Schizophrenia Bulletin,* no. 1 (Fall 1970): 15–20.

13. Nathan S. Kline, *From Sad to Glad* (New York: Ballantine Books, 1975), p. 12; Steven K. Secunda, *The Depressive Disorders, Special Report: 1973* (Washington, D. C.: NIMH, 1973), p. 3; and Ronald R. Fieve, "The Lithium Clinic: A New Model for the Delivery of Psychiatric Services," *American Journal of Psychiatry* 132, no. 10 (October 1975): 1019.

14. Secunda, *The Depressive Disorders, Special Report: 1973,* pp. 1, 41.

15. *Statistical Note 81* (Washington, D. C.: NIMH Biometry Branch, 1973). In 1970, while the number of admissions to mental institutions, including outpatient clinics, was roughly the same for men as for women, the number of men admitted for "depressive disorders" was 119,000; the number of women admitted with such a diagnosis was 277,000. The diagnosis in which men outnumbered women in the greatest proportion was "alcohol disorders."

16. D. Williams, "The Menopause," *British Medical Journal,* no. 2 (April 24, 1971): 208.

17. Sonja M. McKinlay and John B. McKinlay, "Selected Studies of the Menopause," *Journal of Biosocial Science* 5 (1973): 536, 535. Reviewing scores of studies, the McKinlays conclude that "of the research reported, the predominant characteristics are poor planning and design and a general lack of interest in providing comparable or consistent data, with which to augment fragmentary knowledge."

18. Phyllis Chesler, *Women and Madness* (New York: Doubleday, 1972).

19. Pauline B. Bart, "The Sociology of Depression," in Paul Roman and Harrison Trice, eds., *Perspectives in Psychiatric Sociology* (New York: Science House, 1971), p. 149. See also

Pauline B. Bart, "Depression in Middle Aged Women," in Vivian Gornick and Barbara K. Moran, eds., *Women in Sexist Society* (New York: Basic Books, 1971); and Yehudi A. Cohen, ed., *Social Structure and Personality* (New York: Holt, Rinehart and Winston, 1961), pp. 477–85.

20. David L. Rosenhan, "On Being Sane in Insane Places," *Science* 179 (January 19, 1973): 250–58.

21. Ibid., p. 253.

22. Ibid., p. 252.

23. Ibid. For a related discussion, see Scheff, "Schizophrenia as Ideology," pp. 15–20.

24. Arrah Evarts, "Dementia Praecox in the Colored Race," *Psychoanalytic Review* 1 (1913): 396. The report of the Massachusetts Commission on Lunacy is quoted in N. Dain, *Concepts of Insanity in the United States, 1789–1865* (New Brunswick, N. J.: Rutgers University Press, 1964), p. 68.

25. Horatio M. Pollock, "Dementia Praecox in Relation to Sex, Age, Environment, Nativity and Race," *Mental Hygiene* 10, no. 3 (July 1926): 596–611.

26. Bruce P. Dohrenwend and Barbara D. Dohrenwend, *Social Status and Psychological Disorder* (New York: Wiley Interscience, 1969), pp. 9–31. The Hollingshead study is found in August B. Hollingshead and Fred C. Redlich, *Social Class and Mental Illness* (New York: Wiley, 1958).

27. The Midtown Study is reported in Leo Srole et al., *Mental Health in the Metropolis* (New York: McGraw-Hill, 1964); the estimate on family pathology is in N. J. Cole et al., "Mental Illness," *AMA Archives of Neurology and Psychiatry* 77 (1957): 393–98.

28. Dohrenwend and Dohrenwend, *Social Status and Psychological Disorder,* pp. 61–68.

29. Ibid., p. 77.

30. Ibid., pp. 171, 175, 60.

31. The literature on black-white differences is reviewed and analyzed in Joel Fischer, "Negroes and Whites and Rates of Mental Illness: Reconsideration of a Myth," *Psychiatry, Journal for the Study of Interpersonal Processes* 32, no. 4 (November 1969): 428–46.

For analyses of bias in diagnosis and treatment, see Thomas J. Scheff, "Social Conditions for Rationality: How Urban and Rural Counties Deal with the Mentally Ill," in Thomas J. Scheff, ed., *Mental Illness and Social Processes* (New York: Harper and Row, 1967); Lowinger and Dobie, "The Attitudes of the Psychiatrist About His Patient"; and Gross et al., "The Effect of Race and Sex."

The Baltimore study is reported in Benjamin Pasamanick, "Some Misconceptions Concerning Differences in the Racial Prevalence of Mental Disease," *American Journal of Orthopsychiatry* 33 (1963): 72–86; and the observation about changing social conditions, based on another literature review, is from Melvin L. Kohn, "Social Class and Schizophrenia: A Critical Review and a Reformulation," *Schizophrenia Bulletin,* no. 7 (Winter 1973): 73.

**32.** A. J. Rosanoff, "Survey of Mental Disorders in Nassau County, New York: July–October 1916," *Psychiatric Bulletin* 2 (1917): 109–231; G. M. Carstairs and G. W. Brown, "A Census of Psychiatric Cases in Two Contrasting Communities," *Journal of Mental Science* 104 (1958): 72–81.

**33.** Milton Mazer, "Two Ways of Expressing Psychological Disorder: The Experience of a Demarcated Population," *American Journal of Psychiatry* 128, no. 8 (February 1972): 48. See also Milton Mazer, "Parapsychiatric Events as Expressions of Psychiatric Disorder," *Archives of General Psychiatry* 27 (August 1972): 270–73; and Milton Mazer, "Characteristics of Multi-Problem Households," *American Journal of Orthopsychiatry* 42, no. 5 (October 1972): 792–802.

**34.** Milton Mazer, "Concepts of Prevention in Rural Mental Health Services" (Paper read at Summer Study Program in Rural Mental Health, University of Wisconsin Extension, Madison, June 3–7, 1974), pp. 2, 4.

## Chapter Four

**1.** *Alameda County (California) Plan for Mental Health Services, 1975–76* (Oakland: Alameda County Health Care Services Agency, 1975), p. 237.

**2.** *Returning the Mentally Disabled to the Community* (Washington, D.C.: U. S. General Accounting Office, 1977). See also

Pam Moore, "GAO Urges Greater Effort on Community Care," *APA Monitor* 8, no. 2 (February 1977): 1, from which my summary is quoted.

3. *Alameda County Plan,* p. 238.

4. Jack Parker is a pseudonym. The case is from a hearing before a judge of the California Superior Court in Oakland. In theory, such hearings are closed, but until I sat unnoticed through a session involving ten or a dozen cases, the issue had never been raised. Apparently no reporter has ever tried to cover such proceedings.

5. Joan Smith is a pseudonym. The quotation is from a letter to *Madness Network News* 3, no. 4 (December 1975): 4. The *News* is a publication of the Network Against Psychiatric Assault (NAPA), an organization of ex-mental patients, psychiatrists, and others.

6. *In re Union Camp Corporation and International Brotherhood of Pulp, Sulphite and Paper Mill Workers, Local 435,* 59 LAB. ARB. 127, 127–34 (1972). Matt Collins is a pseudonym; the other names are real.

7. Ibid., p. 133.

8. The Robert Friedman story is from *Mental Health Law Project: Summary of Activities* (Washington, D.C.: Mental Health Law Project, December 1975): 1; " 'Wealthy Beggar' Asks $350,000 in Suit Against Psychiatrist," *Chicago Daily News,* 3–4 January 1976; " 'Wealthy Beggar' Buried," *Chicago Tribune,* 8 April 1976; and Joel Klein, "In His Best Interest: Robert Friedman and Involuntary Psychiatric Hospitalization" (Unpublished paper available from Mental Health Law Project); the story of the enuretic woman in New York is from Bruce Ennis, *Prisoners of Psychiatry* (New York: Avon, 1972), pp. 148–62; the story of the applicant for public housing in Oakland is from interviews with workers at the Alameda County Mental Health Service; and the quotation about suicides is from an internal report of the same system.

9. Lucy D. Ozarin, Richard W. Redick, and Carl A. Taube, *Psychiatric Care: A Quarter Century of Change* (Rockville, Md.: NIMH, n. d.).

10. The Bellak quote is from Bellak, "Toward Control of Today's

'Epidemic' of Mental Disease," p. 41. The Kubie quote is from Lawrence S. Kubie, "Commitment," *Psychiatric News,* 21 March 1973, p. 2.

On psychiatric screening, see, e. g., Seymour F. Kuvin and David B. Saxe, "Psychiatric Examination for Judges," *The New York Times,* 21 December 1975; and Alan C. Elms, *Personality and Politics* (New York: Harcourt Brace Jovanovich, 1976).

On Goldwater, see "The Unconscious of a Conservative," *Fact* 1, no. 5 (1964): 55.

On the environmental impact proposal, see Ralph Catalano and John Monahan, "The Community Psychologist as Social Planner," *American Journal of Community Psychology* 3, no. 4 (December 1975): 327–34.

11. *Alameda County Plan,* p. 97.

12. Richard A. Cloward and Frances Fox Piven, "Notes Toward a Radical Social Work," in Roy Bailey and Mike Brake, eds., *Radical Social Work* (New York: Pantheon, 1976), pp. xlii, xxvi.

13. Perpich, *Behavior Modification in Institutional Settings: A Critique,* 17 ARIZ. L. REV. 33, 35–36 (1975).

14. For the Evanston program, see "Employment Agency Gets MH Help," *Innovations* 1, no. 4 (Fall 1974): 31; for the New York City recreation program, see Cloward and Piven, "Notes Toward a Radical Social Work," pp. xlii–xlvi; for the Denver program, see Richard R. Polak et al., "Prevention in Mental Health: A Controlled Study," *American Journal of Psychiatry* 132, no. 2 (February 1975): 146–48. The data on the program in San Jose are from interviews.

15. Most of these categories are standard items on diagnostic schedules of symptoms of recent psychiatric events: the *Schedule of Recent Experience,* the *Global Assessment Scale,* and others.

16. Cole, "Institutional Racism in a Community Mental Health Center," p. 254. Jose Ramirez is a pseudonym.

17. The McGuire story is from a case record in a California clinic. The name and some other details of her personal history have been changed to conceal her identity. The medical history and the quotations from the clinicians' entries are taken directly from the record.

18. Polak et al., "Prevention in Mental Health: A Controlled Study," p. 147.

19. B. L. Bloom, "The Evaluation of Primary Prevention Programs," in L. M. Roberts, N. S. Greenfield, and M. H. Miller, eds., *Comprehensive Mental Health* (Madison: University of Wisconsin Press, 1968), p. 167.

20. Melvin J. Steinhart, "The Selling of Community Mental Health," *Psychiatric Quarterly* 47, no. 3 (1973): 331; Albert C. Cain, "The Perils of Prevention," *American Journal of Orthopsychiatry* 37 (1964): 640. For a general discussion, see also Musto, "Whatever Happened to 'Community Mental Health'?" pp. 53–79.

21. For the Tacoma program, see "Had Your Yearly Stress Checkup?" *Innovations* 1, no. 4 (Fall 1974): 21. The "Sane Asylum" proposal was made by Darold A. Treffert at the annual meeting of the American Psychiatric Association, May 1976, and reported in *Behavior Today,* 17 May 1976, p. 5. The quotes about "psychic tension" are from current advertisements in the *American Journal of Psychiatry.*

22. Interview with Szasz, May 1976.

23. For a general review of commitment laws, see S. Brakel and R. Rock, *The Mentally Disabled and the Law* (Chicago: University of Chicago Press, 1971); and Alan A. Stone, *Mental Health and the Law: A System in Transition* (Rockville, Md.: NIMH, 1975), pp. 43–82.

24. Thomas J. Scheff, "The Societal Reaction to Deviance: Ascriptive Elements in the Psychiatric Screening of Mental Patients in a Midwestern State," *Social Problems* 11 (1964): 401–13. The conclusions about the dedication of attorneys and other professionals in hearings are from my own observations of such hearings and from interviews with participants.

   For the study of visitors to the "Patient's Rights Office" (itself an unusual institution), see David S. Jensen, "Personality Characteristics of State Hospital Patients' Rights Office Visitors," *Journal of Clinical Psychology* 30, no. 3 (July 1974): 347–49.

25. On the prediction of dangerousness, see E. Wenk, James O. Robison, and Gerald Smith, "Can Violence Be Predicted?" *Crime and Delinquency* 18 (1972): 393; Jeanne M. Giovanni and Lee Gurel, "Socially Disruptive Behavior of Ex-Mental

Patients," *Archives of General Psychiatry* 17 (1967): 146–53; Horatio M. Pollock, "Is the Paroled Patient a Menace to the Community?" *Psychiatric Quarterly* 39 (1965): 236–44; and Henry J. Steadman and Gary Keveles, "The Community Adjustment and Criminal Activity of the Baxstrom Patients," *American Journal of Psychiatry* 129 (1973): 304–10.

26. Harry L. Kozol, Richard J. Boucher, and Ralph L. Garafalo, "The Diagnosis and Treatment of Dangerousness," *Crime and Delinquency* 18 (1972): 371–92.

27. Stone, *Mental Health and the Law: A System in Transition,* p. 32.

28. Henry J. Steadman, "The Psychiatrist as A Conservative Agent of Social Control," *Social Problems* 20, no. 2 (1973): 263.

29. Stone, *Mental Health and the Law: A System in Transition,* p. 33; Bernard L. Diamond, *The Psychiatric Prediction of Dangerousness,* 123 U. PENN. L. REV. 439, 447 (1974).

30. Robert A. Burt, *Of Mad Dogs and Scientists: The Perils of the "Criminal Insane,"* 123 U. PENN. L. REV. 258, 278 (1974).

31. Cross v. Harris, 418 F.2d 1095 (1969).

32. Interview with Dershowitz, May 1976.

33. David L. Bazelon, "Follow the Yellow Brick Road," *American Journal of Orthopsychiatry* 40, no. 4 (July 1970): 562–67.

34. D.R. Lunts, "The Theory and Practice of Forensic-Psychiatric Diagnosis," cited in Bukovsky and Gluzman, *Manual of Psychiatry for Political Dissidents,* p. 7.

## Chapter Five

1. On drug maintenance, see Lester Grinspoon et al., "Psychotherapy and Pharmacotherapy," *American Journal of Psychiatry* 126 (1969): 1641–52, which concludes that while the drugs reduce symptoms, "all of these patients are still schizophrenic, and there is no evidence that any enduring or fundamental change has been achieved by medication."

   On the comparative effects of drugs and talking therapy, see E. H. Uhlenhuth et al., "Combined Pharmacotherapy and Psychotherapy," *Journal of Nervous and Mental Disease* 148, no. 1 (1969): 52–64, which reviews controlled studies published between 1950 and 1969 comparing the two modes. "From a practical point of view," the authors conclude,

> these studies consistently suggest that combined treatment is superior to psychotherapy alone, but not to pharmacotherapy alone. From a theoretical point of view, these studies suggest that the effect of two treatment interventions combined is the same as the effect of the more effective intervention alone. Unfortunately, this point remains highly tentative because of limitations in the design and execution of the available studies.

2. See, e. g., Leo E. Hollister, "Uses of Psychotherapeutic Drugs," *Annals of Internal Medicine* 79 (1973): 88–98.

3. Lennard et al., *Mystification and Drug Misuse,* p. 81. For the "radical" position on drug effects see, e. g., David Richman, "Dr. Caligari," in *Psychiatric Drugs* (San Francisco: The Network Against Psychiatric Assault, 1976). The "establishment" viewpoint is ubiquitous in the major psychiatric journals and in periodicals like the *International Drug Therapy Newsletter.*

4. Henry L. Lennard et al., "Hazards Implicit in Prescribing Psychoactive Drugs," *Science* 169 (July 31, 1970): 439. See also David J. Greenblatt and Richard I. Shader, "Rational Use of Psychotropic Drugs, III. Major Tranquilizers," *American Journal of Hospital Pharmacy* 31 (December 1974): 1229; and David J. Greenblatt and Richard I. Shader, "Rational Use of Psychotropic Drugs, II. Antianxiety Agents," *American Journal of Hospital Pharmacy* 31 (November 1974): 1079. Greenblatt and Shader reflect the conventional view about the differing effects of various drugs. Major tranquilizers, they say, "are no more effective than [minor tranquilizers] in patients with neurotic anxiety. Furthermore, the side effects of major tranquilizers are much more serious and frequent" and can "influence the function of almost every organ system in the body." Many other writers believe that the major tranquilizers have no effect on anxiety other than their general tendency to sedate anyone who takes them and, in so doing, may actually exacerbate anxiety by reducing the individual's ability to function.

5. Testimony of Janet Gotkin and Wade Hudson Before the Senate Subcommittee to Investigate Juvenile Delinquency, August 18, 1975, in *Drugs in Institutions: Hearings Before the*

*Subcommittee to Investigate Juvenile Delinquency* (Washington, D.C. Government Printing Office, 1977), pp. 14–15, 33. For other accounts, see also Theodore Van Puten, "Why Do Schizophrenic Patients Refuse to Take Their Drugs?" *Archives of General Psychiatry* 31 (July 1974): 70.

6. Frederick H. Meyers et al., *Review of Medical Pharmacology* (Los Altos, Cal.: Lange Medical Publications, 1968), pp. 298, 300; Frank M. Berger, "Depression and Antidepressant Drugs," *Clinical Pharmacology and Therapeutics* 18, no. 3 (September 1975): 243.

7. *DAWN 2 Analysis,* p. 5.

8. Pierre Deniker, "Introduction of Neuroleptic Chemotherapy into Psychiatry," in Ayd and Blackwell, eds., *Discoveries in Biological Psychiatry,* p. 157.

9. Ayd, "The Impact of Biological Psychiatry," pp. 232–33.

10. Frank M. Berger, "Meprobamate: Its Pharmacologic Properties and Clinical Uses," *International Record of Medicine and General Practice Clinics* 169 (1956): 184–96; Frank M. Berger, "The Chemistry and Mode of Action of Tranquilizing Drugs," *Annals of the New York Academy of Science* 67 (1957): 685–700; Frank M. Berger, "The Tranquilizer Decade," *Journal of Neuropsychiatry* 5 (1964): 403–10; V. G. Laites and B. Weiss, "A Critical Review of the Efficacy of Meprobamate (Miltown, Equanil) in the Treatment of Anxiety," *Journal of Chronic Diseases* 7 (1958): 500–19; J. C. Borrus, "Study of Effect of Miltown on Psychiatric States," *Journal of the American Medical Association* 157 (1955): 1596–98.

In reviewing just the literature for meprobamate alone, Greenblatt and Shader found that various writers had claimed the drug would provide symptomatic relief for alcoholism, allergies, angina pectoris, appendicitis, asthma, behavior disorders in children, depression, dermatologic disorders, glaucoma, hypertension, intractable pain, labor and delivery, menopause, menstrual stress, motion sickness, petit mal epilepsy, stuttering, typhoid fever, and a half dozen other ailments. David J. Greenblatt and Richard I. Shader, "Meprobamate: A Study of Irrational Drug Use," *American Journal of Psychiatry* 127, no. 10 (1971): 34.

11. The ads are ubiquitous in the *American Journal of Psychiatry, Psychiatric News* (both publications of the American Psychiatric Association), and in many other psychiatric journals. For

discussions of the issue, see Robert Seidenberg, "Drug Advertising and Perception of Mental Illness," *Mental Hygiene* 55, no. 1 (January 1971): 21–31; and Frank A. Smith et al., "Health Information During a Week of Television," *The New England Journal of Medicine* 286, no. 10 (March 9, 1972): 516–20.

On drug promotion generally, see Silverman and Lee, *Pills, Profits and Politics,* pp. 48–80; Lennard et al., "Hazards Implicit in Prescribing Psychoactive Drugs"; and Lennard, *Mystification and Drug Use.*

12. Allen Raskin et al., "Differential Response to Chlorpromazine, Imipramine, and Placebo," *Archives of General Psychiatry* 23 (1970): 172. Raskin's study, involving some 535 patients in ten hospitals around the country, also found that women under 40 were helped most by placebo and concluded that for "many depressed patients, drugs play a minor role in influencing the course of their illness." Improvement was judged on the basis of a battery of scales which, like most such scales, are based on ratings of staff and self-ratings by patients. The collaborative studies are reported in the National Institute of Mental Health, Psychopharmacology Service Center, Collaborative Study Group, *Archives of General Psychiatry* 10 (1964): 246; and in Albert Di Mascio and Richard I. Shader, eds., *Clinical Handbook of Psychopharmacology* (New York: Science House, 1970), pp. 343–86.

On the effects of Thorazine and other phenothiazines on relapse rates and recidivism, see W. Tuteur et al., "The Discharged Mental Hospital Chlorpromazine Patient," *Diseases of the Nervous System* 20 (1959): 512–17; M. Gross, "The Impact of Ataractic Drugs on a Mental Hospital Outpatient Clinic," *American Journal of Psychiatry* 117 (1960): 444 – 47; and George Gardos and Jonathan O. Cole, "Maintenance Antipsychotic Therapy: Is the Cure Worse Than the Disease?" *American Journal of Psychiatry* 133 (January 1976): 32–36.

For a review of research on antidepressants, see Jeffrey B. Morris and Aaron T. Beck, "The Efficacy of Antidepressant Drugs," *Archives of General Psychiatry* 30 (May 1974): 667–73.

13. Gardos and Cole, "Maintenance Antipsychotic Therapy," pp. 33–34. In reviewing a number of studies, Gardos and Cole

noted that "drug failures appeared to have a considerably higher rehospitalization rate than placebo relapsers," a phenomenon they suggest may be attributable to the fact that "patients who relapse on medication are sicker than placebo relapsers." If one neglects the redundancy of the inference, the question is why? Are they "sicker" despite the drugs or because of the drugs?

14. William T. Carpenter, Jr., Thomas H. McGlashan, and John S. Strauss, "The Treatment of Acute Schizophrenia Without Drugs: An Investigation of Some Current Assumptions," *American Journal of Psychiatry* 134, no. 7 (1977): 14 –20.

15. Maurice Rappaport et al., "Schizophrenics for Whom Phenothiazines May Be Contraindicated or Unnecessary" (Unpublished study, Agnews State Hospital Research Department, San Jose, Cal., 1975). A summary of the study is available from the Network Against Psychiatric Assault, 2150 Market Street, San Francisco, California 94114. The interview with Rappaport was conducted in the spring of 1976.

16. George E. Crane, "Clinical Psychopharmacology in Its 20th Year," *Science* 181 (July 13, 1973): 125.

17. Ibid.

18. Albert Di Mascio, Richard I. Shader, and Donald R. Giller, "Behavioral Toxicity," in Richard I. Shader and Albert Di Mascio, eds., *Psychotropic Drug Side Effects* (Baltimore: Williams and Wilkins, 1970), p. 133.

19. Robert W. Wildman and Robert W. Wildman, II, "An Investigation into the Possibility of Irreversible Central Nervous System Damage as a Result of Long-Term Chlorpromazine Medication," *Journal of Clinical Psychology* 31, no. 2 (April 1975): 340 – 44. The Wildmans concluded that chlorpromazine (Thorazine) appeared to produce no permanent impairment, but that while they were on it, "patients . . . were impaired." The question was first raised in the early sixties by S. C. Porteus, the psychologist who developed the Porteus Maze Test, a test of concentration and tracking ability, and who concluded that while patients on the drug had an average deficit of 1.89 years, his data threw no light on the question of permanent effects. The list of other side effects is taken from package inserts and entries in the *Physician's Desk Reference*

*(PDR)* provided by the manufacturers of the drugs.

20. J. Sigwald et al., "Quatre cas de dyskinesie . . ." [Four cases of dyskinesia . . .], *Review of Neurology* 100 (1959): 751–55, quoted in George E. Crane, "Tardive Dyskinesia in Patients Treated with Major Neuroleptics: A Review of the Literature," *American Journal of Psychiatry* 124, no. 8, Supp. (February 1968): 40.

21. Ibid.; and George E. Crane, "Persistent Dyskinesia," *British Journal of Psychiatry* 122 (1973): 395– 405. An FDA-required package insert for antipsychotic drugs says the syndrome "is characterized by rhythmic involuntary movements of the tongue, face, mouth or jaw. . . . Sometimes these may be accompanied by involuntary movements of extremities. There is no known treatment for tardive dyskinesia."

What is striking is that the syndrome frequently appears in people treated with only moderate doses. See, e. g., L. Uhrbrand and A. Faurbye, "Reversible and Irreversible Dyskinesia After Treatment with Perphenazine, Chlorpromazine, Reserpine and Electroconvulsive Therapy," *Psychopharmacologia* 1 (1960): 408–18.

22. Gardos and Cole, "Maintenance Antipsychotic Therapy," p. 35. Even among those who are firm believers in the efficacy of antipsychotic drugs, there is general agreement that the drugs are used excessively. There is also a considerable amount of anecdotal information—though no studies—indicating that doctors continue to administer drugs to mask their side effects. "Every chronic schizophrenic outpatient," said Gardos and Cole, *"should have the benefit of an adequate trial without drugs."* (Italics in original.)

23. Brian M. Learoyd, "Psychotropic Drugs—Are They Justified?" *Medical Journal of Australia* no. 1 (March 30, 1974): 478. The fear of side effects also prompts many physicians to prescribe the so-called anti-parkinson drugs automatically despite the fact that they have been found to be ineffective or unnecessary in 80 percent of the cases. See, e. g., Leo E. Hollister, "Choice of Antipsychotic Drugs," *American Journal of Psychiatry* 127 (1970): 104.

24. Crane, "Clinical Psychopharmacology," p. 128.

25. *A Critical Look at the Drug Industry* (Chicago: Concerned

Rush Students, 1976), pp. 1, 2. The publication is available from Concerned Rush Students, Box 160, 1743 West Harrison Street, Chicago, Illinois 60612. Students at other medical schools report similar gifts from drug firms.

For a general review of drug company promotion, see Silverman and Lee, *Pills, Profits and Politics,* pp. 48–80; Arthur S. Waite, "The Future of Pharmaceutical Drug Promotion," *Medical Marketing and Media* 9 (June 1971): 9; and T. Donald Rucker, "Economic Problems in Drug Distribution," *Inquiry* 9 (September 1972): 43.

26. Paul Lowinger, "Statement for the U. S. Senate Subcommittee on Monopoly," mimeographed (Washington, D. C., May 3, 1974).

27. Schrag and Divoky, *The Myth of the Hyperactive Child,* pp. 95–105.

28. Paul Lowinger, "Statement for the U. S. Senate Subcommittee on Monopoly," mimeographed (Washington, D. C., December 18, 1968).

29. Hollister, "Uses of Psychotherapeutic Drugs," p. 88.

30. Much of this information is based on interviews with patients, attorneys, and staff members of clinics, and on reviews of client files, which are theoretically confidential. In one survey of some 400 psychiatrists in New York and California, all said they would use drugs on a hypothetical patient "who was experiencing an acute paranoid schizophrenic break." Charles Sheppard et al., "Comparative Survey of Psychiatrists' Treatment Preferences: California and New York," *Comprehensive Psychiatry* 15, no. 3 (May/June 1974): 213–23.

In a study at Rockland State Hospital (N.Y.), a study of the 3,204 patients diagnosed as schizophrenic found that 88 percent were medicated (94 percent of the women; 83 percent of the men). Eugene Laska et al., "Patterns of Psychotropic Drug Use for Schizophrenia," *Diseases of the Nervous System* 34 (August/September 1973): 294–305. Similar data, founded on scattered local studies, are available for mental-health clinics and crisis centers, prisons, and other settings. Laska, who is a member of the staff at Rockland State, concluded that his study showed that "high standards of psychopharmacological practice were not being followed."

**31.** William S. Appleton, "The Snow Phenomenon; Tranquilizing the Assaultive," *Psychiatry* 28 (1965): 88–93. Appleton points out that "snowing" with drugs appears to be a substitute for "barbiturate sedation, ice packs, prolonged baths, seclusion rooms," and routine use of electroconvulsive shock. Appleton studied all patients at the Massachusetts Mental Health Center who received over 1,500 milligrams of Thorazine daily, although many would be heavily sedated on far lower doses. Among them were several who suffered convulsions and coma, or who were lying "asleep or groggy for days, avoided by the staff and in a kind of chemical seclusion." The anecdotal recollections of former patients are from interviews and from statements published in *Psychiatric Drugs,* pp. 5, 22.

On the use of drugs to control aggression, see Russell H. Monroe, "Anticonvulsants in the Treatment of Aggression," *Journal of Nervous and Mental Disease* 160, no. 2 (1975): 119–26; and Turan M. Itil and Abdul Wadud, "Treatment of Human Aggression with Major Tranquilizers," *Journal of Nervous and Mental Disease* 160, no. 2 (1975): 83–99.

On the use of drugs to control hyperactive children, see Schrag and Divoky, *The Myth of the Hyperactive Child,* pp. 68–107.

On the use of drugs with delinquents, see Barry M. Maletsky, "D-Amphetamine and Delinquency: Hyperkinesis Persisting?" *Diseases of the Nervous System* 35, no. 12 (1974): 544–47.

On the control of sexual deviants, see M. A. Rivarola et al., "Effect of Treatment with Mderoxyprogesterone Acetate (Provera) on Testicular Function," *Journal of Clinical Endocrinology* 28 (1968): 679–84; J. Money, "Use of an Androgen-Depleting Hormone in the Treatment of Male Sex Offenders," *Journal of Sex Research* 6 (1970): 165–72; and "Male Prisoners Get Female Hormones," *Science News* 95 (1974): 16. (The practice of "treating" sex offenders with drugs, hormones, castration, or psychosurgery appears to be more prevalent in Europe than in the United States. Castration is legal as a means of preventing repeated offenses by sex criminals in Germany, but researchers there recently developed an experimental drug which they claim may make castration unnecessary.)

On drugging prisoners, see Joe P. Tupin et al., "The Long

Term Use of Lithium in Aggressive Prisoners," *Comprehensive Psychiatry* 14, no. 4 (1973): 311–17; and Dorothy Geroch, "Chemical Straightjackets (sic) That Last and Last," *Oregon Times,* December 1972, pp. 7–9. Again, there is no hard prevalence data; yet, reports of former inmates, doctors, and others make it clear that the phenothiazines and other tranquilizing drugs are frequently administered to prisoners, retarded children, and others.

32. Monroe, "Anticonvulsants in the Treatment of Aggression"; Tupin et al., "The Long Term Use of Lithium in Aggressive Prisoners"; Michael H. Sheard, "Lithium in the Treatment of Aggression," *Journal of Nervous and Mental Disease* 160, no. 2 (1975): 108–16; "Sex Offenders Getting Drug Treatments," *Criminal Justice Digest,* December 1975, p. 5. In addition, California has experimented with Anectine to control prisoners; those experiments are discussed in Chapter One.

33. Monroe, "Anticonvulsants in the Treatment of Aggression," p. 120.

34. Report of the Comptroller General, *Controls on the Use of Psychotropic Drugs in Veterans Administration Hospitals* (Washington, D.C.: U.S. General Accounting Office, 1975), p. 8.

35. Quoted in *Psychiatric Drugs,* p. 22.

36. U.S. Senate Special Subcommittee on Aging, *Drugs in Nursing Homes,* p. 254.

37. Ibid., p. 261.

38. *International Drug Therapy Newsletter* 10 (October/November 1975): 29–30; and Wendy J. Cohen and Norman H. Cohen, "Lithium Carbonate, Haloperidol, and Irreversible Brain Damage," *Journal of the American Medical Association* 230, no. 9 (1974): 1283–87.

39. Ibid., pp. 29, 36.

40. *International Drug Therapy Newsletter* 10 (September 1975): 28. See also Frank J. Ayd, Jr., "The Depot Fluphenazines: A Reappraisal After 10 Years' Clinical Experience," *American Journal of Psychiatry* 132, no. 5 (May 1975): 491–500.

41. The Dumont and Kupers statements are from interviews in the spring of 1976; the data on staffing of community mental-

health centers are from the Biometry Branch of NIMH, and particularly from *Statistical Note 94: Outpatient Treatment Services in Federally Funded Community Mental Health Centers–1971* (Washington, D. C.: NIMH, 1973).

The caution that drugs sometimes exacerbate the problems they are supposed to mitigate is frequently expressed by the established writers in psychopharmacology, but it appears to be followed only in rare instances. See, e. g., Crane, "Clinical Psychopharmacology"; Gardos and Cole, "Maintenance Antipsychotic Therapy"; and James E. Groves and Michel R. Mandel, "The Long-Acting Phenothiazines," *Archives of General Psychiatry* 32 (July 1975): 895–900.

42. A. D. Richards, "Attitude and Drug Acceptance," *British Journal of Psychiatry* 110 (1964): 46 –52; Donald F. Klein and J. M. David, *Diagnosis and Drug Treatment of Psychiatric Disorders* (Baltimore: Williams and Wilkins, 1969), pp. 17–32; J. D. Wilson and M. D. Enoch, "Estimation of Drug Rejection by Schizophrenic Inpatients . . ." *British Journal of Psychiatry* 113 (1967): 209–11; and Van Puten, "Why Do Schizophrenic Patients Refuse to Take Their Drugs?" pp. 67–68.

43. Ayd, "The Depot Fluphenazines: A Reappraisal After 10 Years' Clinical Experience," p. 499; Groves and Mandel, "The Long-Acting Phenothiazines," p. 898.

44. E. N. Vovina, "Prolonged Action Psychotropic Drugs as Part of a System of Rehabilitation and Readaptation of Schizophrenics," *Soviet Neurology and Psychiatry,* 5, no. 3–4 (Fall/ Winter 1972–73): 66.

45. See note 10.

46. Hollister, "Uses of Psychotherapeutic Drugs," p. 90. Significantly, there are studies which indicate that for some people —particularly hard-driving activists—tranquilizers may exacerbate anxiety or generate hostility by frustrating activity or the individual's ability to cope with problems in conventional ways. See, e. g., Carl Salzman et al., "Chlordiazepoxide-Induced Hostility in a Small Group Setting," *Archives of General Psychiatry* 31 (September 1974): 401–05.

47. "Study Finds Valium Most Abused Drug; Many Deaths Cited," *The New York Times,* 19 October 1975, p. 63. See also *DAWN 2 Analysis.*

On Valium in pregnancy, see L. Milkovich and B. J. Van Den Berg, "Effects of Prenatal Meprobamate and Chlordiazepoxide Hydrochloride on Human Embryonic and Fetal Development," *The New England Journal of Medicine* 291 (December 12, 1974): 1268.

On addiction and withdrawal, see David J. Greenblatt and Richard I. Shader, *Benzodiazepines in Clinical Practice* (New York: Raven Press, 1974), pp. 244–45; and L. Covi et al., "Length of Treatment with Anxiolytic Sedatives and Response to Their Sudden Withdrawal," *Scandinavian Archives of Psychiatry* 49 (1973): 51–64.

On abuse potential, see Arthur Kaufman and Philip W. Brickner, "Tranquilizer Control," Letter to the *Journal of the American Medical Association* 224, no. 8 (1973): 1190; and M. J. Finer, "Habituation to Chlordiazepoxide in an Alcoholic Population," *Journal of the American Medical Association* 213 (1970): 1342. The minor tranquilizers are often used in alcohol treatment programs, and there are reports that for some people they become equally abused alcohol substitutes or supplements. "Chlordiazepoxide (Librium)," wrote Kaufman and Brickner,

was the drug most requested by our alcoholic patients. . . . This tranquilizer was used as an addition to, rather than as a substitution for, alcohol. The sight of inebriated patients appearing at the clinic seeking chlordiazepoxide was commonplace.

The combination of minor tranquilizers and alcohol is known to be extremely dangerous, since one potentiates the effects of the other.

The data on prescribing patterns at Los Angeles County–USC Medical Center is from Robert F. Maronde et al., "Physician Prescribing Practices," *American Journal of Hospital Pharmacy* 26 (1969): 566–73; Robert F. Maronde and Milton Silverman, "Prescribing Hypnotic and Anti-Anxiety Drugs," *Annals of Internal Medicine* 79, no. 3 (1973): 452; and interviews with Maronde. The Los Angeles–USC Center is among the few which now process and analyze all pharmacy prescriptions with computers and which can determine which doctors prescribe what medication. As a consequence, overprescribing has been reduced.

**48.** Parry and Balter, "National Patterns of Psychotropic Drug Use," *Archives of General Psychiatry* 29 (June 1973): 777–79. "Long-time daily use of prescription sedatives and minor tranquilizers is most prevalent *not* among well-to-do and well-educated women, whether working or full-time housewives, but among housewives who are poor and ill-educated." Parry and Balter found that of women from the lowest fourth of the economic scale, one out of eight was a "high level" user of tranquilizers *(i. e.,* regular daily use for at least two months before the survey).

**49.** C. M. Brodsky, "The Pharmacotherapy System," *Psychosomatics* 11 (1971): 24–30; and L. S. Linn and M. S. Davis, "The Use of Psychotherapeutic Drugs by Middle-Aged Women," *Journal of Health and Social Behavior* 12 (1971): 331–39.

**50.** Carl D. Chambers, *Differential Drug Use Within the New York State Labor Force* (Albany: New York State Narcotic Addiction Control Commission, 1971). Since then, Chambers has done similar studies in other states: Chambers et al., *Chemical Coping* (New York: Spectrum, 1975). The only other such work, to my knowledge, is a project now being conducted by Khalil A. Khavari of the Midwest Institute on Drug Use at the University of Wisconsin in Milwaukee; but as of this writing the data have not been analyzed.

**51.** CWA Executive Board Meeting, *Joint Report: Job Pressure Study Committee; Job Pressures Implementation Committee* (Washington, D. C.: Communications Workers of America, 1973), p. 7.

**52.** Testimony of Lincoln Merrill at Hearing Before the U. S. Senate Subcommittee on Alcoholism and Narcotics, 1 October 1971, in *Amphetamine Abuse Among Truckdrivers* (Washington, D. C.: U. S. Government Printing Office, 1972), p. 14.

The same subject has been extensively discussed in articles in various issues of *Overdrive,* an independent magazine for truckers, among them "Amphetamines, Friend or Foe?" November 1967, pp. 87–89, and "Truckers Labeled as Dopers by Large Insurance Company," October 1971, pp. 58–59. The story included a reproduction of an advertisement for an insurance company which appeared in *Transport Topics,* an industry magazine, urging the industry, among other things, to "make the detection of drugs and alcohol users a part of all physical examinations" and to "have your dispatchers and supervisors mingle with the drivers . . . and keep their ears open." Mike Parkhurst, editor of *Overdrive,* is convinced that drug use is down in the industry but that it hasn't disappeared.

53. The low estimates are Parkhurst's (see note 52), who believes that only one in twenty is a regular user. But some truckers believe it remains much higher. There are no hard data.

54. The physician's license was suspended in October 1973. He had stipulated to charges that he had prescribed Seconal and other sedatives without "either a prior examination or medical indication for such drugs." The stipulation did not mention amphetamines or farm workers; but since it focused only on two or three small incidents (probably involving narcotics agents), other, more extensive practices were almost certainly involved.

55. See, e. g., *Industrial Medicine,* June 1971, p. 1. The Federal Aviation Administration continues experiments on the effects of amphetamines. See, for example, D. J. Schroeder and W. E. Collins, "Effects of Secobarbital and d-Amphetamine on Tracking Performance During Angular Acceleration," *Ergonomics* 17, no. 5 (1974): 613–21.

56. By now the story of amphetamine use and abuse should be sufficiently familiar to require little further elaboration. In the period between 1971 and 1976, FDA controls on production of amphetamines and extensive publicity about their dangers have substantially reduced the number of prescriptions written and the number of pills legally sold; amphetamines are still being prescribed, however, particularly in what appears to be a growing grey market which falls between the legitimate and the outright illegal realm of the street pusher. At the same time, the street market has shrunk. The PharmChem Research Foundation, one of several laboratories in the United States which analyses samples of street drugs, reported that in 1973 49 percent of the samples which allegedly contained amphetamines actually did; by 1975, the percentage had shrunk to 5.3 percent. The substitutes contained caffeine, various antihistamines (which are depressants but sometimes mimic some amphetamine side effects), and a host of unidentifiable substances.

*PharmChem Newsletter* 5, no. 1 (January 1976): 3–4. For a more extensive discussion on the use of psychostimulants with "hyperactive" children, see Schrag and Divoky, *The Myth of the Hyperactive Child,* pp. 68–107. On amphetamines generally, see Lester Grinspoon and Peter Hedblom, *The Speed Culture: Amphetamine Use and Abuse in America* (Cambridge, Mass.: Harvard University Press, 1975).

**57.** Ronald R. Fieve, *Moodswing: The Third Revolution in Psychiatry* (New York: William Morrow, 1975); Ronald R. Fieve, "Lithium Prophylaxis in Affective Disorders," *New York State Journal of Medicine* (July 1975): 1219–21; Ronald R. Fieve, "The Lithium Clinic: A New Model for the Delivery of Psychiatric Services," *American Journal of Psychiatry* 132, no. 10 (October 1975): 1018–22.

A Morrow advertisement reads:

> In his groundbreaking new book, [Fieve] tells how the use of lithium carbonate, the "Cinderella drug" in psychiatry effectively controls manic depression. How and why *moodswing* affects twenty million Americans. . . . The *many* glibly stated causes. The *one* true successful cure—and preventative.

In his medical journal articles, Fieve is a little more restrained, but the message is the same. "The success of lithium carbonate is striking," he wrote, "since it not only rapidly calms manic states, but also helps to prevent future occurrence of both mania and depression and attenuates their severity."

**58.** Fieve, *Moodswing,* pp. 223, 201.

**59.** "The Current Status of Lithium Therapy: Report of the APA Task Force," *American Journal of Psychiatry* 132, no. 9 (1975): 997–1001.

**60.** Fieve, *Moodswing,* pp. 200, 201, 213.

**61.** Kline, *From Sad to Glad,* p. 185.

**62.** "Physical Manipulation of the Brain," *The Hastings Center Report,* Supp. (May 1973): 11.

## Chapter Six

**1.** Lloyd H. Cotter, "Operant Conditioning in a Vietnamese Mental Hospital," *American Journal of Psychiatry* 124, no. 1 (1967): 25.

2. Ibid., p. 27.

3. Ibid., p. 28.

4. The anecdotal material is extensive. The quotations in this section are from interviews; from Leonard R. Frank, *The History of Shock Treatment* (San Francisco: Network Against Psychiatric Assault, 1975); and from materials provided by NAPA, an organization of ex-mental patients, a few doctors, and others opposed to forced institutionalization and treatment of nonconsenting individuals.

5. David J. Impastato, "The Story of the First Electroshock Treatment," *American Journal of Psychiatry* 116 (June 1960): 113–14. Cerletti himself later theorized that the shock initiated some biochemical changes in the brain, and several of his followers claimed that they could cure patients by injecting them with serum obtained from people or guinea pigs that had been shocked. The theory is generally discredited. Cerletti's own account appears in F. Marti-Ibanez et al., eds., *The Great Psychodynamic Therapies in Psychiatry* (New York: Hoeber-Harper, 1956), pp. 91–120.

   The terms ECT (electroconvulsive treatment) and EST (electroshock treatment) refer to the same procedure and are used interchangeably.

6. Albert Deutsch, *The Mentally Ill in America: A History of Their Care and Treatment from Colonial Times* (New York: Columbia University Press, 1952), p. 79. The quotation from the English doctor is from James Mason Cox's *Practical Observations on Insanity* (1804), quoted in Elliot S. Valenstein, *Brain Control* (New York: Wiley Interscience, 1973), p. 147.

7. Sylvia A. Riddell, "The Therapeutic Efficacy of ECT," *Archives of General Psychiatry* 8 (1963): 546–56. See also D. T. Templer et al., "Cognitive Functioning and Degree of Psychosis in Schizophrenics Given Many Electroconvulsive Treatments," *British Journal of Psychiatry* 123 (1973): 441–43; and N. O. Brill et al., "Relative Effectiveness of Various Components of Electroconvulsive Therapy," *Archives of Neurological Psychiatry* 81 (1959): 627–35.

   The story of the nonfunctioning machine appeared in Raymond R. Coffey, "Hospital Shocked by Finding No Sock in Its Shock Machine," *Chicago Daily News,* 20 September 1974, and other papers served by the Chicago Daily News Service. It was originally published in *World Medicine.*

8. The estimates are based on projections of local statistics and particularly on George H. Grosser et al., *The Regulation of Electroconvulsive Treatment in Massachusetts: A Follow-Up* (Boston: Massachusetts Department of Mental Health, 1975). The Massachusetts study, which surveyed ECT treatments in 1973–74, covered private and public mental hospitals and came up with some 2,400 people; projecting from that to the national population would produce some 120,000 people. But since the Massachusetts survey did not include outpatient treatment or general hospitals with psychiatric wards (which handle almost as many people as the hospitals surveyed), the figure is likely to be substantially higher.

9. John Friedberg in a letter to *Psychology Today,* December 1975, p. 13; Jonas B. Robitscher, "Psychosurgery and Other Somatic Means of Altering Behavior," *Bulletin of the American Academy for Psychiatry and the Law* 2, no. 1 (March 1974): 12; Robert E. Peck, *The Miracle of Shock Treatment* (New York: Exposition Press, 1974), p. 23.

10. The statement was issued July 28, 1972, during the controversy over Thomas Eagleton's fitness to run for vice-president with George McGovern, and was reported in *The New York Times,* 29 July 1972, p. 11. The figures for the number of shock doctors are consistent with those provided by the American Society for Electrotherapy, an organization of physicians established to defend ECT against its critics.

11. Herbert Goldman et al., "Long-Term Effects of Electroconvulsive Therapy Upon Memory and Perceptual Motor Performance," *Journal of Clinical Psychology* 28 (1972): 32–34; Templer et al., "Cognitive Functioning and Degree of Psychosis in Schizophrenics Given Many Electroconvulsive Treatments," pp. 441–43; Fred H. Frankel, "Electroconvulsive Therapy in Massachusetts: A Task Force Report," *Massachusetts Journal of Mental Health* 3 (1973): 15; A. E. Hotchner, *Papa Hemingway* (New York: Bantam, 1967), p. 308; Beatrice Rosenthal, Statement Before the San Francisco Mental Health Advisory Board, January 1975; the story of "David" is from Constance Paige, "Shock Therapy: Pacification Program," in

Michael Glenn, ed., *Voices from the Asylum* (New York: Harper Colophon, 1974), p. 207. The Marilyn Rice story is from her medical malpractice complaint: Marilyn Rice v. Dr. John E. Nardini, Civ. No. 703–74 (D.C. Sup. Ct. 1974). Attorneys for the doctor replied that if there was any injury or damage, it was caused "by her pre-existing condition or conditions and/or she willingly and voluntarily, with full knowledge, requested and accepted the treatment rendered." Early in 1977, a jury found against Rice and in favor of the doctor. No grounds were given, but her attorney speculated that the jury believed that the physician had adequately explained the risks and that she had given full informed consent.

12. Lonnie Birch and Stuart Kaufer, "Letter to Sisters of Providence . . ." *Madness Network News,* 2, no. 5 (April 1975): 1; Paula Fine, "Women and Shock Treatment," *Issues in Radical Therapy* 2 (Summer 1974): 9–10; Grosser et al., *The Regulation of Electroconvulsive Treatment in Massachusetts: A Follow-Up,* tables 1 and 5; and Jean Dietz, "ECT Study Reveals Disparity . . ." *Psychiatric News,* 6 August 1975, p. 1.

13. The letter to *Psychology Today* was one of several which appeared in December 1975 in response to an attack on ECT. The observation on fear is from B. J. Bolin, "Fear Reactions in Patients Receiving Electroshock Treatment and the Law of Initial Value," *American Journal of Psychotherapy* 21 (1967): 74–85.

14. "ECT Timed with Disturbing Thoughts," *Clinical Psychiatry News,* December 1975, p. 2; Robert R. Dies, "Electroconvulsive Therapy: A Social Learning Theory Interpretation," *Journal of Nervous and Mental Disease* 146, no. 4 (1968): 335.

15. In Wisconsin a few years ago, Dr. Arnold M. Ludwig and his colleagues at Mendota State Hospital used the same principle on an "assaultive" 31-year-old woman, but their only instrument was a cattle prod. Arnold M. Ludwig et al., "The Control of Violent Behavior Through Faradic Shock," *Journal of Nervous and Mental Disease* 148, no. 6 (1969): 624–31. There are, of course, many "therapies" based on aversive conditioning, either with shock or other systematic schedules of punishment. Perhaps the most common are those used to "treat" alcoholics and sex "deviants," including homosexuals.

**16.** Most of this material is from an interview with Dr. Brown in the spring of 1976. The quotation is from the *National Enquirer,* 9 July 1972, but Brown made similar statements in the interview and elsewhere. See note 31.

**17.** Robert H. Moser, "Of Tomes and Tangents," *Medical Opinion and Review,* December 1969, pp. 110–11. The NIMH report is *Psychosurgery: Perspective on a Current Issue* (Washington, D. C.: NIMH, 1973), p. 1. The italics are in the original.

**18.** The best treatment of the subject—its techniques and its limitations—is Valenstein, *Brain Control.*

**19.** Ibid., pp. 239, 276. Among the most comprehensive follow-up studies on operations conducted in the forties was the so-called Columbia-Greystone project, which is discussed in F. A. Mettler et al., *Psychosurgical Problems* (New York: Blaikston, 1952).

**20.** O. J. Andy, "Thalamotomy in Hyperactive and Aggressive Behavior," *Confinia Neurologica* 32 (1970): 324; Vernon H. Mark et al., "The Destruction of Both Anterior Thalamic Nuclei in a Patient with Intractable Depression," *Journal of Nervous and Mental Disease* 150 (1970): 266–72; Peter H. Breggin, "The Return of Lobotomy and Psychosurgery," *Congressional Record,* 92nd Cong., February 24, 1972, E1602–12.

For an extended discussion of other psychosurgery cases, see also Peter R. Breggin, "An Independent Followup of a Person Operated Upon for Violence and Epilepsy by Drs. Vernon Mark, Frank Ervin and William Sweet of the Neuro-Research Foundation of Boston," *Issues in Radical Therapy* (Autumn 1973). The case was reported by Vernon Mark and Frank Ervin in "Is There a Need to Evaluate the Individuals Producing Human Violence?" *Psychiatric Opinion,* August 1968; Vernon Mark and Frank Ervin, *Violence and the Brain;* and Vernon Mark and Frank Ervin, "The Effect of Amygdalotomy on Violent Behavior in Patients with Temporal Lobe Epilepsy," in Edward Hitchcock et al., eds., *Psychosurgery* (Springfield, Ill.: Charles C. Thomas, 1972).

**21.** *Psychosurgery: Perspective on a Current Problem,* p. 7; "Excerpts from the Final Report of a Study of 'The Medical Epidemiology of Criminals'—Neuro-Research Foundation, Boston, Mass.," in *Individual Rights,* pp. 319–21. *Psychosurg-*

*ery,* the NIMH report, was in part an attempt to explain the government's involvement in supporting the work of the Neuro-Research Foundation. The report hedges on the issue of future support for such ventures. However, to be fair to NIMH, its own $500,000 appropriation did not come from an NIMH program but directly from the action of a congressional committee which had been persuaded by Sweet's testimony.

22. Within a period of a few months in 1972 and 1973, a number of people independently began to discover and report on what Peter Breggin called the second wave of psychosurgery, among them a Washington science writer named Dan Greenberg, now publisher of *Science and Government Report;* Sharland Trotter, at the time a researcher for Ralph Nader; and Leroy Arons, a *Washington Post* reporter who broke the story of the psychosurgery experiments in California prisons. Breggin, however, is the person who led the crusade.

The Rosenthal quote is from "Heredity in Criminality" (Paper delivered to the American Association for the Advancement of Science, Washington, D. C., December 27, 1972). In the past five years, NIMH has funded at least five research projects on the relationship of chromosome anomalies and violence, including projects conducted at Johns Hopkins, the University of Wisconsin, the Educational Testing Service, and Boston Hospital for Women.

23. National Commission for the Protection of Human Subjects of Biomedical and Behavioral Research, *Psychosurgery: Report and Recommendations,* 77– 0001 (Washington, D. C.: U. S. Government Printing Office, 1977), p. 38. See also Sharland Trotter, "Federal Commission OK's Psychosurgery," *APA Monitor* 7 (November 1976): 4.

24. *The New York Times,* 12 September 1971, Sec. 4, p. 9. Rensberger's representation of Delgado's claims is more accurate than his description of fighting bulls.

25. Robert G. Heath, "Electrical Self-stimulation of the Brain in Man," *American Journal of Psychiatry* 120 (1963): 571–77; Robert G. Heath et al., "The Pleasure Response: Studies in Stereotaxic Techniques in Patients," in Nathan Kline and Eugene Laska, eds., *Computers and Electronic Devices in Psychiatry* (New York: Grune and Stratton, 1968); "The Lobotomists

Are Coming Again," *Medical World News,* 15 January 1971, p. 34; Delgado, *Physical Control of the Mind,* p. 145. Jose Delgado, Vernon Mark, William Sweet, Frank Ervin et al., "Intracerebral Radio Stimulation and Recording in Completely Free Patients," *Journal of Nervous and Mental Disease* 147 (1968): 329–40.

26. Valenstein, *Brain Control,* pp. 112, 110, 98. Delgado's "propensity for dramatic, albeit ambiguous demonstrations," Valenstein said, "has been a constant source of material for those whose purposes are served by exaggerating the omnipotence of brain stimulation." The claim that stimulation can evoke long-forgotten memories has been adduced as a possible electrochemical correlate (and confirmation) of psychoanalytic theory. The difficulty is that much of the memory evoked was vague and fragmentary, that fear or the trauma of surgery may have played a part, and that often no memory is evoked at all.

27. Delgado, *Physical Control of the Mind,* p. 257.

28. In *Violence and the Brain,* Mark and Ervin argue that violence is associated with psychomotor epilepsy, but they offer no evidence other than a handful of cases in which violence is more easily traceable to brain surgery or other brain damage —or in which psychosurgery "cures" the violence without affecting the epileptic seizures—than it is to epileptic seizures. See, e. g., Peter Breggin, "Psychosurgery for the Control of Violence," *Congressional Record* 92nd Cong. March 30, 1972, E3380, and Valenstein, *Brain Control,* p. 262. Breggin, for reasons that should be obvious, has been more successful in getting sympathetic congressmen to put his psychosurgery material in the *Congressional Record* than in placing it in established psychiatric journals.

29. Ralph K. Schwitzgebel, "Issues in the Use of an Electronic Rehabilitation System with Chronic Recidivists" (Unpublished paper, 1967), quoted in Barton L. Ingraham and Gerald W. Smith, "The Use of Electronics in the Observation and Control of Human Behavior and Its Possible Use in Rehabilitation and Parole," *Issues in Criminology* 7, no. 2 (1972): 45; *Anthropotelemetry: Dr. Schwitzgebel's Machine,* p. 403; Robert L. Schwitzgebel, "A Belt from Big Brother," *Psychology Today*

2, no. 11 (1969): 45; Ralph K. Schwitzgebel, "Electronic Alternatives to Imprisonment," *Lex et Scientia* 5 (1968): 99–104.

For background, see also Robert L. Schwitzgebel and Ralph K. Schwitzgebel, eds., *Psychotechnology: Electronic Control of Mind and Behavior* (New York: Holt, Rinehart and Winston, 1973).

30. Ingraham and Smith, "The Use of Electronics," p. 44.

31. Interview with Hunter Brown, spring 1976. Brown said his patients also come "very well documented."

32. Jose Delgado, "Brain Manipulation: Psychocivilized Directions of Behavior," *The Humanist,* March/April 1972, p. 10; Mark and Ervin, *Violence and the Brain,* p. 161; A. E. Bennett, "Anti-Psychiatrists Threat to Society," *San Diego Union,* 11 July 1975.

33. *U.S. v. Karl Brandt, Trials of War Criminals Before the Nuremberg Tribunals: The Medical Case* (Washington, D. C.: U. S. Government Printing Office, 1948).

34. Kaimowitz v. Department of Mental Health for the State of Michigan. The *Kaimowitz* case is a long and revealing story in itself. Significantly, Dr. Ernest Rodin, an official of the Lafayette Clinic in Detroit who, as an advocate of the proposed psychosurgery program, was a defendant in the case, had visited Vernon Mark in Boston:

> When I informed Dr. Mark of our project, namely, doing amygdalotomies on patients who do not have epilepsy, he became extremely concerned and stated we had no ethical right in so doing. ... I retorted that he was misleading us with his ... book [*Violence and the Brain*] and he had no right at all from a scientific point of view to state that in the human, aggression is accompanied by seizure discharges in the amygdala, because he is dealing with only patients who have susceptible brains, namely, temporal lobe epilepsy. . . . He stated categorically that as far as present evidence is concerned, one has no right to make lesions in a "healthy brain" when the individual suffers from rage attacks only.

Elsewhere Mark has said that psychosurgery should not be done on prisoners "because of the difficulty in obtaining truly informed consent."

35. Stone, *Mental Health and the Law,* p. 101.

36. Wyatt v. Hardin, Civ. No. 3195–N (M. D. Ala. June 26, 1975);

and United States v. Codina, Crim. No. 75–10–N (M. D. Ala. June 26, 1975).

37. The Alexander quotation is from a statement he made at the annual meeting of the Society of Biological Psychiatry, San Francisco, June 9, 1976; the quotation on the "ritual" informed consent is from *The New England Journal of Medicine* 287 (August 31, 1972): 466.

38. Szasz, "From the Slaughterhouse to the Madhouse," *Psychotherapy: Theory, Research and Practice* 8 (1971): 64–67.

39. M. Harvey Brenner, *Mental Illness and the Economy* (Cambridge, Mass.: Harvard University Press, 1973).

40. Kenneth B. Clark, Presidential address to the annual convention of the American Psychological Association, 1971; Frances Fox Piven and Richard A. Cloward, *Regulating the Poor: The Functions of Public Welfare* (New York: Pantheon, 1971), p. 347.

## Chapter Seven

1. *Security World* is crammed with advertisements and articles dealing with the theories, practices, and technology of industrial "loss control" and surveillance. On surveillance of workers off the job, see also *Heights Funeral Home,* 159 NLRB 723 (1966); *GTE Lenkurt, Inc.,* 204 NLRB 920 (1973); and *GTE Automatic Electric Co.,* 204 NLRB 716 (1973).

   On bugging washrooms, see *The Privacy Report* no. 11 (June 1974): 4.

2. *Security World,* April 1976, p. 11. A still more interesting device, recently developed by the navy, is the "Hidden Knowledge Detector," which "relates to the field of hidden knowledge detection in . . . psychology, criminal investigation, and social science [and] encompasses covert mental processes." The patent is available for licensing and development. *National Technical Information Service Weekly Government Abstracts,* 8 March 1975, p. 79.

3. Jerry L. Wall, "What the Competition Is Doing: Your Need to Know," *Harvard Business Review,* November/December 1974, p. 36.

4. The estimate for the number of polygraph examinations is

derived from interviews and industry literature, among them *Polygraph: The Journal of the American Polygraph Association.* In 1974, the APA predicted that between 250,000 and 350,000 tests would be given in 1975 by some 1,500 practicing examiners; one member of a major polygraph-testing firm estimated, however, that the average examiner gives between 500 and 750 tests a year, raising the total substantially. Other industry sources estimate that by 1970, more than 200,000 tests were being given annually; and nearly all sources agree that despite the passage of restrictive legislation in some states, the number has grown dramatically since then. The estimate for the percentage of tests devoted to nonemployment situations is based on a report in *Business Week,* cited in *American Bar Association Section on Labor Relations Law, Committee Report* (New York: American Bar Association, 1965), p. 289; and on industry sources. The basic text in the field is John E. Reid and Fred Inbau, *Truth and Deception: The Polygraph ("Lie Detector") Technique* (Baltimore: Williams and Wilkins, 1966).

5. *The Reid Report* (Chicago: John E. Reid Associates).

6. *The Reid Report: The Search for an Honest Employee* (Chicago: John E. Reid Associates); and "Predicting Dishonesty with the Reid Report," *Polygraph* 4, no. 2 (June 1975): 141.

7. Clarence H. A. Romig, "State Laws and the Polygraph in 1975," *Polygraph* 4, no. 2 (June 1975): 95–107. Some fifteen states have also passed licensing laws for polygraph examiners, generally with the encouragement and approval of the APA. The polygraph has often been challenged in labor arbitration cases, and it has frequently been attacked by labor organizations, particularly the Retail Clerks and the Teamsters. *In Re Bowman Transportation, Inc.,* 59 LAB. ARB. 283 (1972); "A False Lie Detector Nearly Cost Local 31 Member His Job," *Retail Clerks Advocate,* January 1976, p. 22; and *The Lie Detector—Guilty Unitl Proven Innocent* (Washington, D. C.: AFL-CIO Maritime Trades Department, 1970).

8. The industry claims that when a test is given by an experienced examiner, the conclusions are likely to be between 90 and 95 percent accurate. See, e. g., Frank S. Horvath and John E. Reid, "The Reliability of Polygraph Examiner Diagnosis of Truth and Deception," *Journal of Criminal Law, Criminology*

*and Police Science* 62, no. 2 (1971): 276–81; and Douglas E. Wickander and Fred L. Hunter, "The Influence of Auxiliary Sources of Information in Polygraph Diagnoses," *Journal of Police Science and Administration* 3, no. 4 (1975): 405–09. Others have argued that even if the tests were 90 percent accurate as claimed, that would still mean that of every 1,000 innocent people tested, 100 would unjustly be found dishonest.

9. Philip Ash, "Predicting Dishonesty with the Reid Report," *Polygraph* 4, no. 2 (June 1975): 141; Ash, "Screening Employment Applicants for Attitudes Toward Theft," *Journal of Applied Psychology* 55, n.2 (1971): 162.

10. J. Kirk Barefoot, ed., *The Polygraph Story* (Washington, D. C.: The American Polygraph Association, 1974), p. 9.

11. The statement about "starvation or submission" is from a letter appealing the denial of unemployment compensation to an Idaho woman who refused to take a second lie detector test. She had "passed" the first test, was required to take a second during an investigation of a shortage of money in the store where she worked, refused, and was fired. "When I agreed to work at the store," she wrote,

> I was faced with the choice of starvation or submission. . . . I did not know that the polygraph examination included personal questions in many instances unrelated to employment. The test included giving the examiner a list of my bills and expenses per month. It also included questioning work habits and ethics of other employees—a practice I considered highly unethical. There were also questions of a legal nature—have you ever written a bad check? Do you use marijuana or narcotics? Have you ever driven while drunk?

*Congressional Record,* 92nd Cong., December 20, 1973, 42680.

12. *Criminal Justice Information and Protection of Privacy Act of 1975: Hearings Before the Senate Subcommittee on Constitutional Rights, July 15 and 16, 1975* (Washington, D. C.: U. S. Government Printing Office, 1975), p. 231.

13. The Miller testimony is quoted in Committee on Government Operations, U. S. Senate, *Materials Pertaining to S.3418 and Protecting Individual Privacy in Federal Gathering, Use and*

*Disclosure of Information* (Washington, D. C.: U. S. Government Printing Office, 1974), p. 25.

**14.** Elizabeth Wickenden, "Notes on HR 1," mimeographed (New York: The National Assembly for Social Policy and Development, 1971). This is one of several mimeographed reports issued by the National Assembly on the proposal in September and November of 1971. See also "Back to the Poor Law via Section 1115," mimeographed (New York: The National Assembly for Social Policy and Development, May 4, 1971).

**15.** *Monthly AFDC Eligibility and Income Report* (Sacramento: California Health and Welfare Agency, 1975), p. 2.

**16.** The Skinner quote is from my interview in May 1976; the statement of the court is in Piven and Cloward, *Regulating the Poor,* p. 167.

The stories are common. Ever since the early seventies, there have been state and federally sponsored attempts to convert the sporadic efforts of local welfare officials to reduce the costs of public assistance to more systematic programs of work incentives, mandatory training, and cost accounting. The budget, said a California welfare official, "is the most effective form of behavior control we have."

**17.** The standard literature on operant conditioning includes Theodore Ayllon and Nathan N. Azrin, *The Token Economy* (New York: Appleton Century Crofts, 1968); Albert Bandura, *Principles of Behavior Modification* (New York: Holt, Rinehart and Winston, 1969); and Skinner, *Science and Human Behavior.*

In specialized areas, see, e. g., E. L. Phillips et al., "Achievement Place: Modification of the Behaviors of Pre-Delinquent Boys Within a Token Economy," *Journal of Applied Behavior Analysis* 4 (1971): 45–59; Ogden R. Lindsley and B. F. Skinner, "A Method for the Experimental Analysis of Behavior of Psychotic Patients," *American Psychologist* 9 (1954): 419–20; C. B. Foster and M. K. DeMyer, "The Development of Performances in Autistic Children in an Automatically Controlled Environment," *Journal of Chronic Diseases* 13 (1961): 312–45; R. A. Winett and R. C. Winkler, "Current Behavior Modification in the Classroom: Be Still, Be Quiet, Be Docile," *Journal of Applied Behavior Analysis* 5 (1972): 499–504; C. L. Thorne et al., "Behavior Modification Techniques: New Tools for Probation Officers," *Federal Probation* 31 (1967): 21–28; and M. Clark et al., "A Pilot Basic Education Program for School Dropouts Incorporating a Token Reinforcement System," *Behaviour Research and Therapy* 6 (1968): 183–88.

18. Under pressure of law suits and protests from civil-liberties organizations, the Bureau of Prisons terminated the formal START program in 1974. See, e. g., Clonce v. Richardson, Civ. No. 373-S (W.D. Mo. July 31, 1974); and "Project START—Bureau of Prisons Operations Memorandum," in *Individual Rights*, pp. 240–73. Similar programs, however, are common in juvenile detention homes and other state correctional facilities. START itself was patterned on the federal Morgantown (West Virginia) Youth Center, a "model" correctional facility designed along operant conditioning principles by Harold L. Cohen of the Institute for Behavioral Research; Cohen has also created extensive behavior modification programs for schools. See, e. g., Harold L. Cohen and James Filipczak, *A New Learning Environment* (San Francisco: Jossey-Bass, 1971); and *Programming Interpersonal Curricula for Adolescents* (PICA) (Silver Spring, Md.: The Institute for Behavioral Research, 1971).

19. See, e. g., Thomas S. Ball, *The Establishment and Administration of Operant Conditioning Programs in a State Hospital for the Retarded* (Sacramento: California Department of Mental Hygiene, 1969). In recent years, a number of law suits based on the minimum wage provisions of the Fair Labor Standards Act have attacked the common practice of requiring patients to work at low wages or no wages in closed institutions. In 1976, however, the Supreme Court held that the minimum wage provisions of the act cannot be constitutionally applied to state and local governments, leaving the challengers of what is usually called institutional peonage without their most important legal weapon. National League of Cities v. Usery, 44 U.S. L.W. 4974 (June 22, 1976). The practice, needless to say, remains common in most public institutions. See also A. Lebar, "Worker Patients: Receiving Therapy or Suffering Peonage?" *American Bar Association Journal* 62 (1976): 219; and D. Safier, "Patient Work Under Fair Labor Standards: The

Issue in Perspective," *Hospital and Community Psychiatry* 27, no. 2 (1976): 89.

20. Edgar H. Schein, "Man Against Man: Brainwashing," *Corrective Psychiatry and Journal of Social Therapy* 8, no. 2 (1962). Schein later denied that he advocated the Chinese technique of using cell mates as psychological agents to abuse prisoners in order to break down their personal identity and concept of self; but the text of the original speech, which described how "false confessions or insincere attempts to comply with cell mates' pressures were met with renewed hostility" and how "periodic interrogation, general physical debilitation, sleeplessness and a very exacting prison regimen all added to the stresses" suggested otherwise.

21. Singer, *Psychological Studies of Punishment,* 54 CAL. L. REV. 405, 415, 423 (1973).

22. A.M. Kellam, "Shoplifting Treated by Aversion to a Film," *Behaviour Research and Therapy* 7 (1969): 127–28. This is a case of a woman in Wales, a "habitual shoplifter," who was shown a film in which a woman "entered a cooperating store" in which she shoplifted several items while other shoppers watched in disgust. At the moment the woman in the film did the shoplifting, the real shoplifter—the "patient"—was given an electric shock. "Hospital personnel [nuns] administered the treatment. . . . The patient finally stopped shoplifting, and she reported uneasy feelings of being watched whenever she entered a store. The therapist planned to repeat the treatment every few months." Ibid., p. 432.

    For reports on aversive therapy in other areas, see F. Lemere and W. Voegtlin, "An Evaluation of Aversion Treatment of Alcoholism," *Quarterly Journal of Studies on Alcohol* 11 (1950): 199–204; C. H. Farrar et al., "Punishment of Alcohol Consumption by Apneic Paralysis," *Behaviour Research and Therapy* 6 (1968): 13–16; N. I. Lavin et al., "Behavior Therapy in a Case of Transvestism," *Journal of Nervous and Mental Disease* 133 (1961): 346–53; M. J. Raymond, "The Treatment of Addiction in Aversion Conditioning with Apomorphine," *Behaviour Research and Therapy* 1 (1964): 287–91; R. Liberman, "Aversive Conditioning of Drug Addicts," *Behaviour Research and Therapy* 6 (1968): 229–31; Gene G.

Abel et al., "Effects of Aversive Therapy on Sexual Deviants: A Preliminary Report" (Paper presented at the American Psychiatric Association, May 8, 1969); and Gene G. Abel and Edward B. Blanchard, "The Measurement and Generation of Sexual Arousal in Male Sexual Deviates," in M. Hersen et al., eds., *Progress in Behavior Modification,* vol. 2 (New York: Academic Press, 1975), pp. 99–136. By 1974, there were at least twenty-six published studies on the use of aversive conditioning on homosexuals alone.

23. Farrall Instrument Co. Catalog F–72 (P.O. Box 1037, Grand Island, Nebraska 68801). Farrall also publishes *Behavioral Engineering,* a "mini-journal" reporting on "behavior modification techniques using instrumentation."

The "Pants Alert" is made by Lehigh Valley Electronics in Fogelsville, Pennsylvania 18051.

24. Abel and Blanchard, "The Measurement and Generation of Sexual Arousal in Male Sexual Deviates," p. 132. The reports of "successful" cures of alcoholics, as measured by abstinence, range from 10 to 35 percent of those treated with aversive stimuli, while according to one study, standard psychotherapy results in "cures" in roughly 5 percent of the cases. But since the whole matter is such a morass of methodological problems, uncertain definitions, folklore, mythology, and other confounding elements, there is almost no way to evaluate any course of treatment. Almost inevitably, aversive techniques, even when successful, reduce but do not completely eliminate the undesirable behavior; in some cases, moreover, when the treatment is ended, the previously suppressed behavior returns to levels which are as high or higher than before treatment.

25. Claims to the contrary are continuously made; see, e. g., Harold L. Cohen et al., *Contingencies Applicable to Special Education of Delinquents: Establishing 24-hour Control in an Experimental Cottage* (Silver Spring, Md.: Institute for Behavioral Research, 1966). But there is no study which shows any long-term academic difference between students from a behavior modification program and control groups after the behavior modification program has been terminated. The academic programs themselves, moreover, are usually so expensive that they vanish once special funding has been withdrawn, al-

though those portions which deal with classroom order and control are thriving. As a consequence, some educational administrators who advocate behavior modification defend it as a way of maintaining order so that "learning may take place" (*i. e.,* children learn more in an orderly classroom). But there is no evidence to support that argument either.

26. "Report of Resident Abuse Investigating Committee" (Unpublished report), quoted in David B. Wexler, "Behavior Modification and Other Change Procedures: The Emerging Law and the Florida Guidelines" (Paper presented to Symposium on Behavior Control, Reed College, Portland, Oregon, March 6–8, 1975). Wexler was a member of the investigating committee.

27. Goffman, *Asylums,* p. 49.

28. John D. Nolan, "The True Humanist: The Behavior Modifier," *Teachers College Record* 76, no. 2 (1974): 342.

29. Some behaviorists are dreaming of even more extensive ventures. In 1972, Harold L. Cohen, the president of the Institute for Behavioral Research, spoke about his plans to "shape" all of Maryland's Prince George County. What he had hoped to do was train all of the county's agencies—schools, police, courts—to use reinforcing behavior control methods which would reward good behavior rather than punishing bad. Cohen had already established several projects for teenagers in the county, but the more ambitious plans were never put into practice. In addition, in the mid- and late sixties, there was a flurry of efforts to create Utopian communities modeled on Skinner's novel, *Walden Two,* but the fashion has passed.

30. On CPI, see Merriken v. Cressman, 364 F. Supp. 913 (E.D. Pa. 1973). The programs in Orange County are described in the grant applications and reports of projects supported by the California Council on Criminal Justice, an LEAA-funded agency, which are on file in the council's offices in Sacramento.

   For a more extensive discussion of juvenile programs, see Schrag and Divoky, *The Myth of the Hyperactive Child,* pp. 132–74; for a comprehensive critique, see Edwin M. Schur, *Radical Nonintervention: Rethinking the Delinquency Problem* (Englewood Cliffs, N. J.: Prentice-Hall, 1973).

31. *The Privacy Report* 3, no. 3 (October 1975): 5.

**32.** *Behavior Today,* 19 July 1976, p. 3.

**33.** Harold Shane and June Shane, "Forecast for the 70s," *Today's Education,* January 1969, p. 11.

**34.** I owe most of this material to Diane Divoky, who collected it for a report published as "Child Abuse: Mandate for Teacher Intervention?" in *Learning* 4, no. 8 (April 1976): 14–22. *Guidelines for Schools* is available from the Ameｉican Humane Association, P. O. Box 1266, Denver, Colorado 80201. The New York guidelines are based on the New York Child Protective Services Act of 1973 and described in, e. g., "Reports of Evidence of Child Abuse and Maltreatment," Special Circular no. 31 (Brooklyn: The Board of Education of the City of New York, October 26, 1973); for Montgomery County, see *Proceedings: Project Protection Child Abuse and Neglect* (Rockville, Md.: Montgomery County Public Schools, 1974).

**35.** Divoky, "Child Abuse: Mandate for Teacher Intervention?" p. 15.

**36.** Wald, *State Intervention on Behalf of "Neglected" Children: A Search for Realistic Standards,* 27 STAN. L. REV. 985, 993 (April 1975).

**37.** "Model Child Protective Services Act with Commentary," mimeographed (Washington, D. C.: National Center for Child Abuse and Neglect, Department of Health, Education and Welfare, July 7, 1975).

**38.** The estimate is from the American Humane Association in Denver, which monitors, and strongly supports, child-abuse reporting.

**39.** *CBS Evening News,* 1 December 1975.

**40.** "Child Abuse Rate Called Epidemic—U.S. Says Fifth of the Annual Million Victims Die," *The New York Times,* 30 November 1975, p. 14. The background is based on interviews with the UPI reporter who wrote the story and with officials of the American Humane Association. See also *Child Protection Report,* 4 December 1975, p. 1.

**41.** Ibid.

**42.** Divoky, "Child Abuse: Mandate for Teacher Intervention?"

**43.** The name Andrea Martin is a pseudonym, and the birth date has been changed. The policy on general public access to the "bottom" portion of birth records varies from department to department. Most county recorder's offices post a notice stating that the records are not to be used for "scandalous" or improper purposes, and some local health departments show the bottom portion of birth records only to "legitimate researchers." "They're public records," said one health-department official, "with a bit of control." In most agencies, however, almost anyone can walk in and go through them. New York, on the other hand, which requires even more extensive data on birth records, makes serious efforts to keep the medical data confidential and protects the records against even court summons.

**44.** On "suicidology," see generally Edwin S. Shneidman, *Deaths of Man* (New York: Quadrangle/The New York Times Book Co., 1973). The information on practices in Marin County is from interviews with County Coroner Ervin Jindrich and from Jack Viets, "A Psychological Autopsy for Apparent Suicides," *San Francisco Chronicle,* 6 July 1976, p. 5. Between 1966 and 1972, NIMH maintained a Center for the Study and Prevention of Suicide, of which Shneidman was the first director; and for several years thereafter, it supported a number of research projects in suicidology, but the interest appears to have waned. Nonetheless, late in 1976, William E. Bunney, chief of the adult psychiatry branch at NIMH and developer of a test of "suicidal tendencies" which measures urinary steroids, was still promoting the idea of such a test. "It would be tremendously valuable," he told a Washington neurologist, "to develop a highly accurate predictive test. But even with our present test, a clinical suspicion of suicide combined with repeated high urinary steroids should alert a psychiatrist that his patient may be acutely suicidal." Richard M. Restak, "Some Drugs Are Clarifying the Mind," *The New York Times,* 12 December 1976, Sec. 4, p. 5.

**45.** On SPN numbers, see Committee on Government Operations, U. S. Senate, *Privacy: The Collection, Use and Computerization of Personal Data* (Washington, D. C.: U. S. Government Printing Office, 1974), pp. 1646–62; and *The Privacy Report,* no. 4 (November 1973): 2.

In 1976, Representative Edward I. Koch of New York, who

has been the most active member of Congress in the fight against the use of SPN's, said that any individual with discharge papers from which the SPN numbers have been deleted is "instantly suspect." *The Privacy Journal* 2, no. 10 (August 1976): 7.

On the general availability of records to credit investigators or private detectives without official connections, see "The Snooper's Walking Tour," *The Privacy Journal* 2, no. 2 (December 1975): 2–6; and Nicholas Pileggi, "Secrets of a Private Eye," *New York,* 4 October 1976, pp. 38–45.

In the past two years, some voter registrars in California, often under pressure, have become more restrictive about providing access to records which reveal what petitions a particular voter signed; in some places, nonetheless, they are still easily accessible. They have been particularly useful to attorneys in choosing jurors for cases which have political implications. Making access more difficult may—as usual—work more hardship on private citizens or defense attorneys than on official agencies and prosecutors.

**46.** Louise Sweeney, "Testing Drivers to Find Drinkers," *Christian Science Monitor,* 20 August 1976, p. 2; "Snooping on Washington Drivers," *San Francisco Chronicle,* 27 August 1976, p. 19. Mayor Walter Washington ordered the program suspended after stories about it first appeared in the press; by then some 4,000 people had been screened, but there were plans to test 19,000 more in 1977.

**47.** Congress originally mandated EPSDT under Title XIX of the Social Security Act in 1967; in 1972, the law was amended to impose a heavy penalty on states which did not participate; 1 percent of federal welfare (Aid to Families with Dependent Children) funds were to be withheld from states which did not comply. On EPSDT, see Trotter, "Massive Screening Set for Nation's Poorest Children," p. 1; and Diane Divoky, "Screening: The Grand Delusion," *Learning* 5, no. 7 (March 1977): 28.

On the screening of children generally, see Schrag and Divoky, *The Myth of the Hyperactive Child,* pp. 108–31; and Nicholas Hobbs, ed., *Issues in the Classification of Children* (San Francisco: Jossey-Bass, 1975).

**48.** The most comprehensive study on the flow of medical and psychiatric records is Alan F. Westin, *Computers, Health Records and Citizen Rights* (Washington, D. C.: National Bureau of Standards, 1976). Perhaps the major point of the Westin study is the extent to which data are shared and exchanged among the three major sectors of the health-care field: primary providers, private and government insurers and their "fiscal intermediaries," and government health policy agencies.

On the exchange of data between juvenile justice agencies, schools, and welfare agencies, see Schrag and Divoky, *The Myth of the Hyperactive Child,* Chapter VI; on narcotics registers and reporting of patients in drug-abuse programs, see *Privacy: The Collection, Use and Computerization of Personal Data,* pp. 563–81.

Because it makes such exchanges easy, the use of the social security number (SSN) or other "universal identifiers" on almost every form of records has generated enormous controversy. Under pressure some states have passed laws eliminating the SSN from driver's licenses and other documents. Nonetheless, the SSN is probably being added as a requirement more often than it is being eliminated. Moreover, even in those systems where it is not (or no longer) required, clients and applicants are often not informed that they can leave the appropriate spaces blank. Every school-age child on welfare is now required to have a social security number; most colleges and universities now use them as student identification numbers; the military uses them as armed forces serial numbers; some insurance companies use them for policy numbers; and some banks use them for checking account numbers. *The Privacy Report,* no. 7 (February 1974): 2.

**49.** Robert G. Newman and Thomas Newman, "Safeguarding Confidentiality of Methadone Patient Records," mimeographed (Copies available from the New York Methadone Maintenance Treatment Program, 377 Broadway, N.Y., N.Y. 10013.)

In San Francisco, David G. Levine, at the time director of that city's Methadone Maintenance Treatment Program, successfully resisted pressure from state authorities to inspect his agency's treatment records; as a consequence, California law now protects the confidentiality of patient records.

In New Hampshire patients and psychiatrists subsequently learned that the records had been disclosed to the governor's office—they were not informed at the time the records were first turned over—and sued to stop the practice. Doe v. Thomson, Sup. Ct., Merrimack County, N.H., filed March 25, 1975.

The other illustrations of informal exchanges are based on interviews or personal observation.

50. Each year there are more computerized "wanted" lists and blacklists: narcotics registers; registers of wanted persons; a National Driver Register maintained by the Department of Transportation of all Americans who have ever had their driver's licenses "denied, revoked or suspended"; and since early 1976, a Federal Parent Locator Service, an HEW data bank linked to the Social Security System and the IRS to trace some 2.8 million "absent parents" who are not supporting their children.

The Parent Locator Service is described in an HEW press release of February 26, 1976 as "a key part of the recently established Office of Child Support Enforcement. It will be able to contact a variety of federal agencies, including the Social Security Administration, to obtain information to locate an absent parent for a State child support agency." The National Driver Register is described in the *Federal Register* 40, no. 167 (August 27, 1975): 38858. It includes "the reporting jurisdiction, the subject's full name, other names used, date of birth, driver's license number and/or Social Security Number (if used by the reporting jurisdiction), sex, height, weight, eye color, the reason for withdrawal, the date of the withdrawal," and other data.

On narcotics registers, see, e. g., McNamara and Starr, *Confidentiality of Narcotic Addict Treatment Records: A Legal and Statistical Analysis,* 73 COL. L. REV. 1579 (1973). The federal government has adopted relatively strict guidelines to protect the confidentiality of records in federally funded treatment programs, but confidentiality in many other programs is not protected. "Information sought [from centralized state registers]," said McNamara and Starr, "include drug, criminal and medical history, social and demographic data, prior drug treatment information, and employment data." One-third of the states, according to McNamara and Starr, have reporting requirements and a number, including New Jersey, have computerized their registers.

On the reporting of pharmacy prescriptions, see Roe v. Ingraham, 403 F. Supp. 931 (S.D.N.Y. 1975); Whalen v. Roe, 45 U.S.L.W. 4166 (February 22, 1977); and New York Public Health Law Sections 3331 (6), 3332 (a), and 3334 (4). On the reporting of outpatient mental-health records, see Volkman v. Miller (N.Y. Sup. Ct. January 23, 1973), and *Mental Health Law Reporter,* June 1975.

**51.** The largest private medical data bank is MIB, the Medical Information Bureau of Greenwich, Connecticut, which maintains medical and psychiatric data on some 13 million people, all of them quickly available to the 700 MIB-member insurance companies; some states (e. g., Missouri) operate centralized computer networks to store and process data on all state mental patients. On MIB, see "MIB: It has 12 Million Americans at Its Fingertips," *Prism,* June 1974, p. 729; *The Privacy Report* 2, no. 3 (January 1975): 2–8; and *The Privacy Report* no. 9 (April 1974): 5.

On the Missouri system, see George A. Ulett and Ivan W. Sletten, "A Statewide Electronic Data-Processing System," *Hospital and Community Psychiatry,* March 1969, pp. 74–77. A similar system, comprising psychiatric records of patients from six states, is operated as the Multi-State Psychiatric Information System (MSIS) at Rockland State Hospital in Orangeburg, N.Y., which processes the psychiatric records of more than 200,000 people in Connecticut, Massachusetts, Rhode Island, Vermont, and parts of New York and New Jersey. Eugene M. Laska et al., "The Multi-State Information System," *Evaluation* 1, no. 1 (Fall 1972): 66; Eugene M. Laska and R. Bank, eds., *The Psychiatric Information System: Perspectives, Uses and Safeguards* (New York: Wiley Interscience, 1976); and Westin, *Computers, Health Records, and Citizen Rights,* pp. 187–200.

In addition to MIB, many credit bureaus are in the business of collecting medical information for insurance companies, usually as investigators of policy applicants. There is no way to know how much of the medical information collected by the credit bureaus—usually with the cooperation of the subject—is later used in credit reports on loan applications (in connection with which, it may be assumed, the applicant would not have disclosed medical information). But perhaps the most intriguing problem is that posed by Blue Cross and other private medical systems which have contracts in a number of states to process Medicaid claims and which therefore have access to the medical records of millions of welfare recipients. There is no evidence that those companies have misused that data, but they do control the data systems which process it.

52. *Confidentiality and Third Parties, Task Force Report 9* (Washington, D. C.: The American Psychiatric Association, 1975), pp. 55, 56; and *Confidentiality: A Report of the 1974 Conference on Confidentiality of Health Records* (Washington, D. C.: American Psychiatric Association, 1975), p. 24.

53. Volkman v. Miller.

54. Kelley v. Johnson, 425 U.S. 238 (1976); and Paul v. Davis, 424 U.S. 693 (1976). In *Paul*, Rehnquist had limited constitutional protections to "matters relating to marriage, procreation, contraception, family relationships, and child rearing and education." Two weeks later, in *Kelley*, the boundaries had become even narrower. The challenge on the pharmacy prescriptions is Whalen v. Roe.

See also *The Privacy Journal* 2, no. 5 (March 1976): 2.

55. *Confidentiality and Third Parties*, p. 45. (Italics in original.)

56. Alan F. Westin and Michael Baker, *Databanks in a Free Society* (New York: Quadrangle/The New York Times Book Co., 1972), p. 341. "The great majority of organizations," they said, "are not, as a result of computerizing their records, collecting or exchanging more detailed personal information about individuals than they did in the precomputer era. They are not sharing identified information more widely among organizations that did not carry out such exchanges in the precomputer era." Westin's own conclusions in his work for the National Bureau of Standards on medical information systems, however, suggest that the observation in *Databanks* was premature. In the National Bureau of Standards report he concludes, for example, that "while the *character* of personal information

that is being collected for automated patient records is not different from what was recorded before, the automated personal data are being more *systematically collected, more fully recorded and more centralized in permanent files,*" and that automation "of patient data is facilitating . . . the sending out of some automated patient data to organizations outside the primary care sector." Westin, *Computers, Health Records and Citizen Rights,* p. 99.

57. *The Privacy Report,* no. 11 (June 1974): 5.

58. *Description of the Client Information System* (Lansing: Michigan Department of Social Services, 1973); *The Privacy Report* 2, no. 1 (August 1974); "Texas Group Opposes Interagency Data Banks," *Computerworld,* 23, October 1974, p. 3. James T. Bristol and Lawrence Felton, "Social, Legal and Ethical Aspects of Privacy in Computerized Public Welfare Records in Texas," *Law and Computer Technology,* December 1975, pp. 118–32.

## Chapter Eight

1. Richard D. Parlour, "Behavioral Techniques for Sociopathic Clients," *Federal Probation* 39, no. 1 (March 1974): 4. The object of the language here appears primarily to be the infantilizing of the client, to reduce his comprehension and his relationship with the "therapist" to that of a child. "Behavioral therapy," says Parlour, "is like good child-rearing procedure in most respects."

2. Quoted in Perpich, "Behavior Modification in Institutional Settings," p. 34.

3. David L. Bazelon, "The Perils of Wizardry," *American Journal of Psychiatry* 131, no. 12 (December 1974): 1317–18.

4. John R. Seeley, "The Americanization of the Unconscious: Twenty Years Later" (Unpublished paper, May 1976), p. 4. Seeley argues in another paper that since children "might also be defined as those who may—indeed should, indeed must—be molested or tampered with," any person is a child to "the degree that she or he can with impunity, nay commendation, be molested." In that sense, the service network reduces all its clients to the status of children. John R. Seeley, "On Molesting

Children" (Unpublished paper, July 1974), p. 2.

5. The perfect model here is Marcus Welby's clinic—and, to some extent, most of the other medical didactics on television and in the service magazines. The patient who resists the doctor is in trouble; the patient who collaborates is not only cured, but he becomes a better and happier person. Two attempts in 1975 to launch medical series based, at least in part, on the assumption that doctors are human, fallible, and on occasion, venal, careless, or self-serving charlatans both failed.

6. The quotation about the South Italians is from Lewis M. Terman, "The Conservation of Talent," *School and Society,* 29 March, 1924, p. 363. Terman, Goddard, and Thorndike were the patriarchs of testing in America, and all expressed similar fears. All of them were convinced that somehow character was associated with intelligence. "All feeble minded," wrote Terman in 1916, "are at least potential criminals, and every feeble-minded woman is a potential prostitute." For a general discussion, see Clarence J. Karier, "Testing for Order and Control in the Corporate Liberal State," pp. 155–80.

7. Terman, among others, was a leader of the California Human Betterment Foundation, which claimed credit for some 6,200 sterilizations in the 1920s; what he shared with the other testers of his generation was a belief in a genetically based immutability of intelligence. Ultimately, of course, the theory had enormous consequences both in the United States and England; in this country, it justified tracking of schoolchildren—segregation by ability—and in England, largely on the basis of the "research" of Cyril Burt, it produced a rigid three-tier educational system and the famous eleven-plus examinations.

8. Georg Lukacs, *History and Class Consciousness* (London: Merlin Press, 1971), p. 91.

9. The cases have employed two primary sets of arguments: due process and equal protection, on the one hand, and "right to treatment" on the other. For nearly a generation, the Supreme Court enlarged procedural rights in mental health, delinquency, and education. At the same time, lower courts have begun to require that when "treatment" is the reason for depriving a person of his liberty (as an incarcerated juvenile or as a mental patient), some real treatment must be offered. In

O'Connor v. Donaldson, 422 U.S. 563 (1975), the Supreme Court also held that a

> finding of "mental illness" cannot justify a State's locking a person up against his will and keeping him indefinitely in simple custodial confinement. Assuming that the term can be given a reasonably precise content and that the "mentally ill" can be identified with reasonable accuracy, there is still no constitutional basis for confining such persons involuntarily if they are dangerous to no one and can live safely in freedom. . . . Mere public intolerance or animosity cannot constitutionally justify the deprivation of a person's liberty.

In *In re Gault,* 387 U.S. 1 (1967), the court extended certain due-process rights to minors in the juvenile justice system, among them the right to be represented by counsel and to cross-examine witnesses (but not the right to a trial by jury); in Goss v. Lopez, 419 U.S. 565 (1975), the court held that a child cannot be suspended from school, even for a short period, without "written or oral notice of the charges" against him, a "rudimentary hearing" that includes an explanation of the charges, and a chance to present his side of the story; and in another case, Wood v. Strickland 420 U.S. 308 (1975), the court ruled that students may sue for damages school officials guilty of "intentional or otherwise inexcusable deprivations" of a student's constitutional rights. In the meantime, there have been literally hundreds of lower court decisions restricting the arbitrary powers of social-service, mental-health, and educational agencies, and often outlining extensive standards of adequate treatment in mental institutions and juvenile detention homes. See, e. g., Wyatt v. Stickney, 344 F. Supp. 373 (M. D. Ala. 1972); Wyatt v. Aderholt, 503 F.2d, 1305 (5th Cir. 1974); and Morales v. Turman, 364 F. Supp. 166 (E. D. Texas 1973), 383 F. Supp. 53 (E. D. Texas 1974).

10. Bellak, "Toward Control of Today's 'Epidemic' of Mental Disease," p. 41.

11. John R. Seeley, "The Non-Petty Politics of Social Science Policy: Social Problems and Sociological-Psychological Programs" (Unpublished paper, n.d.), pp. 16–21.

12. The dominant pattern in America is to sentence a convicted criminal to a prison term (two to five years, one to ten years)

whose conclusion is set not by the court but by a parole board or "adult authority," theoretically on the basis of the prisoner's state of rehabilitation. (As a practical matter, that pattern probably had more to do with the need for institutional control in prisons than it did with any serious hope of rehabilitation.) In the mid-seventies, however, three states passed laws severely restricting judicial latitude in sentencing and parole board discretion; and by 1977, seven other states and the federal government were considering similar legislation. The federal bill restricting judicial discretion, sponsored by Senator Edward M. Kennedy of Massachusetts, would not only make sentencing more uniform from court to court through the judicial system but would also base the sentence on the offense and not on probation reports or other assessments of the offender's record and character.

13. Obviously it does a little of both: it creates superfluous people and it justifies the exclusion of those already rendered superfluous. (Here again, I am not talking about those who are organically disabled or severely handicapped and who, in some instances, are totally neglected because they are considered hopeless or uninteresting cases.) Yet no one would claim, for example, that the close correlation that Harvey Brenner found between admission to mental hospitals and economic depression can be explained by arguing that the second is caused by the first. Similarly, no one would claim that the vast increase in officially defined categories of social pathology is responsible for the shortage of jobs in the economy.

14. See, e. g., Sharland Trotter, "Psychology Pushes for Recognition by JCAH (Joint Commission on Accreditation of Hospitals)," *APA Monitor* 7 (September/October 1976): 1; Gottlieb Simon, "NIMH Funds Study of Mental Health Utilization and Costs," *APA Monitor* 7 (September/October 1976): 5; and Sharland Trotter, "Insuring Psychotherapy: A Subsidy to the Rich?" *APA Monitor* 7 (November 1976): 1.

# Index

## About the Author

Peter Schrag lived in Europe until he was ten, and came to New York as a refugee in 1941. Educated at Amherst, he returned to teach American studies there after several years of working as a reporter. He has been an editor of both the *Saturday Review* and *Change* magazine, and was also contributing editor to *MORE*, a journalism review. His diverse career has included teaching at the University of Massachusetts and the University of California at Berkeley, and serving on the editorial boards of *Social Policy* and *Columbia Forum*.

Peter Schrag is the author of many books, including *Test of Loyalty, The Decline of the WASP,* and *The Myth of the Hyperactive Child*, which he co-authored with his wife, Diane Divoky. A Guggenheim Fellow in 1971, he was awarded the National Endowment Creative Writing Fellowship for 1976–77.

Schrag is now director of Park Day School in Oakland, California, where he lives with his wife and their two children.

718 589